Nov. 25, 20

Sabrina,

Thank you for joining
us for Thanksgiving Dinner
We enjoy your laughter,
it is so refreshing!

A WAY
Higher
THAN
OURS

Hoping things work out
with your new living
situation & jobs as God
directs your paths

Gary + Karen Price
Prov. 3:5-6
Is 55:9

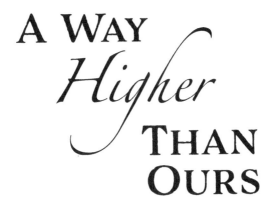

A WAY *Higher* THAN OURS

The Story from a Heart Transplant Recipient,
Her Husband, and Her Family

Heart Failure, a Family's Perspective

Gary and Karen Price

XULON PRESS

Xulon Press
2301 Lucien Way #415
Maitland, FL 32751
407.339.4217
www.xulonpress.com

A Way Higher Than Ours
The Story from a Heart Transplant Recipient, Her Husband, and Her Family

The front cover photo is the Teton Mountains as seen from in the Chapel of Transfiguration.

The back cover picture is a Peaceful Hawaiian Beach - one of Karen's happy places.

Unless otherwise indicated, Scripture quotations taken from (Version(s) used) Scripture quotations taken from the King James Version (KJV) – *public domain.*

Scripture quotations taken from the New American Standard Bible (NASB). Copyright © 1960, 1962, 1963, 1968, 1971, 1972, 1973, 1975, 1977, 1995 by The Lockman Foundation. Used by permission. All rights reserved.

Scripture quotations taken from the English Standard Version (ESV). Copyright © 2001 by Crossway, a publishing ministry of Good News Publishers. Used by permission. All rights reserved.

Scripture quotations taken from the Holy Bible, New International Version (NIV). Copyright © 1973, 1978, 1984, 2011 by Biblica, Inc.™. Used by permission. All rights reserved.

Paperback ISBN-13: 978-1-6628-3313-7

eBook ISBN-13: Z978-1-6628-3314-4

DEDICATED to Timmy, Matthew, Andrew, and Benjamin. We pray that God will bless you, our four sons, as you become more like Christ. Remember that we prayed for each of you before you were born, that you would be saved at an early age and grow to love the Lord your God with all your heart and desire to serve Him in truthfulness and sincerity all the days of your life, and thus be happy people, filled with the joy of the Lord.

Timmy, Matthew, Andrew, and Benjamin – 2021

TABLE OF CONTENTS

Forward ix

Purpose xii

Introduction xiii

Chapter 1   Background.............................. 1

Chapter 2   The Emergency Room 7

Chapter 3   The Harrowing Ordeal Begins 16

Chapter 4   The Long Traumatic Days, Improvements, and
            Discouragements 33

Chapter 5   Witnesses Gone Before 53

Chapter 6   Gary: How Should I Pray? 97

Chapter 7   Terminate Life Support? 101

Chapter 8   Is She Finally Waking Up?............. 105

Chapter 9   God's Miracles Abound 116

Chapter 10 Saints Gone to Heaven Before Us....... 135

Chapter 11 Which Road Will I Choose? 161

Chapter 12 The Great Physician 167

Chapter 13 Well Enough To Leave The Hospital? ...186

Chapter 14 Transplant Decision 213

Chapter 15 Karen's New Heart! 224

Chapter 16 God Is In Control 235

Chapter 17 Emotional Trauma 244

Conclusion 265

Epilogues 273

Forward

BY PASTOR WILL SENN

O n July 3, 2002, our family pulled into Westminster, Colorado. We were quickly met by our new youth pastor, Mike Durrill. We were also greeted by Frank Johnson, who had arrived a day ahead of us with the U-Haul truck. We had several people come to help us get out of the boxes and hopefully into beds for our first night in Colorado. One of the families who were there right from the start was Gary and Karen Price. I quickly learned that Gary is a jack-of-all-trades type of guy. He immediately went to work on some plumbing issues and other things way above my experience level. Also, Clovis Landry was there. I had no idea about his background, but he seemed to be quite gifted in putting beds together. On our arrival, the Prices greatly encouraged us on several levels. We have three sons, and we found out very quickly they have four sons, three nearly the same age as our three.

Also, Gary and Karen grew up in Upstate New York, near Binghamton. This fact was very encouraging to us because my parents have a farm about ninety miles west of them in Prattsburgh, and Allissa grew up ninety minutes southwest of them. So, we shared in our backgrounds: the culture, the cities, and life in the Northeast. Instantaneously, Allissa had a connection with Karen; our boys had a connection with their boys, and Gary and I connected. This new friendship began on July 3 in 2002, and one day later, on the 4th of July, Allissa's 44th birthday, the Prices began a tradition - to come alongside Allissa's birthday and be a blessing to her and a help to me. Throughout our time in Colorado, many of Allissa's birthday celebrations included the Prices, with one of them baking a cake for her birthday. Also, if time allowed on the 4th, we would enjoy a walk to the Westminster recreation center to watch the fireworks.

One of our first outings as the new pastor at Tri-City was to join the Price family for a big night out on the town. We enjoyed going first to Fazoli's for an Italian dinner, and then we spent a great evening at a local historic amusement park in Lakewood, with its infamous rickety rollercoaster. That night when I got home, my stomach was like a concrete truck that spins the ingredients until they are poured out. The rides did me in, but we sure had a great time!

Beginning at the onset of our ministry at Tri-City, our oldest son John and the Price's oldest son Timmy enjoyed much fun together. One of the things they liked doing was making videos. In each movie they produced, they were the stars and uncontrollably laughed as they watched themselves in their cameo performances. They also liked to do pranks together. On one occasion, they had a bike wreck set up in front of our house with a dummy appearing by the bike as if he had been killed. Cars would drive by and look and veer around this hazard while rubbernecking. Likely, someone called the police because they soon came by our house, after I had chided the boys for their shenanigans. Karen homeschooled her boys, and she was a very gifted teacher. She added to her teaching load by becoming our son John's math tutor. He succeeded with her private tutoring.

Over the years, it was fun to watch the boys grow up and the Lord do unique things in all the families in our church. In 2012, things were sailing right along in the work at Tri-City. At this point,

Karen served on staff in our church financial office and the general office as well - a great asset to the church and the team.

My prayer is that God will use Gary and Karen's story to proclaim the gospel to many. As Ezekiel 36:26 states, "A new heart also will I give you," a reference to regeneration, a reference to the new covenant, and a reference to salvation in Christ. My prayer is that this story will go literally around the world, that the good news of Christ will be proclaimed, that people will see the goodness of God, and that will lead them to repentance and knowledge of our wonderful Savior who died for us, was buried, and rose again. We are so thankful for our Savior.

We thank You so much, Lord Jesus, for the Prices and Your grace You gave to them; please use this story for Your glory!

Purpose

The purpose of this book is to share what we have learned, to share what God did in the midst of our trials, and to give Him thanks and praise. Deuteronomy 4:9, "Only take heed to thyself, and keep thy soul diligently, lest thou forget the things which thine eyes have seen, and lest they depart from thy heart all the days of thy life: but teach them thy sons, and thy sons' sons." Through the story told by our immediate family, our church family, and us, we hope to be an encouragement to each one who reads our account.

Introduction

God had plans for us that we did not know, nor did we choose. His way is higher than ours, "For as the heavens are higher than the earth, so are my ways higher than your ways, and my thoughts than your thoughts," Isaiah 55:9. We do not know all that God will accomplish for eternity due to this traumatic time in our lives, but we know His way is best and that we learned much. Gary researched and communicates here the details of the impactful events, especially for the first two months. He also shares his struggles with knowing how to pray, if God will answer, and what God's will is. Gary includes stories of others for whom he prayed in the past. Karen imparts the preparation up to the event and the dramatic changes in her life that ensued from her perspective. We also asked others to share the story from their viewpoint. This book includes writings from our sons (Matthew, Andrew, and Benjamin), friends (Allissa Senn, Debbie Fleming, and Janine Yurka), and two of our pastors: Pastors Will Senn and Pastor Larry Robbins. Also included are excerpts from group emails Karen's brother Kevin sent to keep family and friends updated and some responses. These recollections are broken up and interwoven to where they best fit between Gary and Karen's writings. The name at the start of each section denotes who is writing or compiling each section. Our older son, Timmy, spent many patient hours editing with us. At the end of many of the chapters are "Survival Nuggets." These are lessons God taught

Karen in the past, ones on which she considerably relied to anchor her during the unanticipated trauma and the days since.

Gary: God's Will?

What is God's will? Can we, as God's created beings, know what God's will is for each of us? Can we, by prayer and faith, somehow effect or cause a change of a perceived outcome that is relevant to us?

My writing will try to explain God's maturing process in my life concerning His revealed will and my faith. Can I trust God when my expectations (which are based on my understanding of His will from His Word) do not match or reflect my reality? Through God's maturing process, God's plan is to eventually grow my trust in Him regardless of the circumstances and to have confidence that His ways are best.

My belief is fourfold. First, that my Lord created every person and literally has a unique plan for every person's life. God has a path for us to follow, and He promises to show us this path if we trust Him. "Trust in the Lord [God] with all thine heart; and lean not unto thine own understanding. In all thy ways acknowledge Him, and He shall direct thy paths," Proverbs 3:5-6. The American Heritage Dictionary defines "God" as "A being conceived as the perfect, omnipotent, omniscient, originator, and ruler of the universe, the principal object of faith, and worship in monotheistic religions."

Second, that God is pleased to reveal His initial and ongoing plan (His will) to those who seek after Him. The American Heritage Dictionary defines the word "will" as "1) A mental faculty by which one deliberately chooses or decides upon a course (path) of action: volition, 2) A deliberate decision or conclusion; choice, 3) Something desired or decided upon by a person of authority or supremacy."

Third, that God rewards those people who diligently, through faith (belief and trust), seek after Him. "But without faith it is impossible to please Him: for he that cometh to God must believe that He [God] is [exists] and that He is a rewarder of them that diligently seek Him," Hebrews 11:6.

Fourth, God revealed Himself to His creation, and that revelation is in written form, called the Scriptures. God dictated those Scriptures, face to face as in Exodus 33:1, "And the Lord said unto Moses," and also through His Spirit, "For the prophecy came not in old time by the will of man: but holy men of God spake as they were moved by the Holy Ghost [God]," II Peter 1:21. We call these revelations the Holy Bible or God's Word. It is from this revealed Word that we can learn of God's nature and attributes. God's Word states that human beings were created by God and in His own image. The image we reflect are qualities from God's nature (i.e., reason, intellect, emotions, love, hate, and compassion). We do not, however, and thankfully so, possess the following three of God's attributes: Omniscience - all-knowing, Omnipotence - all-powerful, and Omnipresence - everywhere present.

Believing the revelation we possess, which we call God's Word, or the Bible, is truly the revelation from the actual creator of the universe, then we should and are obligated to trust and follow that revelation. God, as Father, wants His children to grow in their knowledge of Him and their love for Him. God also desires us to grow in our trust for Him, through all the circumstances of

Karen, Timmy, and Gary,
Several Months Before the Life-changing Event

life, for our own good. "And we know that all things work together for good to them that love God, to them who are called according to His purpose," Romans 8:28. In my writings that follow are some of the experiences God has used to grow my knowledge, love, and trust in Him with respect to physical healing.

Chapter 1
BACKGROUND

Karen: The Few Months Before the Big Event

*P*salm 107:15 says, "Oh that men would praise the LORD for his goodness, and for his wonderful works to the children of men!" I experienced God's wonderful works, and I grow to trust Him more through circumstances I did not choose, but circumstances God allowed.

In the spring of 2012, God prompted Gary to put Benjamin, our youngest son, into a Christian school and thus end our twenty-one years of homeschooling our four sons. Before Benjamin started high school at Beth Eden Baptist School, I worked in the office of Tri-City, the church where our family attended for over twenty years. Once Benjamin began as a sophomore in August, I started working more hours at Tri-City. I was also trying to figure out who Karen Price was now. I was born Karen Lilyea to Carl and Marilyn Lilyea in Binghamton, New York. We lived in Vestal, New York, and I attended Ross Corners Baptist Church and Ross Corners Christian Academy. It was at that church where Gary and I met and were married several years later. We attended several colleges and lived in five different states before settling in the Denver metro area thirty years ago.

Who was I now? I was no longer a mom of little ones and no longer a home educator, so what did God have for me now? In September, I remember saying to Gary, "What is coming? Life is so easy right now. What are we getting ready for?" Shortly after that, I directed a wedding, helped with a vow renewal/25th wedding anniversary party, welcomed to the church our new music director and his wife, Pastor Matt and Rachelle Whitcomb, and helped with Debbie Robbins' funeral.

Throughout my life, I had told God I was willing to go to the mission field, but each time something happened to prevent me from going: mission trips canceled, other individuals chosen for teams, or missionaries left the field. Despite these closed doors, I still was willing to go. Yet, I was content to focus on being a wife and on the daily activities of raising and nurturing our sons, serving at church, and encouraging those with whom I came in contact during my everyday life. At the annual missions conference in October 2012, I once again told God that I was willing to go anywhere and do anything for Him. During one of the evening services, I remember singing the congregational song as a prayer, *Lord, Send Me Anywhere.* Little did I know, He would soon place me in a new environment with many opportunities to witness and serve Him.

I flew to New York State to visit my mom, mother-in-law, and other family members and friends. At a wedding reception, I reconnected with many aunts, uncles, and cousins that I had not seen in numerous years. Hurricane Sandy hit the Northeast, the airports were closed, and I was stranded for three additional days; some of my family later thought that those three days were a gift from God – the last they would ever spend with me on earth.

When I arrived back home in Colorado, I had a busy week catching up on projects at both church and home. By Friday, November 9, I was tired, and after finishing work at the church, I decided to go to Costco, so neither Gary nor I would have to go out later and get groceries that evening. While lifting the groceries into the back of our van, including cases of drink, I suddenly felt a wave of heat and dizziness come over me. It ended after only a few seconds, but I still called Gary and told him what had happened and asked him to meet me in the driveway because I did not know what would happen when I stood up again. I drove the half-mile home; Gary was waiting in the driveway and walked me into the house. I felt ok, but I felt different from normal - a little strange. After lying on the couch for about forty-five minutes, I still felt tired but was not experiencing any other noticeable symptoms. I ate, relaxed, enjoyed some time with my family, and went to bed early that evening. The next morning, I was rested and felt normal. I decided to go to Walmart to purchase a gift for a baby shower later that day. While in Walmart, I pushed an almost empty cart approaching the baby section, when suddenly I felt the same sensations as the evening before, only more intense. It was as if a waterfall of heat came over me, accompanied by dizziness, sweating, and a little pain just below my left collarbone. Although it again passed quickly, it alarmed me, and I thought this might be more than the approaching menopause or just being tired.

I wanted to let someone know, so I called Gary while he was at work, then I drove the short distance home. Andrew was planning on attending a retreat for college and career adults, but he was prepared to cancel his plans since he was concerned about me. I did not want him to miss the annual event he was looking forward to, so I encouraged him to go, as I was confident that I would be fine.

I called up the stairs to Benjamin, but it was a Saturday morning, and the heavy sleeper did not respond. I then dialed my doctor's office and was told to go to the emergency room right away but not to drive myself. I attempted to call several friends, but many were at the baby shower with their phones turned off. Allissa Senn did call me back saying that she and Pastor were up in the mountains, but she would contact someone to take me. I again called up to Benjamin, "I'm headed to the emergency room. If you want to go with me, please come down here right away." He got out of bed, dressed, and down the stairs in several seconds. Allissa contacted Skip and Wanda Hunter, who arrived and asked which hospital to go to. At the time, I thought about going to St Joseph's Hospital but didn't know where it was located in downtown Denver, so I asked them to go twenty minutes north to Good Samaritan Hospital.

We arrived at the hospital and told the emergency room desk lady that I had a pain in my chest and immediately was taken back even though the waiting room was crowded. Many tests were run,

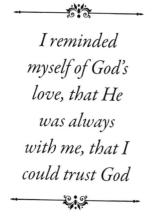

I reminded myself of God's love, that He was always with me, that I could trust God

but nothing was found. I felt a little silly for having gone to the hospital and no longer felt any of the initial symptoms. I was assured that it was wise to go to a hospital and have something like that checked. Benjamin was able to come back to the exam room and be with me. Pastor Rich also arrived and asked what he could do for us. My most important request to him was to get Ben something to eat; being a mom, I was concerned that my growing fifteen-year-old had missed two meals with only two granola bars to eat.

A second doctor was consulted, and they decided I should stay overnight so they could monitor me and then perform a treadmill stress test in the morning. I called Gary encouraged him to finish work before coming to see me since it was near the end of his shift, and I seemed fine. A few hours later, Gary, Timmy, and his wife Gracelyn came for a short visit. The mood was light and jovial, with much laughter. We were aware there might be something wrong, but no one thought it would be anything significant. The medical staff

4

had said that I did not have the typical factors that lead to bigger issues. Gary was told that after a test the next morning at about ten o'clock, he could probably take me home. After everyone left, I reminded myself of God's love, that He was always with me, that I could trust God, and that He would guide the doctors to make the right decisions. I went to sleep and slept well that night!

The following morning came the stress test. I had been regularly attending a women-only exercise center for the past two years, so when I was asked to walk on the treadmill, it was not strenuous for me. Towards the end of the test, the pain I had felt the day before, along with dizziness and heat, suddenly returned but more intensely. The technician administering the test slowed the treadmill down and helped me cross the room and lie down on a cot; I felt very weak. The technician and the nurse were very kind and compassionate to me. I called Gary, but he did not answer his phone. So, I called Timmy between church services and explained a little of what was happening. He then contacted his dad. While Gary was on the way to the hospital, a hospital staff member came to my cot, discussed an angiogram, and wanted me to sign some paperwork. I could not completely process what they were saying, so I did not want to make a decision. Once Gary arrived, he handled things, talked with them, and comforted me. The hospital personnel said they might also have to do an angioplasty if they found something during the angiogram. Most likely, they would keep me overnight, and I would be released the next morning. Like with all medical procedures, there was a minimal risk (as I remember it, they said that there was a 1 in 10,000 chance) of serious complications. After contacting Timmy, Andrew, Benjamin, my mom, and our pastor, Gary prayed with me. I went into the procedure, trusting Jesus and remembering my life verses: Proverbs 3:5-6, "Trust in the Lord with all thine heart; and lean not unto thine own understanding. In all thy ways acknowledge him, and he shall direct thy paths." Little did any of us know how we would have to lean on God and His ways in the next few hours, weeks, months, and years.

Survival Nugget: During the several months spread between the multiple hospitals, I had some very dark days. I searched for the light and could not find it: not in myself, nor in my surroundings, nor in the words I heard, nor in what I sensed or felt. The Bible tells us in I John 1:5, "God is light." While in a class that I had taken from Dr. Jim Berg years earlier, I learned principles called Four Stabilizing Truths. The truths came back to me while in the darkness. I realized I did not have to search for light since I already know THE Light, and He was very close. God had prepared me for that dark time, and His truths were my staying power. Later I re-memorized the Four Stabilizing Truths word-for-word, but they were not just words; they provided a beam of truth that guided my survival. Look for them in following Survival Nuggets. They are also listed in the conclusion of this book.

Chapter 2
THE EMERGENCY ROOM

Gary: Karen with a Chest Pain

Saturday, DAY 1 – November 10, 2012

The phone call came in on Saturday. My wife Karen said she had a pain in her chest; she seemed only somewhat concerned. She decided to have it checked out and had friends drive her to the emergency room, ER. The snow was falling; she encouraged me to wait and, finish my shift at work, and then meet her at the hospital. She felt fine. Although the enzyme test for a heart attack came back negative, the ER doctor recommended that she stay overnight in one of the private ER rooms for observation and have a stress test the next morning.

Survival Nugget: God's Love for Me is Unchanging. I had learned about God's love when I was very young. It was something I knew and did not question. I have never felt God's love more than when amid a crisis. Psalm 18:1-3, "I will love thee, O Lord, my strength. The Lord is my rock, and my fortress, and my deliverer; my God, my strength, in whom I will trust; my buckler, and the horn of my salvation, and my high tower. I will call upon the

Lord, who is worthy to be praised." This time was to be the biggest crisis of my life. Through it, God showed me His unchanging love.

Janine: "Twin" Heart Pains

I received a call from Karen Saturday morning, November 10, but she had to leave a voice mail since I was in a baby shower. I heard the message later and realized that I had arrhythmia at the same time Karen was trying to get a hold of me to take her to the hospital for chest pains. We are often told at church that we look alike, almost like twins. I felt like my heart was telling me my "twin" was having heart trouble. My arrhythmia attack that morning was definitely more pronounced than it had been in a long time. I was very concerned about Karen, and I called to be sure she had a ride to the ER and then called and talked to her Saturday evening at the hospital. I learned that she was being kept overnight in the hospital to do a stress test, but she thought she would be back to work on Monday. Little did we know what was going to happen.

Allissa: God's Hand was Upon Her

Before I begin with my thoughts concerning Karen's great trial, I must say that there are few people with the faith and hope in God that Karen has always exhibited. She was, and, even now, after much tribulation, is still faithful to our local church. In a special way, she always has been right there to help me as we planned and prepared our ladies' Bible studies. Karen was, and I am sure is the same, very caring for visitors at our church and keeping track of ladies who were hurting or just needing a friend. She is very unassuming. When Karen had this trial come into her life, our church family found out more about Karen. There were many "gaps" in the ministry that had to be quickly filled because Karen was not there. Many thanks go to her as a special servant of the Lord.

We were in the mountains when I first became aware of Karen's health concerns regarding her heart. She called me one Saturday afternoon to ask if I could take her to the hospital in Lafayette to have some chest pains checked out. Her doctor had urged her to do that. We were not geographically close enough, and I did not know how severe Karen's situation was, so I called Skip and Wanda Hunter, who were staying with us at the time. They were gracious enough to drop what they were doing to take Karen to the hospital. Later that night, I was informed that she would be kept overnight for evaluation and that the next day they would do the angiogram. I had no idea that the events of the next day, which happened to be a Sunday, would have serious ramifications for the rest of her life. Thankfully, God's hand was upon her, and nothing took Him by surprise.

Karen: Very Little Hope...But GOD, part 1

I wrote the first draft of the "Very Little Hope...But God" less than a year after the initial life-altering incident. Only minor changes were made to this original writing. In August of 2013, I used only a few of my very sensitive fingers to type this, mostly in the middle of the night, when I could not sleep. Some words in the three parts with this title are a repeat, with fewer details, of what I or others wrote. However, it is included to display what I was thinking then and partly to show the immense improvement in brain function between November 2012 and August 2013. There are many times "but God" is included in a Bible story. I now had my time when there was very little hope, and then "but God" events happened.

In the fall of 2012, my life abruptly and dramatically changed! God, however, got us ready in ways we did not know at the time; God cares about even the little details. First, I had homeschooled our boys for over twenty years; we decided in the spring that Benjamin, our youngest, should attend a private Christian school. So we enrolled him, and he began in August. Second, Gary sold an apartment building that we owned, and we paid off our house; this freed up a lot of Gary's time. Third, when clothes shopping, I purchased several blouses that were too big (I planned to wear a belt) or too long. My size was not on clearance, or it was a thrift store item, or one was pretty, and I had not tried it on in the store. God knew I would need them later. Next, I sold textbooks to homeschooling parents and was a senior consultant overseeing many other consultants. I had tried for years to sign up other consultants in places a ways from our home. That summer, three new consultants began, and I began training them to sell in their local areas. When I became disabled, they were able to step in and minister to homeschoolers and hold the meetings I had done for years. Then, we had some home projects done that I had wanted done for years: living room, dining room, and family room painted; new carpet in the downstairs; new vinyl in the downstairs bathroom, kitchen, and a semi-circle by the front door.

Because homeschooling had ended, we disposed of some furniture, and we were slowly sorting through the many boxes of things that had accumulated over the years. Having the house cleared out made it easier to rearrange to accommodate my new needs, and our home is more presentable to the visitors and therapists who come to the house. I even canceled my membership at an exercise facility; I thought I would begin again in a few months when things were a little less busy. Also, our oldest son and his wife, Timmy and Gracelyn, did not go back to China. Gracelyn was planning to look for another job soon. We had not seen much of our second son, Matthew, in the last five years, but he called in August, and Gary and I went out to lunch with him. Andrew, our third son, left a college he was attending out of state, came home, and is attending a local college. So, all our sons were in the Denver metro area – close by when the life-changing event happened.

I had a small chest pain just below the collarbone while shopping on Friday evening. I also felt a wave of heat, and I was briefly dizzy. I had been lifting several heavy things and was very tired from the week, but I was concerned. So, I called Gary on the way home; he met me in the driveway and walked with me to the house. I lay on the couch for a while, and the pain went away. I did a few simple things and went to bed early. The next morning, I quickly went to another store to purchase a baby gift prior to a baby shower that morning. The slight pain and heat came back with a weak feeling, even though I was walking slowly and lifting only light things. I tried to tell myself that all was ok; I have had gas pains more severe than that. The Holy Spirit was prompting me to pay attention to it and seek medical help. I called Gary, and he asked me to go right home and call our doctor's office. So, I went home, lay on the couch, and encouraged Andrew to go to his college and career retreat. Then I called the doctor. The nurse asked several questions and then told me to find someone to take me to the emergency room or call an ambulance. I called several friends, but many were at the baby shower with their phones off, and one was in the mountains. After a short time, Wanda and Skip Hunter came, I woke Benjamin, and the four of us went to the emergency room. The Hunters stayed quite a while at the hospital.

All of the many tests performed in the emergency room showed no problem, and the pain was decreasing. I had Benjamin call Gary and Timmy. We also talked with both my mom and my mother-in-law. Pastor Rich came, prayed with us, and was a big comfort and strength. At my request, he took Benjamin to get some food since he had eaten only a couple of snacks but no breakfast or lunch. When Gary finished work for the day, he came to the hospital to be with me. I felt fine, so Pastor Rich then left and took Benjamin to a youth activity. The doctor decided that I should stay overnight, be observed, and do a stress test in the morning. I felt quite silly for causing concern and wasting time and money for no problem. The medical personnel told me that it was wise for me to come to the hospital; they thought that probably nothing was wrong but wanted to run this last test as a precaution. Gary stayed *with me for a long while and then went home to get some rest. We planned that he would come Sunday and take me home after the test. I had a good night's sleep and felt fine.*

Sunday, November 11ᵗʰ, I failed the stress test. The pain and dizziness came back; I turned pale and was very hot and sweaty. I called Gary, and he came right away. He called Timmy, and he talked to others. It was decided that I should have a heart catheterization and, if needed, a routine angioplasty. It was <u>not</u> routine but dramatic. Those in the hospital still talk nine months later about that day and my case. Others will have to tell the events of the next eleven days and details of the next several months.

Survival Nugget: God's purpose for me is Christlikeness. II Corinthians 3:18, "But we all, with open face beholding as in a glass the glory of the Lord, are changed into the same image from glory to glory, even as by the Spirit of the Lord." God had molded and taught me through years of life events, and now He was ready to entrust me with a greater task – to bring Him glory through suffering. He also had some pruning to do in my life so that He could bear more fruit through me.

Benjamin: As I Remember It

I know that there are other much more detailed accounts of this story in this book, so if my section is confusing, just reference those accounts for timeline clarity. I will only include the details and parts relevant to my story. My story starts on the evening of Friday, November 9, while my mom was out shopping. My dad was exhausted from working overtime and was headed to bed early. At this point in my life, I had only gotten haircuts from my dad, and I NEEDED one that night. I pleaded with my dad, and he so lovingly agreed, but he was so tired he couldn't see straight. I got a haircut - but it did not look good; in fact, it looked really bad. My older brother Andrew decided to try and help me. Right about the time Andrew's attempt on my hair finished, mom came in. When she entered the kitchen, she took one look at me, dropped what she had in her hands, and fell to the floor laughing at me. It was a full two minutes before she regained composure. Once she and Andrew were able to speak, they decided that a buzz cut was the best way to go - it was the last resort. It was only two days later that my mom would start her three-month hospital stay. When I tell people my story, I jokingly tell them it was my haircut that gave my mom a heart attack.

The real serious story truly starts on Saturday morning, the 10th. I had been up late Friday evening, and I was sleeping in. I awoke around 10 am to my mom calling from downstairs for me to get up. I'm a heavy sleeper, and it barely made it through my sleepy fog. A few minutes later she called again, and I will never forget the words she said: "Ben! I need you downstairs now! I need to go to the emergency room!" About 1.7265 seconds later, I was dressed, downstairs, and ready to help my mom however she needed. It was terrifying for me, my strong, healthy, and energetic mother was sick? My world was a little shook. Just a short, blurry time later, we arrived at the ER, and they began to run tests and do their ER thing. There is a lot about that day that I don't remember. But before I knew it, it was 4 pm, and I hadn't eaten all day. Someone from our church showed up at the hospital just a little while before that to be with my mom and encourage her. After a little convincing, they persuaded me it was all right for me to leave my mom alone for a few minutes with them and go get myself some dinner. After this, I had a church activity to attend. After much assurances given by my mom that she would be ok, I reluctantly went to the activity. This would be the last time I saw and talked to her before her coma.

Sunday morning came around, and during choir practice, Timmy pulled me out and told me she was going to have a procedure to open a blocked artery. This news was shocking and pretty scary, to say the least. I did not pay attention during the church service that followed; I just kind of sat there thinking about nothing, kind of in a state of shock as to what was happening. A few people at church already knew about what was going on, and they made sure to encourage me or ask questions. Little did I know that eventually, I would get really used to being bombarded with questions, comments, and encouragement.

At this time, I did not have great relationships with my entire family, but I will get into that more later. When we arrived home from church, I had some sort of event with one of my brothers. I don't even remember who it was or what it was about. I just remember wanting to spend the rest of the afternoon alone on my bicycle. Mere seconds before I stormed out the door, my dad called and told us that we need to be at the hospital ASAP, that something happened with Mom, and we needed to be there because it was so bad she might not survive. When that information entered into my brain, it was so earth-shattering to know my mom, who was perfectly fine, happy, and smiling just less than 24 hours ago, was potentially going to die today; my brain couldn't process it. Not only could it not processes it, but it also did not even try. It was like the emotional weight of that thought just bounced off me. As a survival instinct and partially out of confusion, I felt nothing at that moment. So Timmy, his wife, Andrew, and I loaded into the car. While we were on our way to the hospital, we called my brother Matthew, who we had not talked to in quite some time, to let him know what limited information we knew. It was about 2 pm or 3 pm at this point.

The next thing I remember is when we arrived where my dad was standing in the hospital hallway. To this point, I had zero emotional reaction to the news, but something about how my dad's face looked as he was standing there caused the weight of the situation to finally hit me. I got blindsided like a 250-ton freight train. I think my dad saw this because before he said anything to anyone, he grabbed me and just hugged me as I broke down. He did not let go, not even when people started asking him questions. That one act characterized how the rest of our time as a family in the hospitals would go. This kind of love isn't a new thing for my dad to show. He has always been a very kind and supportive man. I think it just meant the world to me at that moment, and I don't think I had ever seen its true depth before that hug.

Just a few minutes after we met up with my dad, we heard a CODE BLUE over the intercom, meaning Mom's heart had just stopped. It seemed like the entire hospital staff went running toward the room where they were working on her. In all reality, it was probably ten people. It wasn't too long after that the doctor in charge informed us that she needed to be transferred to another hospital where they could potentially save her. They told us that they would try every single thing in their power to save her life, even if there was no guarantee it would work. So they loaded her up in the ambulance for her forty-minute drive downtown, a drive no one thought she would survive.

Chapter 3
THE HARROWING ORDEAL BEGINS

Gary: Code Blue

Sunday, DAY 2 – November 11, 2012
~ Veterans Day ~

Karen failed the stress test, so it was determined she would have an angiogram/heart catheterization to determine if any coronary arteries were blocked. Since it was a Sunday, the cardiologist had to assemble a team before performing the angioplasty; then, stents would be inserted to keep the arteries open. The cardiologist reviewed the potential risks. Since Karen was still considered "young," was not overweight, had no cholesterol or diabetes, etc., the procedure risks for her were considered extremely low. The heart catheterization was performed. The cardiologist met me in the otherwise empty waiting room to show me the images. He was very upbeat, although a little perplexed at how clear Karen's coronary arteries were, with the exception that one of them was closed off. Normally with coronary artery disease, multiple arteries or a single artery would show partial blockages in multiple places. He stated that the angioplasty specialist would complete her work in about fifteen minutes; then, Karen would have to spend the night for observation and be released the next morning. He was pleased with the progress.

Just then, he received a phone call, frowned, and abruptly got up to leave and said he would be right back. A minute or two later, a code blue was announced on the PA system. Then a man walked up to me and introduced himself as the hospital chaplain. I asked the chaplain if that code blue announcement was for my wife. He said, "Yes," and that he was there to wait with me and talk or listen, whatever I felt I needed. He was glad to hear that I would trust God for whatever outcome God would allow. At that time, the cardiologist returned. He no longer was upbeat and stated that the guidewire for the angioplasty balloon/

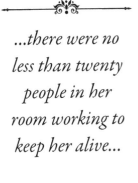

...there were no less than twenty people in her room working to keep her alive...

stent had perforated the artery wall. He further stated that if they could keep Karen alive and stabilize her, they would transport her to a different hospital for immediate bypass surgery to repair the artery. Also, he told me that there were no less than twenty people in her room working to keep her alive. I was stunned at how quickly life can change and what little control I had in the process. I remember asking God, "Is this what you really want?" Sunday church service had just let out. Three of our sons, one daughter-in-law, and two of the pastors arrived. They were apprised of the situation. The angioplasty specialist came out and apologized profusely. She appeared very upset and stated that she had "no excuses" to offer. I felt that she was sincere and had tried her best. The medical team was able to stabilize Karen, and she was transported to a hospital approximately forty minutes away for immediate bypass surgery.

Pastor Larry Robbins – Chaplain and Recent Caregiver

On Sunday afternoon, November 11, 2012, I received a text message concerning Karen Price's medical procedure at Good Samaritan Hospital in Lafayette. Something had gone wrong with a generally "routine" heart catheterization. I was only a short distance away at my home in Broomfield, so I decided to just run up to the hospital to see what was going on.

When I arrived, I was directed a couple of different directions before locating some of the family near the surgery waiting area. Everyone was standing. There was a nervous anxiousness that was subdued but evident. I was only there a short time before a medical team emerged from the surgical wing doors. I had already met the hospital chaplain, briefly chatting with him about my own ministries at Tri-City and the Westminster Police Department, where I serve as chaplain. I do not recall exactly who spoke or what they said to the family, other than to quickly update them as to what had gone wrong. Karen was in poor condition from excessive bleeding due to the cut in an artery just above the heart.

What I distinctly remember, however, was a comment to me privately by the hospital chaplain. There was a grimness in his voice, which also conveyed a familiarity with events such as this one. "This is NOT good." I recall turning in the opposite direction to see the attending physician speaking quickly and obviously frustrated with what had transpired earlier in the operating room. "No excuse! No excuse!"

The staff then explained that Karen was being immediately transported to another hospital in Denver that was equipped to handle open-heart surgery. It was quickly determined who would drive family members to that location. There was an urgency but a protective cloud of ignorance as to just how severe Karen's condition was.

Allissa: Grim, Anxious News

We got to the hospital as soon as we could when we heard that the procedure had gone awry. When we arrived, there was a group of people in the hallway waiting for news. From those first moments, things looked very grim. We did not know if Karen was going to make it or not. Pastor Robbins was there, and it is always encouraging to see his face in the group. Gary and the boys were anxiously awaiting any news. It looked like they were transporting her to a hospital downtown. So off our group went. My husband and I were in our car right behind Gracelyn as we pulled out of the hospital parking lot. He had to preach, but I wanted to go with the family downtown. I jumped out of our car and asked Gracelyn if I could ride with her. So there we were. I have always felt terrible about that because I gave Gracelyn the wrong advice on directions to the hospital, and we arrived late. In those early moments, there was nothing to do but wait for the outcome of all that they were doing for Karen. Will changed his mind and made arrangements for Skip Hunter to handle the evening service, during which they spent some time praying for Karen. Will actually got to the hospital before Gracelyn and me.

Gary: Karen's Bypass Surgery

Shortly after arriving at the second hospital, the waiting room began to fill with immediate family, church family, and the staff from church. I was grateful for the support of so many being there. Our estranged son and his wife were there also. Debbie, one of Karen's good friends at church, spotted the two and immediately engaged them in conversation - small talk at first, then went on to more emotionally uplifting and reassuring conversation. Debbie and Karen had completed a number of Christian counseling courses together. They had shared and prayed with each other over the years, including the challenges each faced in child-rearing. What a blessing it was to me to see this unfold - that God would send this gracious and knowledgeable lady to be an early part of the reconciliation with our son.

The same angioplasty specialist came out to the waiting room. She again apologized for the perforated artery. Later, it was verbally stated that the medical team had to revive Karen five times, using multiple shocks and multiple pressors at a high dose in the first hospital, then approximately five more times during the transport. The medical notes showed that an external heart pump was connected through the femoral artery before transport, and CPR was continuous during transport. Included in the doctors' notes was that the family was given a "very grave prognosis."

I was glad that many from our church family were there, sharing their time, concern, and support with my family.

More circulatory stabilization was required before the immediate emergency bypass surgery could begin. It was noted that the left ventricle wall of the heart was severely compromised [not responsive], fractured sternum resulting from CPR; Principle problem: dissection of a coronary artery, Active problems: cardiogenic shock, cardiac arrest during or resulting from a procedure, C/P CAB G X2 [double bypass], massive swelling, LVAD - Left Ventricle Assist Device [external heart pump].

After surgery, the heart surgeon explained that the double bypass was necessary. Karen had been stabilized enough to move to ICU, but it may be days/weeks/months before recovery, or the extent of injuries is known. He gave us hope stating, "This is what we do here. We pull them back from the brink."

Many from our church family were able to hear the updates directly from the hospital staff in the waiting room. I was glad that many from our church family were there, sharing their time, concern, and support with my family. I thought it was appropriate for them to hear exactly what the family was hearing. It brought a sense of closeness because we were all in this trial together.

Pastor Larry led a song - "Great is Thy Faithfulness." Then Pastor Senn, our senior pastor, prayed, committing Karen to God's care. The church folks then slowly left; at this point, the family went to see Karen in the ICU.

I was glad Pastor had warned us that heart surgery patients are usually very swollen and sometimes do not resemble themselves. This was true for Karen. It was difficult looking at my wife of thirty-two years; just twelve hours earlier, we had been reviewing the potential risks of an angioplasty with the cardiologist. We were confident that this "fairly routine procedure" would go well. Except for slightly elevated blood pressure and some hormone therapy to control migraine headaches, she did not have any of the standard risk factors (diabetes, high cholesterol, old age, overweight, smoker, etc.). I had jokingly told Karen as she was wheeled into the cath. lab, to be careful in there because people named Karen in my family, at age 53, did not fare so well. (My own sister, named Karen, died at age 53 due to complications of corneal replacement surgery.) I then told Karen, "I love you." The thought never crossed my mind that twelve hours after my wife was wheeled away from me that she would have been through so much trauma that Karen would be comatose, connected to life support equipment that would pump blood for her heart and a respirator to breath for her. She was extremely swollen. We then prayed for her, and I encouraged everyone to go home and try to rest as much as possible. It would be better to be rested before facing whatever trials God was going to allow, rather than be fatigued when facing those challenges.

Our son Matthew did stay overnight; the first of three nights that he stayed with his mom. He left a simple note, "Praying for you Mom – Matthew." That was a huge blessing to me because of his four-year absence from the family. Another blessing was Pastor Senn's willingness to share ongoing updates with the church family, which are included in this narrative, italicized and titled "Church's Update."

Church's Update 11/11/12
Pray for Mrs. Price rushed into surgery in critical condition.

Survival Nugget: God's Word for me is the final right answer. All His promises are true. After the coma, when a verse of Scripture or just a phrase made it to the forefront of my foggy brain, I latched on to it. It was like meeting an old friend, and I knew I could depend on the truth of them. My heart was permanently damaged, and my flesh failed. Psalm 73:25-26, "Whom have I in heaven but thee? and there is none upon earth that I desire beside thee. My flesh faileth: but God is the strength of my heart, and my portion for ever." I love the Bible and study it to learn the truth.

Pastor Senn: Standing in the Gap

On one occasion, in November, Karen did not feel really well and had some pain around her collarbone, and she was sweating profusely. At one point, she called us to see if we could give her a ride to the hospital. Unfortunately, we were not in town; but we were able to have Skip and Wanda give her the ride she needed to Good Samaritan. The Hunters had just moved in to live with us temporarily. So, on November 10, 2012, Karen went to Good Samaritan, and they ran some tests. They wanted to keep her overnight to observe her further and to do a stress test the next morning. After taking the stress test, the doctor immediately ordered an angioplasty. It is a normal procedure, one that doctors do quite frequently with little incident, but on this Veteran's Day, things went haywire. We received a phone call that things went very bad for her. It appeared that one of the guide wires actually went through her artery; she was bleeding and was in a life and death situation. When I received the phone call, Allissa and I quickly put everything aside and drove to Superior to the hospital. We just missed seeing her, but we saw some of the family, and we actually talked with the doctor who made the mistake. She was visibly unnerved by her error in the procedure.

We learned that Karen was being taken to St. Joe's downtown. Allissa hopped in with Gracelyn and rode down to the hospital with her; meanwhile, I tried to think through my afternoon and evening and to make all the necessary arrangements and coverage. As I was praying, it was very clear in my mind I needed to get down to the hospital and be with the family. It was very much a life-threatening situation. So I called Skip back at our house and said, "Skip, I am not coming to church tonight. You need to cover the service and make it a unique prayer meeting for Karen Price; here is what has happened." Skip did a fantastic job from all reports of that service and had everyone pray. I think from that point forward, there was an amazing amount of prayer offered for Karen. Truly, God's people stood in the gap between the dead and the living by their prayer life.

My heart was permanently damaged, and my flesh failed.

Pastor Larry Robbins: The Great Physician

I arrived at St. Joseph Hospital; almost everyone arrived at the same time to hear more details as to what was transpiring. The attending emergency room nurses from Good Samaritan, as well as the doctor herself, traveled with Karen in the ambulance. It was also revealed that they had performed CPR the entire trip in an attempt to keep her condition stabilized. The fragile state of Karen's condition and nearness to death was beginning to be understood by others outside the medical staff. In an attempt to present some encouraging news, a nurse indicated that they believed they had, through aggressive CPR, kept blood flowing through Karen's heart, hopefully minimizing damage. It was not determined until later that severe damage to her heart had taken place. But Karen HAD survived the transport, and the doctors HAD still found a heartbeat – although extremely weak. The only course of action the doctors could recommend was to press ahead with open-heart surgery, as dangerous as that would obviously be. The medical "odds" for survival were very low.

NOT MAKE IT?!

The family and several other friends had now gathered and sat about the surgery waiting area in small groups. Much prayer was being lifted up. As time passed that evening, I became aware that God was providing me comfort as well as Karen's immediate family. It had been only a month and a half since I had lost my wife to cancer. I was able to share with Gary and the boys that I had indeed faced similar positions in my own life. To Gary, there was the distinct possibility he would lose his wife. To the boys, they might well lose their mother to a medical procedure that had gone terribly wrong. I had lost my own mother when I was 16 years old to complications – the wrong blood type being administered – following open-heart valve replacement surgery in 1968. We were able to, at least at some level, give a portion of our anxiety to the Lord in prayer that Sunday night. Karen was being watched over and cared for by the Great Physician, Who did what the doctors were unable to do – bring miraculous protection, healing, and recovery!

Karen made it through the surgery! But would she make it through the night? That was only known by the Lord Himself!

Debbie: Profoundly Life-Changing News

Karen was not at choir practice. She had been napping on Sunday afternoons and had overslept on occasion. I decided this must be one of those Sundays.

As choir practice came to a close, I overheard Katie Malik telling someone, "She may not make it." As more questions were asked, it was determined that the <u>she</u> was Karen! Katie shared the information she had gotten from Benjamin, explaining his mom had been rushed from Good Samaritan Hospital after her angiogram procedure had gone terribly wrong. My mind was racing with questions. What angiogram? What was she doing at the hospital on Sunday? It was unlike Karen to schedule any appointments on a Sunday! How is this possible? She might not make it??? Does that mean what I think it means? Literally, NOT MAKE IT?! Katie went on to explain an artery had been perforated, causing it to "bleed out," causing Karen's heart to "crash," requiring CPR and extraordinary revival efforts in order to save her life. She was currently on her way to St. Joseph's Hospital, which was better equipped to handle her situation.

After observing the reactions of shock and horror on the faces of his choir members, Pastor Whitcomb led us in prayer for healing for Karen, comfort for her family, and guidance for the doctors providing her medical care. He closed after asking that God's perfect will be done.

Because we were not expected to sing a choir number that evening, I felt it was my privilege to leave if I wanted to, and I wanted to. I could not imagine being anywhere else but in the waiting room at

St. Joseph's Hospital with Karen's family and the others who felt the same as I did. I needed to be there to find out first-hand what had led to this catastrophe! I was joined by my mom, Barb Upchurch, and Janine Yurka. As we drove to the hospital, each of us shared what we had learned from the various conversations we had taken part in or had overheard that evening at church. We pieced together all of the facts, and we realized Karen would undergo continual CPR during her journey from one hospital to the other. If she survived the trip, it was to be determined when she arrived at St. Joseph's if she would tolerate a heart pump to sustain her life. There were many moments of silence as we tried to put things into perspective. At one point, Janine asked the question that had been on my mind: Would Matthew be there to support his family? I knew God had used extremely hard circumstances to bring families to a realization of their need for one another before, and I prayed the Price family would experience the same results.

It should have been no surprise when we entered the waiting room to find Pastor Senn, Pastor Robbins, Bart McNaughton, Gary, Timmy, Gracelyn, Andrew, Benjamin, Matthew, Christine, and others waiting quietly for news of Karen's prognosis. After scolding us for not staying at church to worship, Gary caught us up to date on the amazing efforts made by the emergency medical technicians to keep Karen alive as she was transported from one hospital to the other. She was in surgery, having a heart pump placed as he spoke. When the operation was complete, Gary told us the doctor was to report his findings and share information that would prove to be invaluable when making intelligent decisions concerning Karen's care.

It looked like there would be a bit of a wait, and I realized where my time would best be spent. I wanted to do something for Karen, and this was my opportunity. After all of the gut-wrenching discussions we'd had about our precious kids, I knew she loved Matthew with all of her heart, and if she had been given the choice to live life without Matthew here on earth or die if it meant reuniting her family, she would have chosen to die. I said a little prayer before approaching Matthew and Christine. I asked all of the questions I thought Karen would ask and took every opportunity to encourage them in their godly endeavors. Matthew, Christine, and I had a wonderful visit, and I could not wait to share the details of our conversation with Karen.

The doctor appeared after a reasonable amount of time, and we all gathered around to hear the news. As shocking as it was to hear Karen's name linked with such profound life-changing news, I adjusted my thinking to the new reality and listened as though the surgeon's words were the last ones I'd ever hear. He explained Karen's heart had sustained damage, but it could repair itself, and we'd have to wait and see. It would be a matter of time before it would be known whether her heart would function well with the pump, but, for now, it was holding its own. There was "quivering" in the portion of the heart, which may have been damaged, which he was interpreting as a good sign. There was hope. We would have to wait and see. They should know within a week or so if the pump could handle the demands of Karen's heart without taking over so much of the work, it would lessen the chances of the heart healing itself. Then, he presented the other possibilities, and the chance of additional surgeries, and the eventual need for a heart transplant. After each comment, there was an opportunity for questions. Gary had such intelligent observations; it was as though he had been through this before. I was amazed at his calm demeanor. Timmy asked his questions until they were answered to his satisfaction. He was clearly preparing himself to come alongside his dad. This would be hard and take some time before anyone would know anything. When the surgeon had finished speaking, Gary looked numb. No one spoke, so I spoke up. "Whew!!" Gary nodded and echoed my sentiment.

When it was apparent the surgeon and his team had done all they could do for the evening, our group began to say their goodnights to Gary and the rest of the family, who promised timely updates on Karen's condition. It was nearly midnight when I arrived home.

Benjamin: Trying to Keep a Candle Lit

At some point, I heard a doctor say that keeping her alive in the ambulance was like "trying to keep a birthday candle lit in the middle of a hurricane" with nothing but your own body to shield the flame from the gale-force winds and the monsoon rains; only God could do such a thing.

We proceeded to chase the ambulance down the freeway and highways, and we finally made it to the other hospital just as they were pulling my mom out of the ambulance and moving her inside. This was the first glimpse I had of her. I did not see much, but I remember thinking that I could not see her through all the machines and wire piled up everywhere, not to mention all the people all over the place around her. They rushed her straight to the operating room, where they would do open-heart surgery. Once again, they told us they could not believe she made it down from the other hospital and said the risk of death is only growing, but they would try their absolute best to save her. It was about 6 pm when they started the surgery. That surgery seemed to last an eternity. My brother Matthew had rushed to the hospital and made it to the second hospital. We had friends and Pastors with us at the hospital. My mom and our family are very involved with our church, and my mom has touched many lives. During the surgery, our Sunday evening church service would stop periodically to pray for her. And as soon as the service was over, more friends and the rest of the pastors showed up to help support us. After about six hours, the surgery finally ended. Miraculously, my mom was still alive; God was watching out for her.

When the doctors told us that she was out of surgery and over that hurdle, they also told us that there were other complications and that her condition was only worsening. It seemed like they wanted to tell us it was hopeless, that all their efforts were futile. It's like they were trying to break it to us gently that there was no real hope. At least that was the message I was receiving. I'm not entirely sure when I took that message to heart, but I think it was on the first day. When I took that message to heart, two things happened; first, I started to make peace with my mother's death even though she wasn't dead yet. After all, it was inevitable, was it not? Secondly, I started to grieve her. Let me take a break from the story and explain a few things. I was 15 at this point, I had never had anything close to this hard happen to me in life, and I had no experience dealing with emotional pain on any level close to this magnitude. Think of a smart car trying to snowplow a parking lot in a blizzard. So when this whole situation happened, I took the road I thought was less damaging to me personally. It ended up being more emotionally and personally damaging than if I had kept up hope and fought through it the entire time. This was the end of my mom's first day in the coma.

From this point until Day Nine of her coma, my memory is spotty. I remember events, facts, and a conversation here and there. I remember a few times our entire family would be gathered around in one corner of the waiting room just telling jokes and cracking up. Once I looked around and realized that there were four other groups of people there, they all looked extremely sad, and most were crying. Don't get me wrong, my family and I were all very sad and on the verge of tears almost every moment of every day. However, we found that being able to tell jokes and laugh, in the times that didn't require us to be serious, really helped us to cope; "If you're not laughing, you're crying."

A random memory that I have is all the friends that would continually pour their love and support into us. Some would come and spend hours and hours with me at the hospital, some would bring food, some would call or text, and most everyone prayed. All of these things helped so much! Personally, I probably would have starved if people had not brought so much food to us. When I experience stress, I lose my appetite and forget to eat. Honestly, eating wasn't anywhere near the top of my priorities. The people that visited us helped to keep me sane and keep my mind off of the situation. The calls and texts were especially helpful in the evenings and when I was alone to help remind me of others and God's support.

I've heard a lot about depression in my lifetime. I've heard some people say it's a mental illness, I've heard others call it a physical problem with one's brain, I've heard some people call it a side effect of PTSD and trauma, and I've heard some call it something "you just need to get over." I've never gone to a psychologist, I've never been diagnosed, and my knowledge of depression is limited. So if in the next couple paragraphs, I say something false or unknowledgeable, it would be because I do not know a lot about the whole thing.

With that being said, I think I had depression. I don't believe it was instigated or started because of the trauma I experienced through this whole ordeal. I cannot pinpoint when it started, but I know that I had some small issues before my mom went into the hospital. It was not until years later that I came to the realization that what I was dealing with was more than normal grief and sadness. I thought it was normal for someone to feel surface happiness but no depth of joy for months on end. I thought it was normal to forget the feeling of living a day with no regrets while lying in bed that evening. I thought it was normal not to want to eat because the sight of food made me sick. I thought that suddenly not enjoying hobbies and suddenly losing interest in people I liked was normal. I thought that living in a mental fog was normal. It was crippling. I would seek out emotional pain just to force my brain into "emergency mode" so that I could get normal daily tasks done. The bigger the task, the more I would hurt myself. It got to the point where I almost had myself convinced that my family did not love me, that I was not wanted by friends or family, that everyone would be better off without me, that I was an unnecessary weight. My brain would then go down that road of how to make that happen, what the implications would be, how people would feel, and what they would think. It was a very dark time for me. This train of thought was a daily path. In fact, it was a good day if I could only go through it once. I lived like this for more than five years before I realized I needed to change.

In early 2018, I realized that the way I was living wasn't right, it wasn't godly, and it wasn't healthy. It took me a long time to understand and learn what God was trying to teach me. I was living on emotional and physical adrenaline. While that does get the job done, and it seems to be the only way to live while I was going through things, I eventually had a meltdown. I lost a bunch of friends, left my job, and God brought me really low so that I could learn some life lessons. I was addicted to the adrenaline high, and learning not to have it and how to go through daily life without it was extremely rough. It took me about two years to figure that out, and I'm still learning some parts of it. My depression has some aspects that I think will never leave. I think it will be a lifelong struggle, and I have peace with that. I'm confident the Lord will carry me through. I have absolute faith that there is nothing He allows to happen to us that He doesn't give us the ability to deal with or give us a way to get away from it, and if I cannot get away from it, then He will continue to help me through it. Another lesson is how to balance God's command to love others and my own emotional health. I will reference this topic of my depression and the struggle with emotional pain as we go through the story.

Pastor Senn: Family Teamwork

I remember arriving down at the hospital that afternoon. The day was one of those overcast days – and had a very, very ominous feel to it. It was very fitting to the circumstance through which we were walking. This evening would be the first and only time that I would ever cancel my participation in a service due to an emergency within the church family. So, this was a very unique day. I remember getting to St Joseph's Hospital and finding the waiting room outside of where Karen had been taken. We heard that they had issued her CPR pretty much the whole way from Good Samaritan to St Joseph's. We knew that she was really on the edge of life and death. As we waited in the waiting room, all the boys showed up and all the different family members that were there in town. I would say that one of the great things God did through this trial was to bring the family closer together. As in most families, there were several strained relationships. I was staring at them in the waiting room. It became very apparent God had designed this trial for the Price family to have their hearts knit together closer than ever through this issue of Karen's health! I began to see the family come together, especially that first afternoon. This spirit would continue through all 110 days that Karen was in the hospital. I watched the family consistently work together to have incredible coverage while Karen was bedridden. I don't ever recall visiting Karen when there was not a Price there, or where they had just stepped out. To see the team-work, the support, the love, and to watch them work together was extremely rewarding. One of the highlights for me was to watch Gary's tender care of his wife and the wisdom he exercised that through all the scores of medical decisions he had to make. Gary was a fantastic testimony of what a Christian husband should be. And to watch the boys support their mom and to love their mom was very, very precious to watch.

Chapter 4

THE LONG TRAUMATIC DAYS, IMPROVEMENTS, AND DISCOURAGEMENTS

Gary: Condition is Tenuous

Monday, DAY 3 – November 12, 2012

The surgeon stated that Karen's kidneys had failed, and dialysis was starting. The worst-case scenario was that she might have only twenty-four hours to live. We were assured that they would do everything they could for her. I believe they did. It was encouraging to see the level of care and compassion from the health care team.

Church's Update 11/12/12

Karen underwent emergency open-heart surgery last night. She suffered a heart attack when the doctor was trying to address a blockage issue and accidentally cut her artery. Her condition is very tenuous. If you are on praying ground, please pray for Karen. Karen was in good health, in her fifties, wife of Gary, and mother of four sons. She also plays a significant role in our church office...We will keep you posted on her progress.

Tuesday, DAY 4 – November 13, 2012

Shortly after I arrived at the hospital, the cardiologist from the first hospital sought me out. Each Tuesday, all of this HMO's cardiologists gather at this hospital to discuss issues and cases. This days' main topic was Karen's case. Why did this happen? What could have been done differently to prevent this? There was no consensus among the doctors. It was perplexing to that group of approximately twenty cardiologists. Their best guess was that the artery had been dissected. The inner wall separated from the outer wall. This condition sometimes occurs in women just after giving birth or possibly when there is tremendous physical exertion, neither of which was Karen's case. When the catheter's guide wire reached that weakened section of the artery, the artery easily tore, resulting in the heart attack. It was not stated to me whether future angioplasty procedures would be postponed and the patient transported to a cardiac surgical center if there was a suspicion of a dissected artery or if there is a better method of identifying dissected arteries. The cardiologist did share the ongoing debate in the medical community of doing procedures at outlying facilities – the pros and cons. The conclusion is that allowing smaller facilities to perform procedures and then transporting patients to larger trauma/surgical centers when needed saves more lives. If all procedures were only performed at the larger centers, the mortality rate would increase due to the additional two or three-day wait period required to schedule patients at the larger facilities. The cardiologist then assured me that this hospital was a very good place for my wife to be. He said that the overall team and the surgical support system make a huge difference. I was thankful for the time he had spent to look for me, explain things, and share his concern. It was noted this day that Karen was "over-breathing" and moving around in bed. The movements were a good sign, but because of her extremely low blood pressure, she needed to be completely still. Even a turn of the head or rolling to her side could drop her blood pressure, and she could expire. More sedatives were administered to put her in a comatose state. Overall, she seemed to have been improving slightly.

Church's Update 11/13/12

The doctor told us yesterday regarding Karen that no news is good news. We have heard no news! We will keep you posted with any current information regarding her condition.

Survival Nugget: God's GRACE for Me is Sufficient. I had heard II Corinthians 12:9, "And He said unto me, 'My grace is sufficient for thee: for My strength is made perfect in weakness.' Most gladly therefore will I rather glory in my infirmities, that the power of Christ may rest upon me." I learned in a new way (what I could only learn through the process of a traumatic trial such as this) that His grace is sufficient. During all I went through, God was with me, providing the grace I needed for this specific circumstance.

Debbie: A Myriad of Machines

It was not until later on Monday that I learned Karen's family had been called back to the hospital to say their final goodbyes. Karen was not doing well at all, and the doctors did not expect her to live through her latest setback. The heart pump was not doing its job, and an immediate choice had to be made to put Karen through another surgery and place another pump, risking her life once again. Praise the Lord, the surgery was a success, but they would once again have to wait and see how her heart would respond to this new pump on a day-to-day basis.

At this point, I had resigned myself to visiting Karen and the family as often as possible. I thought of what I would like my family to experience if I was Karen, and I was determined to help as much as I could. All I had to offer was a listening ear, some food, and some encouragement, but I was willing. Honestly, I could have never imagined what God had in store for each person involved in Karen's journey, but I was about to find out.

In the days to come, each time I had a few hours, I would travel to the hospital, usually alone, talking to the Lord on Karen's behalf all the way. I needed the time to prepare myself for what I might see or find out when I arrived in her room. On my first visits, I found Karen's family gathered around the entrance of her room, talking quietly with various health professionals about her condition and the observations that had been made that day. As I listened intently to what Gary, Timmy, or Gracelyn shared with me, I wondered what they must be thinking and feeling as they faced yet more decisions as to her care. Karen's caregivers were very clear about the chances for her full recovery. Each hour revealed more challenges during the early days of her struggle to adapt to her new life-sustaining mechanism. In order to allow Karen's body to adjust to its "new normal," she was connected to a myriad of machines, each with a specific function, sound, look, and monitor. It was difficult to imagine how she could suddenly be so dependent on such artificial means of support, but she was.

> *It was difficult to imagine how she could suddenly be so dependent on such artificial means of support, but she was.*

Gary: More Ups and Downs
Wednesday, DAY 5 – November 14, 2012

The surgeon stated Karen had a stable night; however, HR [heart rate] went down a little. Also, she has internal bleeding, which for his normal bypass patients, is unacceptable. Due to her extremely fragile state, it is best to continue to transfuse blood, and if there is sufficient improvement, then go back into the chest cavity and stop the hemorrhaging. Her sternum was still open due to the massive swelling. The surgeon suggested that I consider allowing Karen to be moved to University of Colorado Hospital (UCH). He stated that UCH does have more to offer her, although if we wanted Karen to stay here, that would be fine. The surgeon also stated he was going on vacation the next day, and a different surgeon would take over for him. Ironically this very gifted heart surgeon that delicately performed heart surgeries and saved human lives was going on a hunting trip literally to blow the hearts out of the elk he was trying to bag. People do need time off from work, particularly those in high-stress jobs. I was happy for him, but the timing did not seem right for my family.

As a family, we all prayed together over Karen. It was difficult to keep the tears back. Even though she was getting good care, I felt her condition was now in decline. The staff was doing all they could for her. The life support equipment could only deliver a maximum of 3.5 liters per minute of blood flow through her body. We continued to pray and hope for a better tomorrow.

Thursday, DAY 6 – November 15, 2012

Kevin, Karen's older brother, sent out emails starting on the second day of this agonizing period to many family and friends. He received back many emails from people expressing their surprise, concern, and promise to pray. He wrote on this day, "I recently talked with Gary. Last night was not a good night for Karen. She is still sedated and hooked up to a number of machines. Although her numbers were going up some on Tuesday and Wednesday, they were not good last night and this morning. There is a real question on whether she will be able to pull through this." He then thanked the many people that were praying that God's will would be done and requested they continue to pray for Karen and the family.

Along with other responses, one cousin wrote, "Continue to have the faith. I'm so sorry to hear Karen is not showing positive signs of recovery, but that does not mean we should give up. It just means we need to keep praying for her and for all the family to be strong. Love with prayers has no equal, so we all stick together as long as it takes." Another responded, saying she felt so helpless and wished there was something she could do. People we had never met responded. One said that he is sure that Gary is crushed as the psalmist was when he wrote Psalm 56:3 and Psalm 46:1 and asked Kevin to let us know they were praying. Karen's fellow homeschooling consultants and HomeWorks people she worked with and their families and churches were praying.

Shortly after arriving at the hospital, the replacement surgeon came to the waiting area to speak with us. Instead of first introducing himself, he stated that he felt that I really should consider having Karen moved to University Hospital, UCH, because UCH had more to offer and that they (doctors at UCH) do heart transplants. He wanted an answer very soon. My oldest son Timmy and I talked about how the first surgeon seemed so confident that this current hospital was a good place for Karen. We were much assured by his statement, "That's what we do here; we pull them back from the brink!" Now he is on vacation, and immediately we are strongly encouraged to allow this hospital to move her out from under their care to a hospital outside of our health care system. We were in a panic. The first surgeon would not answer his phone. We had questions. Did the new surgeon think this hospital could no longer pull Karen back from the brink? Were they just trying to "clean their own slate" by sending her away and letting her die in transport or at the new hospital? Was this UCH hospital really any better? The BIG Question was in Karen's greatly weakened comatose state, could she survive a transport to a different facility?

We have been very thankful for the support our church family and staff had shown. Each day and evening, church members and someone from the pastoral staff were there almost continuously. Today was no exception. Pastor Senn was there at this point, and we apprised him of the situation. Four of us: Pastor, Timmy, Andrew, and I, found a quiet room to pray. Pastor called a local anesthesiologist friend for counsel. Pastor asked him for five minutes of his time. The friend replied, "No, I will give you two minutes." (We ended up getting ten minutes.) Pastor then asked his anesthesiologist friend what his recommendation would be: have Karen stay at this hospital or send her to UCH? Without hesitation, he said, send her to UCH immediately! They have more to offer! He had a similar situation with his own father. This anesthesiologist had hesitated, and his father died. He said that he wished he had not waited. We thanked him and hung up. We discussed the recommendation and felt strongly impressed to have Karen sent to UCH immediately. Maybe this was the way God was going to preserve her life; apparently, "UCH had more to offer!" The surgeon was pleased to hear of our decision. He already had the approval from UCH for Karen's transfer and continued care. We were again cautioned about the difficulty of having Karen transported. She may not survive the move.

The transport company arrived one to two hours later and started their 3½-hour process of prepping her for the eight-mile trip. Since Karen was on total life support, a large-sized ambulance was needed to accommodate her, the life support equipment, and the six-person crew. I felt some sense of hope, knowing that my wife had been approved for the transfer, that UCH had a plan for her care, and that there must be some optimism on the part of UCH to allow my wife to be transferred to their facility in her critical condition. My decisions for her care over the last four days had been stressful to make and yet easy. Stressful because she was so "critically ill," moment to moment, we did not know if she would suddenly die. When we left the hospital each night to go home, we thought, "Would this be the last time to see her alive?" There was nothing I could do to help her! The easy part was knowing that God was in control; I could pray but do nothing else to help my wife. The decisions were also easy to make. After repeatedly hearing this type of question, "We need to have your permission to do this procedure, or your wife will die," it becomes very "easy" to make those decisions.

I also had a sense of despair. The realization that the current hospital could no longer give my wife the type of care she now required. Even though it had been stated and affirmed to us that this was a very good cardiac hospital and that "they pull them back from the brink." Karen was now slipping over the brink. She now faced a transport to a third hospital in a worse condition. Was this the time God would use to take her home? I had not been confident she would survive the first transport four days earlier. I now was less confident she could survive this transport. Pressure sores had developed on the back of her head because the medical staff was afraid that a slight movement of her body would cause a massive blood pressure drop, and she would die. Now she was prepped and ready for transport, which would require much more movement. Each of the previous four days, I had remained somewhat hopeful. The first two days there seemed to be a very slight improvement in her condition. In the last two days, she definitely was in decline. She was being transported to a hospital that I had never been to and was unfamiliar with except for the statement to me that "they had more to offer."

> *"Would this be the last time to see her alive?" There was nothing I could do to help her! The easy part was knowing that God was in control...*

We would later hear from the ambulance crew that it took 3 ½ hours to prep her for transport because her condition was so fragile. They "could only change one drip out at a time." They "couldn't do anything with any medications because she was already maxed out on anything they could have given her to sustain her life." They were hoping that she would still be alive when they arrived at UCH and not be responsible for losing her. They did not think she would survive the transport.

My hope for Karen's survival was all but gone. God gives us comfort and grace during our trials. There had been so many people visiting us at the hospital. They prayed, talked, brought food, and even played games. People were there each day until late each night. Our youngest son's high school principal and his family visited several times. The principal promised to help keep Ben's studies "on track" after Ben returned to school, whenever that would be. Life does not totally stop when in the midst of a crisis. It is comforting when others have an understanding spirit and do what they can to bring relief to those in distress.

We were allowed to pray over Karen just before she was transported to UCH. It took approximately thirty minutes to get her to the ambulance and loaded into it. There was a continued sense of uncertainty about whether she would survive the trip. We left just before the ambulance; eventually, the ambulance passed us. Lights were flashing, but no siren. We were in sight of each other the whole trip. That sense of uncertainty continued. Was she struggling? Were they losing her? Did UCH really have more to offer? When someone is so critically ill, hopes are for survival, but thoughts start to focus on funerals instead of the future.

After arriving at UCH, we were sent to a large but empty surgical waiting area. The ambulance crew and the previous hospital's staff slowly wheeled Karen through this dimly lit and very quiet waiting area. I was struck by how slowly and carefully this crew of six moved her. She was still alive. We were thankful that God had allowed her to survive the transport. My realization was, however, that this was only another small piece of her health care puzzle that had been put in place. The continuing reality was that we could lose her at any time. While this was a victory, my optimism for her recovery was small. Later we would read from the UCH medical notes about the initial physical examination, "On presentation, she had a mean arterial pressure of 70 with no pulsatility, heart rate of 100 in sinus rhythm. She had LV apical and aortic cannulas connected to a CentriMag with an oxygenator. She had two liters of flow. Her extremities were mottled [marked with spots or smears of color]; in fact, her fingertips were black,

I asked God, "Is this what You really want?"

and so were her toes and forefeet. They were cold to the touch. She was paralyzed without any neurologic function. She was Edematous [excess of watery fluid collecting in the cavities or tissues of the body] throughout. Assessment and Plan: Fifty-three-year-old female in severe cardiogenic shock, with inadequate mechanical support and unknown neurologic function. We will plan tonight to convert her to venoarterial ECMO to provide flow, and we will see what her brain does, to see if she is salvageable." SALVAGEABLE!

A few minutes later, an assistant came out of the Surgical/ICU and informed us that the surgeon would be meeting with us shortly. He wanted to be able to make a preliminary assessment of Karen's life support needs. When asked what the surgeon's name was, the assistant replied, "Babu." I had not heard of this surgeon, but upon hearing his name, my heart sank! All I could think of was the cartoon characters: Yogi Bear and Booboo Bear. After what Karen had been through, now her care is assigned to Booboo!?! Yes,

I felt discouraged because of my wife's declining condition. Yes, I should just have given thanks to God for all things. No, I should not let name associations control my thoughts. Yes, it was late; I was tired, and frankly, I had not expected my wife to survive this long. Once again, I realized that I had little or no control over the events going on. I was just a spectator. I could, however, try to control my thoughts and cast my burdens on the Lord. Again, I asked God, "Is this what You really want?"

A short time later, Dr. Babu appeared and introduced himself (pronounced bah'-boo). His voice was hoarse, and I thought he was sick. I was, however, very glad that a surgeon was there at 10 p.m. to evaluate and hopefully stabilize my wife. Dr. Babu stated that he would change the type of life support equipment to allow better blood flow through the body. This would take a few hours. He would then return and give an update. Less than two hours later, he returned and stated that Karen had been successfully transferred to the UCH Life Support Equipment and was for the time stable. He noted that she continued to lose blood internally. If she remained stable, he said he would soon like to go back into the still open chest cavity, locate and then repair the leak. Later, we found out that Karen had received 178 units of blood up to this point and would eventually receive 254 units of blood or blood products (i.e., platelets, plasma, or red blood cells). With this different circulation method and different types of equipment, her blood flow rate had increased from the 2 to 3.5 liters per minute to now five liters per minute!

The staff believed they could already see a change in Karen's skin tone, a slight pinking in color. Dr. Babu invited us to come back to see Karen in her ICU room. Karen's color did look better, not quite so ashen as two hours earlier. Dr. Babu told us he was going to stop all the meds (medications) that were keeping her in the comatose state. He hoped that in a few hours, or at most twenty-four hours

Karen, would be conscious. At that point, we could start to make a determination of brain activity. I told Dr. Babu that I was "flabbergasted." I felt overwhelmed. I started to feel a sense of hope. After just two hours at UCH, my wife looked better than she had the previous two days. Perhaps in a few hours, she would be conscious after the four days of unconsciousness. Maybe God was going to allow Karen to live. And maybe UCH really did have more to offer!

We would later read from Dr. Babu's notes, "Briefly ... sustained left main dissection during diagnostic catheterization with V Fib arrest ... Transferred to [second hospital] placed on bypass and underwent CABG. The LV [left ventricle] did not move ... and was placed on LVAD support ... lungs did not work ... oxygenator placed ... not able to generate much flow due to small LV apical cannula ... poor right ventricular function. Remained in cardiogenic shock postoperatively ... developed multiple organ failure ... on high dose drugs ... now has ischemic [inadequate blood supply] necrosis [death of most or all of the cells in an organ or tissue due to disease, injury or failure of the blood supply] of the fingers and toes, along with other organ function. She was sent to UCH to see if she could be salvaged at this late stage. Unfortunately, she has been in severe cardiogenic shock for an unknown duration, potentially four days. I do not know what potential her brain, kidneys, and liver will have for recovery. Only time will tell. We will support with VA ECMO until she can show us what her neurologic function is. If she recovers neurologically, we may move toward centrally cannulated LVAD or BIVAD, continuing if necessary to allow time for the rest of the organs to recover. I have spoken with her family at length about her very guarded prognosis and the potential need to turn things off if the brain is not intact." ECMO stands for Extracorporeal Membrane Oxygenation; it is a type of life support.

Church's Update 11/16/12

Last night was a big night for Karen Price and the family. They were able to move her successfully to University Hospital. The new set of doctors immediately took her into surgery. Her blood flow since the surgery has improved. They also have taken her off many of her meds and desire for her to wake out of the induced coma. They want to see how her other organs will respond. Every day she is lingering between two worlds. She has been right on the bubble. If the Lord takes her forward to His heavenly city, we will rejoice for her sake, but we are praying that today she will take a step back into our world.

Pastor Senn: Bonding Hearts

Early on, there was a judgment call that needed to be made to transfer Karen from St. Joe's to University Hospital, where there was better cardiological care for her situation. I remember us asking people to pray that the transfer be safely accomplished, knowing that each transfer was life-threatening. So she was taken there, and additional care was given to her that sustained her life. But during this time period, it was very nerve-wracking to watch. Watching all the equipment hooked up to Karen's body to realize how weak she was and how much damage was done to her heart as reports were forwarded. And then to sit there with the family as Karen was in the comatose state and hearing directly or indirectly through the whispers the possibilities that she would not come out of her coma state or if she did there would be severe brain damage or other horrific consequences. I watched the family pray and trust God. There were also those from the church that came and would sing, would sit, would read Scripture, and would just be with the family. These were some special times to get to know Gary and the kids better. We all wish it were under different circumstances. God bonded our hearts further together through the trial.

45

Also, at this time, there was a family from a sister church here on the Front Range, Beth Eden, who had a family member going through some severe health issues. I remember visiting the Prices, and then I would go over to the Pollocks and be with them and pray for their daughter-in-law, who actually would not go home, at least not to their home in Arvada. She would go home to be with her Lord in Heaven. That was very challenging to see two life-threatening situations. In the one, the Lord chose to preserve, and in the other, the Lord chose to take someone home. That just points to the sovereignty of God that He will do what He wants to do for His own glory.

Gary: Karen Remains in the Coma
Friday, DAY 7 – November 16, 2012

I returned to the hospital half expecting to see that Karen would be conscious; she was not. Dr. Babu had stated that it could take up to twenty-four hours. It was agreed that he would go back into the still open chest cavity, locate the leaks (hemorrhaging) and repair them.

After that surgery, he reported that all looked well, and the chest cavity was now dry. The swelling had diminished; the chest cavity was now closed, which was good news. A CT scan of Karen's brain was performed, and a 5 pm meeting was planned with the neurologist, Dr. Babu, our family, Pastor and Allissa, Pastor Bart, and Kasey (our youth pastor and his wife), and a church intern, Patrick Reilly. The neurologist was "very, very concerned" and gave us a very dismal report. The CT scan showed evidence of two strokes in the frontal lobes, which would affect her ability to walk. Because she had not regained consciousness at this point, it may be indicative of additional brain damage. A 24-hour test called an EEG would be performed to monitor brain wave activity. The results of this test would help determine a more accurate prognosis. The neurologist stated that Karen's condition was similar to being "brain dead," but she did not meet the technical description.

The following are the positives. Her skin color continues to improve, with some of the purple areas receding. Eyes are glassy; one is half-open. After the meeting concluded, I asked my estranged son and his wife to stay a few minutes so the three of us could talk. Karen had only seen this son one time in the previous four years. I told them how much of a blessing it was to have them with us at this time. I asked their forgiveness for anything that I had said or done in the past. I told them that I would like to begin to develop a relationship with them. It is encouraging to believe that God can restore relationships. It is more encouraging to see God working in hearts (figurative and literal) to allow restoration. Maybe God planned this event and when it should occur. Despite the negativity of the "dismal neurological report," I had a sense of joy believing and seeing this relational restoration continuing to unfold.

Saturday, DAY 8 – November 17, 2012

Kevin's update included, "Her color has come back, and swelling is significantly reduced. Gary is really happy with the University Hospital and the care she is receiving. The big concern now is when she will come out of the coma and if there is any brain damage. So far, she is not responding. The next step is waiting on God." One responded that they were earnestly praying for Karen to come out of the coma completely well and normal. Another went to talk with her pastor, and they prayed for Karen. More and more people are praying as people tell their friends and family requesting prayer."

EEG brain wave test was started. Skin color continues to improve slightly each day. Swelling continues to go down. But Karen is still in a coma.

Sunday, DAY 9 – November 18, 2012

There is mounting concern for Karen. She is still comatose and non-responsive. The EEG test was still in progress. The EEG monitor displays approximately 16-18 graph lines; only two were active. The others were almost a flat line, almost no response. The ICU nurse stated that they personally were not qualified to give an interpretation from that test equipment but believed that all the graph lines should be active. Likely, there is some type of neurological abnormality.

Church's Update 11/18/12

Karen Price's condition remained the same yesterday. The internal bleeding appears to have been corrected. Now, it all hinges on the condition of her brain, if it was damaged or not, and if damaged, how badly. Pray that she opens her eyes and begins to move her hands and feet with purpose. Thanks for your prayers.

Monday, DAY 10 – November 19, 2012

Arm movement is seen. This has generated excitement for the family. Maybe the comatose fog is lifting, and Karen is starting to move her arms with "purpose." I asked the medical staff, hoping they could affirm our observation. Instead, they seemed disappointed, explaining that this is called "posturing." This movement was not a good sign. Posturing shows that the brain is impaired, that a person is struggling, and likely to have a negative outcome.

Posturing, as defined by Wikipedia, "is an involuntary flexion or extension of the arms and legs, indicating severe brain injury. Posturing is an important indication of the amount of damage that has occurred to the brain; it is used by medical professionals to measure the severity of a coma. On patients with decorticate posturing (which Karen was displaying) present with arms flexed or bent inward on the chest, the hands are clenched into fists, and the legs extended and feet turned inward ... An ominous sign of severe brain damage." Needless to say, we, as a family, church family, and friends, were saddened to hear of these things. While Karen's skin tones and body swelling had daily showed signs of improvement, we now were seeing more clearly the extent of the damage to her brain and extremities. This experience reminded me of the proverbial roller coaster ride with all the ups and downs, a continuous cycle of good news followed by bad news. We would clear one hurdle and find another one looming in front of us that seemed more insurmountable than the last one. I would just like to see the ups – the positive things, the "good things" occurring. My questions to God were: "Is this what You really want?" and "Can we just see continued improvement without all this trauma?"

I prayed, "Father, if it is Your plan to take her home, why do we continue this cycle of seeing some improvement in one area, immediately followed by more negative news in another area? I believe You can heal her if that is Your desire. Healing Your child Karen is my desire, but I do not know Father if that is Your desire. I know that all things work together for good to them that love God, but right now, I am not seeing the 'good.' My definition of 'good' is that You Father have allowed this bad thing to happen. Now, we should see You working and causing a 'good' thing to happen, namely full restoration of Karen's health." Despite the roller coaster of events, we were blessed by the many people coming to the hospital and the many more who were praying.

It had been our practice to talk to Karen while she was in the comatose state. Some of the medical staff had recommended this, stating that sometimes people are able to hear and understand. The family would share with Karen events and activities, hoping that if she could hear, our voices may, in some way, bring her comfort. Today, I felt the need to again talk to her about her condition. I told her that we had been praying for her and that our church family had been praying for her and that our extended families and their churches had been praying for her. Also, we had received communications that others unrelated to our families and their church families were praying for her. With all these prayers, she surely had God's attention. I shared that the doctors were now at a standstill. They had done everything they could to support her life. They could not proceed any further with other medical procedures without her becoming conscious. I told her she had been in a coma way too long. God had not brought her out of the coma, and that the medical staff had tried but were not able. I told her that she could not be left on life support indefinitely, and soon we would have to make the decision to terminate her life support. Although many people had prayed, her time was running out. We had done everything we could. There was nothing else anybody could do. Only God could bring her back. I told Karen that I had nothing to offer her. Perhaps she had a glimpse of Heaven and did not want to come back. That would be ok. I would probably desire Heaven if I were in her place. The decision was hers. If she decided to go, I would be happy for her knowing that she was in a much better place - a place filled with joy and happiness with no more pain, sickness, or suffering.

The doctors were now at a standstill. They had done everything they could to support her life.

We, as a family, would be saddened at losing her, and I would miss her terribly. I told her that it was difficult for me to go home to a quiet house. I was lonely, and that her presence was greatly missed. Each of our four boys was also saddened and expressed the same desire that God would allow them to communicate with her at least one more time. They would be supportive of any decision made regarding life support, but they did not want to lose their mother. Again, I told her that her time was running out, and I had nothing to offer her compared to the glories of Heaven. If she wanted to go, I would understand. However, if she wanted to stay, she needed to talk to God, tell Him her desire, and then ask Him if He would allow her to remain on earth a while longer before going with Him to Heaven.

There was nothing more I could do. I then prayed with Karen telling my Heavenly Father what had just been said. I do realize that God is all-knowing and knows the thoughts and intents of my heart even when I do not know those things. I believe God wants to have a relationship and desires to commune with each of us as a loving earthly father does with his own children. To tell God what has just been said is totally unnecessary for His knowledge but important for a relationship with Him. I continued by telling my Heavenly Father that Karen may share her desire with Him concerning going to Heaven now or staying here a while longer. I thanked Him for the time He had allowed us to be together and asked that His will be done.

Emotionally this was a difficult time for me - a time of letting go - ten days filled with uncertainty. Once again, the overwhelming realization was that we were losing her. I was thankful that this was not sudden, like somebody unexpectedly dying in an automobile accident. God had allowed us some time to try to come to grips with this situation and start to let go. I did not want to let go. Was there some way I, or all that were praying for Karen, could somehow intercede or pray in some fashion as to "move God's hand?" At this point, we would need a miracle! Would God be pleased to perform something that was considered outside the bounds of normal medical science? We read in God's Word that Jesus, God's Son, or God in the flesh, performed miracles of healing. Jesus told his disciples that they would do "greater works than these" (healings included in John 14:12) or greater works than what Jesus was doing. Jesus also said, "if you [as his followers] ask anything in My name I will do it," (John 14:14 NASB). Should I ask God to heal Karen completely, and would I have the expectation (faith) that God would perform this "good" work based on this understanding of Scripture? This brought to my mind several people I had known and prayed for in the past.

Chapter 5
WITNESSES
GONE BEFORE

Gary: People for Whom I Had Prayed

Mrs. Snyder

*I*t made me remember Mrs. Snyder from the Ross Corners Church during the late 1970s. She was married, mother of four children, and the two youngest were still in elementary school. She had contracted cancer. The church earnestly prayed for her. The hope was that God would heal her and allow her to continue to raise her children, particularly the two younger ones: Mark and Mary. God did grant a reprieve and allowed her approximately two more years before calling her home. I had hoped that the healing would have been for a longer-term but was glad for the extra time God had allowed that family to be together.

Bob Botkin

Also from that church was a man named Bob Botkin. Bob was an engineer with General Electric in the Aerospace division, in his late forties, a wonderful soul-winner, and a sold-out Christian. The church had earnestly prayed for Bob, but God took him home a few years later.

Over the years, there have been many other people with health issues that I had prayed for at the churches I attended. Also, there are people I have heard about that were outside the church (unsaved) with health issues and for whom seemingly no one was praying. In my mind, I had done an unscientific, qualitative type survey (the quality not the quantity of something, very general). I concluded that those in the church fared no better than those outside the church with respect to physical healings. What I observed, though, was that those trusting God were more at peace about their own passing. They displayed much less anxiety. I had been taught that God wants us to pray for each other. That God delights in our prayers, and we may possibly move the hand of God, by our prayers, to heal the sick person of their infirmity. We could not know with certainty that God's will is to heal or that God would, in fact, heal, but it is OK to ask for healing. We could not, however, expect healing to occur just because we asked for it. To be safe, we needed to ask for God's will to be done. Whether or not God so chooses to heal is God's business, not ours. God sees the whole picture and can make perfect choices for the edification and growth of individual believers. It may better serve God's purposes if an individual believer is not healed. That was my overall outlook regarding the responsibility to pray for the sick and what my expectation of God actually healing the sick should be. I recognize that healing related teaching is quite different from the salvation teaching in that same church. When we believe that Jesus is the Christ, the Savior of the world, sent to be our sacrifice for sin, and ask God to save us from our sins, then God saves us immediately. We do not have to wonder if it is God's will to save us, or if we need to wait and continue asking for salvation but never really knowing if God is going to grant salvation, and If God does grant salvation will that salvation be short term or long term?

In 1986, Karen and I moved to the San Francisco Bay area for work. After being raised in church and having attended a Christian college in the Bible belt, she felt like she was now on the mission field in California. Rarely did we hear English spoken outside of work and church. The church we settled into had a Christian day school and was doctrinally similar to the previous churches we had attended in New York, South Carolina, and Oklahoma. I had a work commute of approximately two hours each day. During this time, I would listen to Christian radio preaching and teaching programs. Many of the programs were more of the "faith" based variety. The speakers taught us that God wanted us to trust Him for more than just salvation. God has other promises that He would be delighted to give us if we ask Him and believe that He, the creator of the universe, would, in fact, joyfully give us those things that we needed. God had given us promises of physical healing in His word. Sometimes God's people would need to ask in faith personally or have someone of faith ask for their healing. God's desire is to grant healings and is pleased when his people trust and expect Him to heal, based on His promises and our faith to appropriate those promises. Medical Science is a help to people, but it is more desirable if, by our faith, God is then able to supply all our needs, including physical healings. These theological concepts were different from what I had previously and then currently been taught at the churches Karen and I attended. It sounded very exciting for God's people to have the ability to ask for and receive healings and therefore bring glory to God. By believing (trusting) God for those promises, any Christian could, in fact, appropriate (cause to happen/receive) healings from God.

People, in general, viewed sickness as a "bad" thing. Healing or the cessation of sickness was viewed as a "good" thing. They said that God viewed sickness as a "bad" thing. If one remained sick, they were not experiencing the blessing from God that He (God) so desired to give them. Christians should recognize that sickness or infirmity was supposed to be a very temporary event. If there was sin, they needed to deal with that first; then ask for their healing. To remain in a sickened or infirm state was not God's desire and showed there was either a lack of knowledge concerning God's plan for healing or a lack of faith, [belief or trust] in God to perform those healings. By my simple childlike faith of believing that God had sent Jesus into the World to save sinners from hell, then asking God to save me; and trusting that God did save me, I had appropriated (caused to happen, received) God's free gift of eternal life called salvation. With this salvation, I had been adopted into God's family, where I would spend eternity with Him in Heaven. I could never have this relationship with God severed by anything or anyone, including myself. God was holding me securely in the palm of His hand. Likewise, by simple childlike faith, they taught me that I could trust God and appropriate healings for myself and for others for whom I would pray. Usually, however, the sick or infirm person, if already a Christian, would need to have some measure of faith for God to perform the healing. The healing aspect just mentioned was a composite of the teachings I had received primarily from the radio preachers and generally not taught at the churches I attended. I was eager to see God working in this area of more complete trust, referred to as faith. There had to be the belief that God would honor His Word and perform the healings. If that were questioned, then there would be no faith and potentially no healing.

In 1989, several months before moving from California to Colorado, I felt impressed by God to pray for a man with a head injury. This man was a distant relative to a couple of our church members. Karen, Timmy, and baby Matthew had traveled to New York State for Christmas; I would join them there later. Despite an invitation from the pastor to spend the holiday with him and his family in California, I made an approximate 500-mile round trip to Reno, Nevada, to pray for this man, with the head injury and associated complications, for God to heal him. I hoped that eventually, I would hear of the results. The Intensive Care Unit (ICU) in Reno was different from any that I had ever visited, but I had not been too many. This ICU allowed visitors once every four hours at specific intervals, to visit for ten to fifteen minutes. Even though this man had not had a visitor that day, I was still required to wait almost two hours until the next four-hour interval occurred. He was semi-comatose and seemed delirious. I prayed for him and left, thanking God for the opportunity to have prayed for this man and the safety provided while I drove in snow over the mountain passes in a rear-wheel-drive car with summer tires.

I could never have this relationship with God severed by anything or anyone, including myself. God was holding me securely in the palm of His hand.

Later, I had heard that this man recovered enough to be moved to a home situation but still had challenges. I had hoped initially to hear a considerably more positive report, then later to hear of continued improvements.

Ken Fagan

After moving to Colorado in 1990, we joined the Tri-City Church. I remember praying for Ken Fagan, a heavy equipment operator in his forties. He had contracted leukemia and succumbed to it after approximately two years. Ken had stated to me that if God wanted to heal him, that would be OK, or if God wanted to take him home, he would be fine with that. It would be difficult for his family if God took him, but whatever God wanted to do would be OK with him. Ken just did not seem too concerned about what God was doing or what God was going to do. He seemed to have just turned the matter over to God and was not going to be stressed about it.

Usually, people desire to be healed if they have something to live for and if they believe their pain levels will diminish. Ken's attitude seemed to defy some of this logic. There was no question that he loved his family and was devoted to them, and they to him. Again, he stated to me that he would miss them, and he knew they would miss him. He was involved in the church activities, and he appeared to be well-liked. Why did he seem so unconcerned? Had his trust in God grown to a level that allowed or caused him to appear unconcerned? One thing was for sure; Ken Fagin was trusting God and at peace with Him!

Wendy Wasey

Also, during the early 1990s, I remember praying for Wendy Wasey. Wendy was married with three children living at home. Wendy was first diagnosed with breast cancer in 1989 and underwent a mastectomy. It was believed, at that time, that the cancer had been caught in time, and no further treatment was needed. It was early 1990 when Karen and I moved to Colorado and met Wendy at the Tri-City church. In late 1990, Wendy relapsed. As I remember, the church was praying very diligently for Wendy's healing. Karen and I also prayed for her. Wendy was another person I hoped God would use to show His omnipotent hand and heal her body. Whether it would be by God's intervention or man's intervention did not matter to me. Prior to the relapse, Wendy had acquired new health insurance and a new physician. After much testing was completed, the new doctor determined that the cancer had metastasized to the liver and had been there at the time of the original diagnosis but had not been found. Prayers continued for Wendy Wasey, and the continued hope was that God would grant this healing so that she could remain on earth as a wife and mother to her three children. She died August 14, 1991, from cancer and is now with the Lord in Heaven. Wendy no longer experiences the pain, sickness, and suffering she endured in her earthly body. Wendy's daughter Kim recently shared, "It took me many years to come to grips with what happened [to my mom] and why the [original] doctor didn't bother searching for answers! Unfortunately, by this time, it was too late, and the cancer was terminal. A lesson learned is never just take the doctor's word ... for it. If you aren't well, keep searching for answers! Thanks for remembering my mom."

Cinthy Midkiff

During 1999, Karen became a very close friend to Cinthy Midkiff. Cinthy, her husband, and two children moved back to the area from Kansas City and started attending Tri-City, where Cinthy's parents (Bill and Joan) attend. Early in 2001, Cinthy first became aware that something was not right. She sometimes had trouble speaking. She knew what she wanted to say but could not communicate it verbally. Cinthy was diagnosed as having a non-cancerous brain tumor that could have been growing for seventeen years. She underwent a six-hour brain surgery on March 6, 2002, at Colorado General Hospital. This surgery removed as much of the tumor as possible, approximately 99%. Cinthy did improve after the surgery; however, the tumor started to regrow. In 2004, she went to Loma Linda Hospital in California for proton therapy. Proton Therapy is a highly focused radiation proton beam that irradiates diseased tissue and is most often used in the treatment of cancer. The beam is very precise and stays focused on the tumor. It delivers only low-dose side effects to the surrounding tissue, causing less damage to the patient's body. This painless, non-invasive treatment allows patients to maintain their quality of life and resume normal activities more quickly when compared with other traditional radiation therapies. Cinthy did recover and was soon able to do things she used to do. Cinthy and her family decided to avoid chemotype therapies and instead use more natural nutritional-based therapies to control or suppress the growth of any existing or new tumors. Cinthy had attended a seminar and met a number of Chemo survivors. She felt that many of them reminded her of walking zombies, and she wanted to avoid that type of outcome. There was no proof that chemo would be effective on her type of brain tumor.

Cinthy's cancer did return, and in April of 2005, she was taken to the Burzynski Cancer Clinic in Houston, Texas. The founder of the clinic, Dr. Stanislaw Burzynski, a Polish immigrant, was trained as a biochemist and a physician. The treatment he developed involves a gene-targeted approach using non-toxic peptides and amino acids, known as antineoplastons. This clinic's belief is that every patient requires a unique treatment plan and that the "one size fits all" approach does not work. The treatments, based on the natural biochemical defense system of the body, are capable of combating cancer with minimal impact on healthy cells.

The strategy involves studying the patient's entire cancerous genome, analyzing some 24,000 genes to identify the abnormal genes. Then drugs and supplements are used in very specific formulations for each individual patient to target specific genes. The antineoplastons act as molecular switches. They turn off the oncogenes that cause cancer and turn on or activate the genes that fight cancer. Cinthy did receive the one-month cancer therapy regimen from the clinic as an outpatient. Cinthy was in a semi-comatose state, and her husband, father, and mother spent the month nursing, transporting, and learning to care for her, including administering intravenous treatments. During this month, Cinthy did have a lucid moment. Seeing and recognizing her husband, she said, "Bobby, I love you." Cinthy was transported back home to the Denver area.

She later became unresponsive and was admitted to Colorado General. Approximately one week later, Cinthy went home to be with the Lord, May 6, 2005.

Her dad would later share these memories. "Joan [her mom] and I stayed all night with her on May 5, and I shall never forget the moment I saw Cinthy's soul leave her body and knew she was gone." Nine days after Cinthy was born, she was placed in her (earthly) father's hands for him to completely care for her since her mother had to return to the hospital. Nine days after Cinthy's 46 birthday, she was placed in the hands of her Heavenly Father. "Many, many people across the nation prayed for her, and there were 750 people at her funeral. Cinthy never, never once complained the three years she fought the tumor. We always thought that we would beat the tumor, and we never gave up. In 2002, we did call for the [church] elders to lay hands and anoint her with oil for healing. We prayed that it was God's will for healing but wanted God's will and were willing to accept whatever was God's will... I know Cinthy, Joan, and I were in God's will when He chose to take her home. Sadly there came a day when I realized that Cinthy was not going to make it and that it was God's will to take her to Heaven, and therefore CINTHY IS ALIVE AND WELL AND WE WILL SEE HER AGAIN SOMEDAY!"

When asking Bill if he ever felt angry or let down by God for not healing Cinthy even though he had expected the healing, he replied with this answer, "After three years [of fighting the tumor], I had to accept that she was not going to make it. I had to accept that everything we tried was not going to work. I wished it would have been different. But I was not angry with God. I accepted it as His will."

From my personal exposure to Bill and Joan, I know there has been much disappointment over the loss of their daughter. When asking Bill how long it had been since Cinthy passed away, he immediately stated the number of years, months, and days it had been. It is something that he thinks about daily. How can it be that something so emotionally difficult as the hoping, believing, and trusting for this healing and then not experiencing healing did not lead to frustration and disappointment with God? Cinthy was also frustrated. Her dad provided this excerpt from her diary recorded on October 2, 2002. It was written less than seven months after the surgical removal of the brain tumor and immediately after the tumor was discovered to be growing again.

> *"I was disappointed, to say the least! I cried ... I feel so helpless. I've done what Dr. Ruby has recommended [nutritional approach] and drank my tea faithfully, and it [the tumor] has still grown. I know the Lord has reason for it coming back. I was hoping so badly for this chapter in my life to be behind me, but apparently, God has other plans. My story is not finished yet. He may want me to go thru radiation and Chemotherapy like the patients I talked to at the seminar. I could not relate to them because I hadn't gone thru radiation; maybe He will use me to reach them. Whatever He wants, I'm willing to go through. I've been praying that God will do anything He chooses to see my family walk with God; if this is how He plans to accomplish it, I TRUST HIM COMPLETELY."* The caps are Cinthy's.

Although frustrated and disappointed, Cinthy was not letting those setbacks derail her trust in God. She recognized that God has an ongoing plan and that she was a part of that plan. God's plan may have been to use her cancer to draw her family closer to Him, and she was willing to be a part of that plan even if God allowed her own health to be sacrificed.

I, too, shared frustration. Never before or since have I prayed so intently and with the expectation for a person's healing. I believed

God wanted Cinthy healed; I believed God wanted many people involved in the praying for her needed healing. God could use this healing to build the faith of Christians by building their trust in God and His promises, having witnessed her healing. Christians could know with certainty that when they needed healing, they could appropriate that healing by asking and believing. They could point to Cinthy's healing and know that God had either caused or allowed it. Christians could know that when they exercised their faith and belief, through prayer, that God would hear and perform healings.

Karen and I had prayed for Cinthy regularly. Before Cinthy went to the Burzynski clinic in 2005, Karen and I went to Cinthy's home with a meal, to help out, and to pray. Cinthy was losing the use of one of her arms due to the tumor's regrowth. Karen and I laid our hands on Cinthy, establishing a point of contact, and prayed for her healing. From that point in time, God could act on the faith/belief that was evident in at least one of us and start the healing pro-

> *Whatever He wants, I'm willing to go through. I've been praying that God will do anything He chooses to see my family walk with God...*

cess. "The effectual fervent prayer of a righteous man availeth much," James 5:16. We did not need to keep asking, but now believed that God would start the healing process, or continue the process if already started, and we could now "receive" or witness the healing.

Because we had asked in faith, God would now honor His word and "do it." "If you ask anything in my name, I will do it," John 14:14 ESV. "Ask and it will be given you," Luke 11:9a. "For every one that asketh receiveth," Luke 11:10a. We were asking for a "good" thing, the healing of Cinthy's body, one of God's dear children. "If a son [or daughter] shall ask bread of any of you that is a father, will he give him a stone? Or if he ask a fish will he for a fish, give him a serpent? Or if he shall ask an egg, will he offer him a scorpion? If you then being evil, know how to give "good" gifts unto your children: How much more shall your heavenly Father give the Holy Spirit to them that ask Him?" Luke 11:11-13. These verses tell us that we as fathers (by extension – parents), despite the fact that we are sinners, still know how to (and do) provide "good" gifts to our children. The examples use food. Food is requested by the son (and by extension – children) bread, fish, egg. It was absurd to think that stones, serpents, and scorpions would be offered as substitutes for edible human food. In our culture, parents would be cited for abuse if their children were not given proper food. In like manner, if children are sick and require medical care, parents again are held responsible for withholding the medical attention that would allow the healing of their children's bodies. Withholding proper food and medical attention are considered "bad" things.

We had asked, believed, and I had expected that now was the time for God actually to perform the healing in Cinthy's body and for God to receive the glory. Cinthy's health continued to decline. My continued belief was that God was still going to heal her body, albeit in the twelfth hour. Then God took her home to Heaven! My next thought was that maybe God's plan is to resurrect Cinthy sometime prior to burial, similar to the raising of Lazarus. The funeral service was the largest attended funeral I had ever witnessed. During the service, my continued expectation was that God was going to raise her up, assuming His plan had been to heal her. My silent prayer was a reminder to God that we had asked for Cinthy's healing. Time was running out; soon, she would be buried, and it then would be too late for the physical healing of her earthly (mortal) body. Cinthy was buried. We look forward to seeing her in her glorified body in Heaven, where there is no more pain, sickness, or suffering. Those words are comforting, and I believe them to be completely true. However, my faith was shaken with respect to my expectation of God performing physical healings. I did not question the authorship of God's Word, but something was not right. Could my understanding and personal interpretation of God's Word be that far off from the actual meaning of God's Word in the area of healing? If my understanding was correct that God was obligating Himself to His Word to perform or fulfill the promises contained in His Word, why then did Cinthy not receive her healing? Some would say, "God does not have to do anything He does not want to do." I would say God is not a liar. Romans 4:4, He is truthful and can be trusted. God will fulfill or honor His Word. Questions remained. Could my understanding of God's Word concerning healing be inaccurate? Could God's Word really be teaching something vastly different from my simple interpretation concerning healing? How could God be using this event in my life and in the lives of others to bring honor to Himself if there was a seeming contradiction? Were my views regarding healing being tempered?

Amy Bixby

Jon Bixby had been pastoring a church in Steamboat Springs, Colorado. He and his wife Amy moved to the Denver area with their children and became active with our church. In October 2008, Amy found out two things in one week: she was pregnant with their seventh child and had stage III metastatic breast cancer. No family history of this was present. Amy was a healthy person and did not possess any evident risk factors. Being pregnant is the worst possible complication to cancer treatment and survival.

The medical recommendation was to terminate the pregnancy and immediately start chemotherapy, or both Amy and the baby would die. Jon and Amy received much information to help make some complex decisions. Jon and Amy were strongly opposed to having an abortion, wanting to continue the pregnancy, and trust God for the outcome. Amy wrote in her blog, "The Lord has made Himself so near to us during the very difficult moments of the last week. Please pray that I will keep my focus on Him; everything else is too overwhelming. Our church and friends have leapt to our assistance. We are amazed at the care and love that everyone is offering to us."

Amy went to see another physician for a second opinion. Jon, Amy, and this physician agreed to a treatment plan that would allow the pregnancy to continue. An oncologist told them that in Denver, a couple of years prior, a new kind of chemo was developed for pregnant mothers. It was still experimental, but they were in the right place to receive it. She could not have radiation until after the baby's birth. The baby was to be taken as early in the third trimester as safely possible for the baby, and then Amy was immediately to start the intense chemotherapy treatments for cancer. The Susan G. Komen Foundation (the pink ribbon people) agreed to provide funding for this high-risk case.

Amy wanted life to be as normal as possible for the children. She shared in her blog many humorous stories like this. That November, the resident tooth fairy slept late and had to recruit help getting treats to the de-toothed children, for three Bixby children had recently lost teeth. Many people in the church began to help: people brought meals, ladies - two at a time - began to clean the house each week, some sent gifts and cards, one man took pictures of the family together, others picked up laundry each week and returned it ready to be put away, and Benjamin, a teenager, made cakes for them that year for their birthdays - almost once a month. I, Karen, was struggling with the thought that I should offer to homeschool their children since I had many years of experience and only had Benjamin at home. I did not want the children to miss school or have to begin at a traditional school when their mother's and baby brother's lives were in such danger. But the thought of adding five more to our home was overwhelming. After a few days of prayer, I called Amy. She told me that Diana, a lady in the church, had already offered to homeschool the children with her own. Amy suggested I call Diana as she needed help. Diana and I worked out that I would homeschool the one Bixby child that was not in the same grade as Diana's children as well as help her oldest son, a friend of Benjamin, with math. My step of faith in responding to God's prompting ended up being a blessing and just the amount I could do.

Every doctor and medical person to whom Jon and Amy talked (traditional and alternative) confirmed that she needed to have a mastectomy soon. The biggest concern was that Amy could miscarry due to the anesthesia required. Amy wrote, "Many people are praying. That is the best of all. Until you are facing something like this, you don't know how good it is to know that others are praying."

The surgery went well, and the doctor reported that they got all the tumor, but fifteen lymph nodes tested positive for cancer. Amy's risk of cancer returning was now about 50%, and if the cancer returned, it would probably be fatal. Ten days later, Amy entered in her blog, "I bet some of you are wondering how I can continue to trust in a God whom I believe arranged this cancer and its complicating factors." "Everything I understand and control could be contained in a drop of water compared to the ocean of knowledge and power that God has. Also, I have become absolutely convinced of God's love for me." "When those 2 points of faith are combined, what's left to worry about?"

About a week later, on December 1, Jon posted, "I can't help but be renewed in my commitment to give thanks in everything. One [of] the realities that has been impressed on our hearts is that this experience is not just about us. It is about all who surround us and observe, with whatever degree of curiosity or care, what God is doing. Amy and I have been filled with a passion to reflect on what

God has been doing for us. For those who know Him, our prayer has been that somehow through our experience, you might see that God is everything that He claims to be. It may be impossible to experience outside of the fire – but if we can somehow serve as surrogates and share with you even a small taste of the greatness of God, that would thrill our hearts. For some of you, we pray obsessively that our experience would bring to the surface of your conscience those pesky questions about life, death, God, and His love. We love all of you – and want to communicate that if there is something worse than facing death – it is facing death without the one true God."

That December, Amy had the opportunity to speak to the ladies at Tri-City. Her topic, given to her months before, was *Peace*. Amy appreciated the opportunity to tell of the wonderful comfort of God's peace surrounding her heart and mind. Philippians 4:7, "And the peace of God, which passeth all understanding, shall keep your hearts and minds through Christ Jesus."

Chemo began on December 18; it was to happen every twenty-one days if her blood counts were high enough. We were praying that God would protect the baby from the side effects of the chemo. People the Bixbys did not even know reached out to them, provided help, and prayed. In January, the family learned that the baby was a boy. His growth was not slowed down by the chemo; he was ahead of schedule. The oncologist had a different opinion than the obstetrician about when the surgery to deliver their boy should be. Amy wrote, "This appears to be a competition between my health and our son's. God has shown that he can and will guide circumstances that are entirely beyond our ability to handle. I don't know why he has let things happen the way they have, but I'm thankful for years of experience that back up what the Bible says about trusting him." "Trust in the LORD with all thine heart; and lean not unto thine own understanding. In all thy ways acknowledge him, and he shall direct thy paths." Proverbs 3:5-6.

Amy blogged in February 2009, "I've had so much difficulty breathing over the past week that we were beginning to get worried. The blood work showed that I've become very anemic." Her doctor scheduled her for another round or two of chemo so that three months would not lapse without any chemo. This gave the baby time to grow and then Amy to recover for a month after the c-section. The technicians assigned to do a CAT scan were uneasy about doing the doctor-ordered scan on a pregnant woman. They talked to the doctor, told Amy all the risks for the baby, and then proceeded. It was a difficult time not to worry. The scan showed no tumors nor any site where the cancer was recognizably growing. After other test results, she was told that her health was reasonably good; she was less anemic, and her lungs have some scarring. Two days later, she was feeling nauseous and exhausted and having trouble breathing. The doctors are now planning for the baby to be born around Mother's Day.

April 1 entry is, "Next week we meet with the neonatologist and tour the neonatal intensive care unit. I'm looking forward to having my list of questions answered. If you could look at my list, you'd never guess I've already had six children. There are so many details about this situation that are new to me that I almost feel like an inexperienced mom again. And I'll probably act like one too." Gilead was born on May 10, 2009, Mother's Day at 9:06 in the morning. Jon wrote, "He had a healthy voice," and was "18.25 inches long and weighed in at 5 lbs. 2 oz. That was an exciting answer to many prayers." Jon and Amy chose the name Gilead from the verse in the Bible about a balm in Gilead, liking its meaning – a monument of testimony. This healthy little boy is a testimony to God's love and care. Gilead continued to grow, develop, and gain weight while Amy healed and started more intense chemotherapy drugs along with radiation.

Because the Susan G. Komen Foundation provided grants to cover all medical costs for Amy and Gilead, Amy agreed to an interview; the story of her and Gilead was in a local magazine, *5280,* and on Channel 9 news. "I can't believe how much has changed since last October. My family continues to grow up even though I sometimes feel like my life has been placed on hold. I still can't believe we have another precious baby," Amy recorded in July. Just as the last round of chemo was finishing, a test showed some spots on her liver, but after a PET scan, it was determined that they are not cancerous, another answer to numerous prayers! Now she had only radiation left lasting through August.

On September 2, 2009, Amy wrote in her blog, "When I finished radiation almost two weeks ago, I had no idea that one of the most uncomfortable stretches of treatment was still ahead. My skin was red from the radiation, and my arm felt a little tight, but I wasn't experiencing any pain. The radiation oncologist commented that my skin had held up remarkably well during this process but warned that it would get worse for the next ten days or so before it began getting better. I'm glad she warned me, or I would have been very worried. By the following Tuesday, my skin was blistering, peeling, and very painful. The pain spread to my muscles and deep inside the tissues; I've taken more Advil over the past ten days than I did after either the mastectomy or the c-section. Of course, I haven't been in bed recovering from the radiation like I was after the surgeries, and I'm sure my constant activity has only aggravated the radiated area."

I sometimes feel like my life has been placed on hold.

"Less than a week after the radiation was finished, I found another enlarged lymph node just below my collarbone. The oncologist had me come in right away, but she didn't have any definite answers. She hopes I am just reacting to the radiation but can't promise that's the case. My next appointment is near the end of September, and we'll be making some decisions about more biopsies and tests."

"I've been struggling with fear that the cancer is making a comeback already. But it's been strengthening to constantly remind myself that life on earth is temporary, even in the best of health, and that God has already proven Himself loving and trustworthy."

"The biopsy results came back negative." Life in the Bixby home was getting closer to normal. Homeschooling was going well; Amy's hair grew back in.

Jon spoke at Tri-City on March 6, 2011, about his thoughts back on this time in their lives. Included here are excerpts from his talk.

"Be careful what you pray for. As Christians, we have sung these words, "God make me Christ-like whatever it takes." Those could be dangerous words. God might answer your prayers."

"As a child, I read the book *The Martyr of the Catacombs*. I prayed to the Lord that God would give the grace and the privilege of earning a martyr's crown. He can now retract that request. I'm not interested in suffering that way."

"More than one time as an adult, we have prayed to God to allow our children to personally see and experience God's provision when there were no other means. I think of the Jew's exodus from Egypt. The first-generation children that lived during Moses' time actually saw and experienced God's provision when there were no other means available: the plagues, the parting of the sea, forty-year supply of manna, shoes that did not wear out, etc. The second-generation children that outlived Joshua only heard what God had done but never personally experienced it. They started to wander from God. The third generation did not hear all that God had done and stumbled around in the dark."

"As an MK [Missionary Kid], I saw God work in supernatural ways of provision and protection. Today, when reviewing what I had witnessed God doing when I was a kid, I scratch my head, saying, "Did God really do that?" I did not want my children to be second-generation Christians, only hearing the stories of what God did. I wanted God to allow my children to see God's power first hand, where only God had the solution and the answer."

"Just prior to Amy's cancer being detected, we desperately wanted to see God work in the hearts of our children. I felt like I was stuck in a rut. I wanted to rekindle the flames and see God miraculously answer prayers. If there is healing, it will come from God's hand; it's not about which tool is used; it's about the Healer. We pray to God, 'Take us to that place where we trust You!'"

"Nothing God has promised is untrue. God is always there. Cancer is a horrible thing, but God used it in the lives of the children to show His provision. God provided:

- Cancer treatments and care and additional grants from Susan G. Komen Foundation,
- Oncological/obstetrical care team for safe delivery,
- Family and church family support: financial, domestic, childcare, etc.,
- Financial gifts from strangers,
- Alternate treatment in Arizona, treatments covered, house and utilities – no charge,
- And job opportunities."

Even for things they did not think about ahead of time, God provided! "Philippians 4:6, 'Be anxious for nothing, but in everything by prayer and supplication, with thanksgiving, let your requests be made known to God; and the peace of God, which surpasses all understanding, will guard your hearts and minds through Christ Jesus.' Supplication – the noun form is supplicant, a beggar, totally dependent on someone else to live. It's been a very humbling experience because we were totally relying on God using people and organizations to supply all our needs."

"In Arizona, the kids wrote on an outside chest of drawers. 'This is our clubhouse, made for our entertainment while we are stuck here in Arizona. It is never to be used wrong. We will use it for the glory of our heavenly Father, who, for some unknown reason, has placed us here. May we live to His honor and glory.' To me, there is nothing more precious than seeing my children view God this way."

"I Peter 1:7, 'That the trial of your faith, being much more precious than of gold that perisheth, though it be tried with fire, might be found unto praise and honour and glory at the appearing of Jesus Christ.' The trial of your faith is more precious than gold. I encourage everyone to embrace your trials; do not shun them. You may be surprised when God puts you in a trial, thinking this is what happens to other people! Why me? Do you try to bury or reject the trial? I could have said, 'God, I'm serving You; I've got seven kids, and you are going to take my wife?'"

"God makes you realize that the trial is an investment for God's glory. Then we see the trial as a privilege God has allowed us to have. The trial is a wonderful thing to go through. It should be embraced, not rejected."

On January 28, 2010, Amy entered in her blog, "Last Sunday morning, as I was sitting in church, I watched my wrist swell up, and a slight pain that had been there for weeks spread over my hand and arm. My oncologist looked at the area and was very concerned. Her instructions were to go straight to the emergency room if the swelling and redness got worse. Or if the Augmentin she had prescribed did not begin to improve

> *"...the trial is an investment for God's glory. Then we see the trial as a privilege God has allowed us to have. The trial is a wonderful thing to go through. It should be embraced, not rejected."*

the problem in a few hours. It did get worse over the next 24 hours, so I went, rather reluctantly, to the emergency room."

"After a brief examination and review of recent medical history, the doctor decided to admit me. Evidently, I have a kind of staff infection called merca (MRSA – antibiotic-resistant staph). It was caused by some unknown intrusion into my left arm, which has been weakened by the lack of lymph nodes. I got a round of IV antibiotics and some hefty oral medication. The infection seems to be responding well to the treatments, so (much to my relief, I was discharged yesterday evening with prescriptions for bit-gun antibiotics."

Gilead had been healthy and doing well until that February; Amy wrote in her blog, "Gilead began to show slight cold symptoms on Friday. On Sunday morning, we noticed he seemed to be struggling to breathe, so we took him to an urgent care clinic near us." "He was admitted into Children's Hospital on Sunday evening. Monday morning, he was moved to PICU since he was not responding to breathing treatments." "His oxygen levels kept dropping into the 70's so he was kept at Children's until he could hold his own oxygen levels up. That happened Thursday night for the first time – he didn't need oxygen all night. He was very much improved in every other way." "We are glad to be home. We're all sleeping better and hope to be done with all this drama for a while."

The entry of March 12, 2010, is "I found another lump under my arm in February, so on Monday afternoon, I went to the oncologist to have it checked out. She was able to get me right in for an ultrasound and then (amazingly) a biopsy too. Usually, they would have required three separate appointments. Then she shooed me on over to the emergency room for a round of tests on my heart and lungs." "In the emergency room, a series of tests were performed on my heart and lungs, all of which came back resoundingly normal." "I'm still having pressure in my chest and a cough, but now the assumption is that my heart, or the muscles on the chest wall, have been affected by the chemotherapy or the radiation. From what I've learned, these symptoms may come and go over the years."

Amy blogged October 27, "Last Friday, I had a routine visit to the oncologist's office for blood work. I also had my annual mammogram. Dr. Cook (the oncologist) told me that my blood work looked better than it ever had since I've been her patient. My red blood cell counts have doubled, and otherwise, the lab results were beautiful." "Dr. Schoeder (the doctor who handles mammograms) scared me when he said more imaging needed to be done." "Monday morning, Dr. Cook called me with further results from the blood work. A tumor marker (that's the blood count that indicates a growing tumor) has risen from about 30 to over 200. Barring a mistake in the blood work, that means the cancer has returned. I will be having a PET scan at 8:00 a.m. tomorrow." "Chemotherapy is her recommended course of treatment, but I'm not interested in doing that again."

Two days later, Amy wrote, "The news we got this afternoon was not good. The oncologist reviewed the PET scan results with us." "The scan showed that the cancer has spread to my liver, spine (T2), hips, and possibly my ovaries. The suggested treatments offer a 10% survival for 5 years. There is no hope offered for a cure. Isn't it astounding that being deathly ill, I feel better than I've felt for years? I've continued to make my spinach-lettuce-carrot juice three times each day and eat mostly raw food." "I have not given up, but I am constantly aware of the probability that I won't live for very long. I pray for a miracle or for some unsung yet successful treatment, but I'm ready to accept moving to the next life. I ask all of you to pray for my family. I've got the easier load to carry right now."

Neither life nor death shall ever
From the Lord His children sever;
Unto them His grace He showeth,

And their sorrows all He knoweth.
Lisa Sandell – translated from Swedish by
Ernst W. Olson

O the deep, deep love of Jesus,
Love of every love the best!
'Tis an ocean full of blessing,
'Tis a haven giving rest!
O the deep, deep love of Jesus-
And it lifts me up to glory,
For it lifts me up to Thee!"
O the Deep, Deep Love of Jesus, by S. Trevor Francis

Amy said, "I completed nine rounds of chemotherapy, twenty-five radiation treatments, and took Tamoxifen until October 2010. After the fifth round of chemotherapy and various other treatments and tests, Gilead Victor was born six weeks early on Mother's Day, 2009. He is a healthy little guy and a joy to us all. In October 2010, tests showed that the cancer had returned in my liver and bones. This is now considered stage IV, terminal cancer."

The Bixbys decided to move temporarily to Arizona for some natural cancer treatments for Amy that were having success with others. God provided for them in incredible ways: a home, Jon's work, assistance, gifts, etc. At the clinic, they administered different medicines and treatments that had beneficial consequences. Amy took advantage of many chances to witness there and to encourage others in the treatment center. She experienced a variety of side effects from the treatment but saw much improvement, including her tumor markers steadily going down.

As Amy finished her treatment and prepared to return to Colorado in February 2011, she entered in her blog, "My blood work results were disappointing today; my tumor markers remained basically the same – 76. We were really hoping for another drastic drop, but we knew it wasn't guaranteed. Through this past week, the Lord has reminded me constantly through a variety of sources that He always works perfectly, and I can continue to trust Him without reserve when things don't go the way I thought I wanted them to. What peace. I hope and pray that every one of you can have the same peace. The difficulties it usually takes to learn this are worth it."

"I've been doing a lot of reading lately. I won't do a review of the following books, but they both deal with trusting our Shepherd and King and have been a powerful blessing to me. I hope some of you will enjoy them too, <u>Hinds Feet On High Places</u> by Hannah Hunard and <u>Edge of Eternity</u> by Randy Alcorn."

By April, Amy wrote, "My blood work all came back entirely normal – even the tumor markers, which are now 24! My oncologist told me she was surprised to see that. However, I still have active cancer. I have a new lesion on my liver, but it is small."

"The other lesions in my liver have either continued to shrink or have stabilized. One of the lesions no longer shows any abnormal metabolic activity, which means that although the lesion is still there, it is no longer considered malignant. The lesions in my hip bones also no longer show abnormal activity. The lesions in my spine have not changed since my last scan. We praise God for these results."

On June 29, 2011, Amy blogged, "I haven't been feeling as well lately. Most days, I have periods of nausea, and I've been losing weight again." "Meanwhile, while we hope for healing, I realize that's probably not what's happening. As I've watched this year's beautiful springtime, I've enjoyed imagining what this would look like if it were all truly perfect. And I have such an anticipation about what God has prepared for His children. I feel like I've been given the most incredible travel package, but my family won't be able to join me yet. I feel a little bad for not being more hesitant to begin my eternity." "Although this summer has not been the smooth sailing I would have asked for, we have been having a good time. I sat down last week with the summer's schedule and the master calendar. Cancer doesn't stop swimming, soccer, art or piano lessons, dentists, orthodontists, pediatricians, employers, youth groups, or libraries. And the kids are involved in it all. I'm glad their lives are rolling along – it's a pleasure to watch them grow. In July, we may be able to enjoy a special week in the mountains, and I'm looking forward to that possibility."

Three days later, an entry said, "Thank you for your prayers. Amy's tumor markers have jumped, and her health is rapidly declining. Hospice has been called in, and Amy is anticipating her journey Home. During this time, we would ask you to pray:

1. That God would be merciful to Amy;
2. That He would give strength, comfort, and peace to Jon, Amy, and the children; and
3. That He would be honored and glorified in the dark days ahead. That His light would be clearly seen by all who come into contact with the family. That people would be compelled to ask the 'reason of the hope' that lies within us."

Amy made one final post four days later, "Most of you probably thought I had posted my last update, and I thought I had too. Last week there were days when I was sure I wouldn't live 'till the end of the day, although I can't describe what's going on as physical pain. My body is beginning to shut down. We were able to find a couple of simple ways to relieve the toxic buildup in my body, and although I can still feel that I am quickly coming to the end of my life here on earth, my eyes and skin are no longer yellow, I can think very clearly, the swelling I was beginning to have has gone away, my nausea is somewhat decreased, and I can eat and drink a little. My oncologist said that as long as we can keep the toxin drained and keep a little food in me, this process will be eased considerably. One thing that has helped has been ionic foot baths. I've seen those things advertised and thought they were a bunch of baloney, but I felt immediate relief when I had one."

"I began having a marked decline at the end of May." "I began having trouble with regular nausea and could not chew my raw food without getting sick. The oncologist couldn't see why I would be having these problems since my blood work was showing normal results, and my liver ultrasound didn't show anything new. She scheduled a PET scan. Just last week, she called me to say that my labs were not as good as she had thought. A portion of them had been signed by another doctor on the team, and she had not seen that part. But my tumor markers had quadrupled in May, and my liver enzymes were messed up. I felt relieved in a way to know that what I was experiencing had an explanation – even though it was the cancer. The PET scan was canceled at my request." "Once this process starts, only God could stop or reverse it, and He doesn't usually choose to do so."

"I realized right away that we had entered the final phase of my life, and I am very, very ready for it. I've wished, as I've faced the surprising battles of the last few weeks, that someone could tell me what to expect, what I might struggle with, what to be prepared for. I'm so accustomed to researching and preparing for what is ahead. But people don't come back from the dead to guide us, and Jesus Christ is the only one who has done it perfectly anyways. So I'm glad to say I have that Someone I need, and He is daily making Himself more dear to me. I truly cannot wait to see Him."

...I do want to share some of my experience in this valley of the shadow of death...

"All that said, I do want to share some of my experience in this valley of the shadow of death before it's too late. I want to acknowledge the struggles and let you know that God has over-come them. I want to tell all of you that He is doing and will do the same for you. Whether or not you see, it is between you and God, but I want to shout from the rooftops that if you will just believe Him, even though you can't understand now, even though some things hurt now, He will never truly hurt you. The pain we feel is a reminder that He is making it more than better – He's redeeming things so perfectly that the pleasure He is preparing for me is beyond my comprehension, and so, even the pain is a grand evidence of His grace."

"I have been blind-sided by some of my battles since the end of May. I went through a few days of being terrified that what I had placed my faith in was not real, that I had missed the truth somehow. God took my heart, my eyes, and my mind and made me see how everything I have learned about Him, everything that has become dear and a comfort to me, is reinforced in every single area of our lives. He is constantly showing us His truth through what He gives us – the earth, people, and especially His Word. And suddenly, all those seeming contradictions we struggle with, all the whys, the unlikely reconciling of the effects of evil with the omniscient good, all those questions about ultimate truth, popped into focus. That is not the end. God has been preparing for what comes next. And if trouble is part of the preparation, then I can view it as painful training, but not as ultimately powerful evil."

"Another difficulty was the weight of my regrets. Everyone who knows me would say that I've lived a good life. And I have. I have been faithful to my husband; I haven't abandoned myself to drugs, I tried to do what's good for others, I've gone to church regularly, I've prayed and read my Bible, I've invested in my children, I've striven to honor my parents, I've apologized when I was wrong. But it's not enough. *It's not enough.* My regrets were overwhelming me. Why did I yell at the kids? Why did I rip at my husband? Why didn't I invest more in that lady? Why did I say those cutting things? Why didn't I just resolve that bitterness I was carrying? As well as I lived my life, it wasn't anywhere near good enough. And the weight is heavy because no, there isn't time to re-do or fix. Jesus Christ took my memory and reminded me of the Scripture that my mother and others have poured into it. "Truly, I tell you, he who hears my word, and believes on Him who sent me, has everlasting life, and shall not come into condemnation, but is passed from death into life." John 5:25 "For I am persuaded, that neither death, nor life, nor angels, nor principalities, nor powers, nor things present, nor things to come, nor height, nor depth, nor any other creature, shall be able to separate us from the love of God which is in Christ Jesus our Lord." (Romans 8:38-39) "There is therefore now no condemnation to them which are in Christ Jesus." (Romans 8:1) These Scripture reminders washed over me and reminded me that Jesus has taken care of all my regrets for me." "I thought of the people who have regrets that we all recognize for what they are – big, ugly, havoc-wreaking, self-centered, world-altering mistakes. How do you deal with your regrets when you get to where I am? Because you will be here. The most healthy diet in the world will not help you avoid this moment. Look at God's word and be comforted even more deeply than I have been. You also can have no condemnation in Christ Jesus. He doesn't care how bad you or others think your mistakes are. Any mistake of any size is enough to separate you from God in your death, but no mistake of any size is enough to keep Christ from rescuing you just as He has done for me."

"As I've become more and more unable to handle what have been my responsibilities, I have struggled viciously with giving up control. I am ashamed to say how many times in the last few days, I have lost control of my temper as my duties were handled by someone else or not handled at all. I've felt panicked that I won't be able to prepare my family for what's coming, to live life without me. I have dragged my family through this emotional rollercoaster of trying to control. But God is getting a hold of my fears and helping me to trust Him – that whatever He allows during this time is part of my preparation and the preparation of those around me to enjoy Him. My house and family do not have to be handled my way in order to accomplish God's goals." "I've thought often of John Bunyan's *Pilgrim's Progress*. That man must have lived in the valley of the shadow for a long time in order to be able to describe it so well. His description of Christian's soul-scraping struggles and fears, and then victory, is the most accurate picture of what's been raging inside me that I can think of. I'm so thankful that ultimate victory is waiting."

"I am aware that many people from different perspectives read my blog. I have atheist, agnostic, Hindu, Jain, Wiccan, Mormon, Jewish, Buddhist, Christian, and wildly searching friends and acquaintances. I don't know the spiritual persuasions of many of you. But I know this. You will all face what I am facing now. I want for every one of you to be blessed with the peace and confidence that Christ has given me. I wish that everyone could see during their whole lives what I am seeing so clearly now. God loves us all so completely. His plan has never been to destroy us but to redeem us and all of His creation perfectly. There is another someone who hates us completely because we are the creation of his Enemy, and he never stops trying to deceive and destroy us as long as we are on this earth. Christ has offered the solution, but we have such a hard time trusting that He truly is the way. We are afraid that if He even is who He claims to be, He is just waiting to slap us into judgment, or at best, to take us to a

> *I want for every one of you to be blessed with the peace and confidence that Christ has given me.*

place where we will sit around and sing for eternity. (Sorry, but singing has never been one of my great pleasures, although I do love the words to songs. So I had a hard time getting excited about that view of Heaven.) He tells us so clearly what He wants for us, yet for some reason, we usually don't see it. But it's there, and you will see it too. I hope you will embrace it when you do, that you will search for it when you don't, that you will plead with God to prepare you for eternity with Him. Eternity is real, and you don't want to live it without God and His redemption of all your mistakes. You don't want to miss what is waiting for those who choose to trust God's love. For God so loved the world, that He gave His only begotten Son, that whosoever believes in Him should not perish but have everlasting life, John 3:16."

On August 19, 2011, Jon wrote, "Finally Home, Amy crossed the river very gently at 6:55 AM MDT. Praise God for His grace to her and to us."

Before her passing, Amy had help from some friends to make videos. One was for her family to watch after she was gone, and one to the church. I was thankful for those who used their talents to help fulfill Amy's wishes. The one played at her service was a blessing to many.

Amy's prolific and humorous blog is at http://amycaldwellbixby.blogspot.com. We look forward to reading the book that Jon said he has plans to write with more details, thoughts, things he learned, and what God has done.

Debbie Robbins

Karen and I met Debbie Robbins in early 1990 at the Tri-City church, then located in Arvada, Colorado. She was the church pianist and wife to Pastor Larry, the music pastor. They had two children: a daughter and a son. Debbie wrote and directed children's choirs, and her smile, sense of humor, and her laugh/cackle were both enjoyable and humorous.

It was late in September 2011 when we heard the news that Debbie had developed pancreatic cancer. Below are excerpts from Pastor Larry's journal entitled, "I Think I Can Help You," A testimony of the sovereignty of God through the valley of pancreatic cancer. It is written by Pastor Larry and is used with permission. The full copy may be downloaded at https://smile.amazon.com/ Think-Can-Help-You-ebook/dp/B006ZMCAMS/ref=smi_ www_rco2_go_smi_g3905707922?_encoding=UTF8&%2AVer-sion%2A=1&%2Aentries%2A=0&ie=UTF8

While vacationing in early Sept 2011, Debbie first noticed some discomfort and thought she might be "experiencing some gall bladder related problems." An ultrasound test was completed, and the results were given that day: more tests needed, "We see no problem with the gall bladder, but there might be a problem with the pancreas." Pastor Larry states, "The very mention of the word pancreas brings shivers to our family, as Debbie's brother Bill is a ten-year pancreatic cancer survivor himself – another miracle in the family already!" Pastor Larry did research on his own and determined the problem is likely pancreatitis – an inflammation or irritation of the pancreas. He was confident that everything would be fine with a prescription antibiotic to fight off pancreatitis. Later Debbie had a CT scan that revealed "a mass on her pancreas." A needle biopsy was scheduled then canceled by Debbie for fear that cancer cells could be released into other areas of her body. After conferring with other knowledgeable people about this decision, she immediately was comforted and sensed an overwhelming peace from the Lord. Unknown to Debbie and Pastor Larry, at the time, was that this cancellation actually moved the medical treatment process forward by perhaps two weeks. The timing of this was another evidence to them of God's sovereign hand working on their behalf. Despite the feelings of emptiness and despair, the two of them shared; they started to process the news. Pastor Larry stated, "Each day is filled with more dialog with friends and family as to what course would be the most advantageous should the mass turn out to be cancerous."

Understand at this point, we have been in ministry for more than thirty-five years. I have also been a police chaplain for well over a dozen years. I have dealt with major trauma! Within our own families, we have faced the cancer issue with at least four different members. Debbie herself has helped in the care of her brother through cancer surgery and recovery. She spent many days and weeks alongside her mother's bedside as she battled cancer. We know the pattern. We know the complications and the painful stages of development both physically and emotionally.

Now we have to decide for ourselves. Do we participate in chemotherapy? Might we agree to radiation therapy? Also in the equation are numerous friends who have successfully chosen to take different paths of alternative treatments – natural, immune system strengthening programs. Ultimately, as we have already experienced the previous week, we must (1) carefully consider the options, allow the Lord to bring into our path those who might further inform and educate us – good counsel. And then, (2) give time and meditation to the Lord and His word, praying and seeking a peace about what course we should take, and how we should proceed.

Wednesday, September 28. Our anticipated meeting with Dr. Mehan, the surgeon, arrives. The doctor takes more than forty-five minutes to carefully show us the CT scan photos, which reveal the mass in the tail of Debbie's pancreas - of significant size. He also explains the "cloudy area" surrounding the pan-creas, which in all likelihood is cancer that has metastasized into the tissue. A couple of lymph nodes nearby also seem to be somewhat enlarged, but that is really inconclusive. There is a possibility that the cloudy area is only inflamed tissue and not cancerous. After all the bleak prognosis, and explanation of how the surgical team at the hospital has reviewed Debbie's case, he pauses and then says, "I think I can help you." My immediate thoughts were, "Well, I should think so! Getting that tumor out is bound to help!" The underlying meaning of the doctor's statement has only become clear to me over the past 12 hours. We leave the office with new anxieties. Cancer is likely. It may have already begun to spread. How much time do we have to prepare for surgery?

What is happening? Deb and I are now in the midst of "white-water rapids" as we descend, tossed around now with abso-lutely no previous warning. Only three weeks ago, we were enjoying the Sight and Sound production of Noah in Branson, Missouri! How were we to know we were about to face an over-whelming flood of our own! Unbelievably, it was only a couple of hours later that we received the call." "You are scheduled for surgery next Monday morning at 7:30 AM." Again the thought of, "How can all this be happening so quickly?" con-sumes us! With calls to our children and other family members, as well as our church staff, word spreads quickly. Requests to be "my friend" are coming in almost every minute from Facebook. A network of prayer overwhelms us with support and concern.

Word was sent to family members, and travel plans are made for Debbie's son, daughter, son-in-law, and Debbie's sister. "Wow, that was easy! Obvious to us is the blessing and direction of the Lord in the details as well as the timing of every part." After the surgery, Dr. Mehan reported that:

The mass was definitely cancerous – of the typical pancreatic nature, as was the surrounding tissue. Approximately ½ or a little more of her pancreas had been removed along with the spleen. The "distal pancreatectomy" has gone very well. Nothing unusual accounted for the extended length of time in surgery." "He considers it "successful cancer surgery," meaning all visible evidence of cancer had been removed. Testing of the spleen has also revealed that it was clear of any cancer. "Although, in no way should you take that as meaning she is cured of cancer." There were some seven lymph nodes in the tissue that were removed. A pathology report would be forthcoming as to the presence of cancer in the nodes.

On Wednesday, during Dr. Mehan's regular patient 'rounds,' he sits on the edge of the bed. Literally hundreds of friends are praying and waiting to hear via the internet the conclusion of the pathology report on the lymph nodes that had been removed during surgery. "Are you ready to hear it?" the doctor asks. "The news is not good." As it turns out, the news is not as bad as it might have been. In fact, the tests reveal to me once again the significance of God's timing and the expediting of the surgery itself. Of the seven nodes that were in the cancerous tissue surrounding the tumor, three of the seven had cancer cells. This is bad. Four of the nodes had no cancer. This is good! What would the delay of another few days have meant? What of another several weeks' delay? The aggressive nature of pancreatic cancer would no doubt have spread through the lymph node system to all parts of Debbie's body. Was this God's way of showing us His control over events? There are moments of emotional struggles. We have a day of hugs and tears on Friday, but the recovery is progressing well. She is up and walking, gradually gaining strength each day.

It is now some two weeks later. I continue to read and learn as much as I can about the intricacies and details of what is really known about pancreatic cancer. Deb and I seemingly take turns day to day, with brief emotional 'melt-downs.' We regard these more as 'cleansing' than frustration with circumstances, or even with God. For years I have counseled others through traumatic events as a pastor and police chaplain. Now more than ever, I am committed to dispensing answers to life's most challenging questions. Why would a loving God permit such suffering? Why do bad things happen to good people?

Follow-up doctor's visits begin. We meet with our general practitioner.

He is pleased that Debbie's sugar levels are remaining low, with only a portion of her pancreas remaining. At this point, it looks like no form of insulin will be necessary to stabilize normal glucose levels – another blessing from the Lord. The doctor is also pleased and somewhat surprised at the speed of Deb's recovery to this point. The surgeon is also "very pleased with Debbie's progress." Then the first meeting with the oncologist. We view this meeting with anticipation of what we know we are going to hear – the accepted "standards of medicine" advice to begin radiation and chemotherapy. We are skeptical, primarily due not only to our personal research but also our

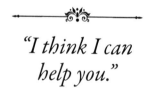

"I think I can help you."

experience with family members and dozens of friends who have followed this path of therapy. Why damage the immune system – God's wonderful design to fight all maladies in the body – in an attempt to fight this particular disease? Are the side effects more costly than cancer itself?

As we expect, he [oncologist] recommends that we begin chemotherapy, but not for at least six weeks, to allow Deb to fully recover from surgery and for her immune system to be as fully restored as possible. With a dismissal of our thoughts about alternative treatments, the oncologist shares with us documented clinical studies about Debbie's specific cancer. Out of a study of 368 patients, one-half of the patients received no chemotherapy, while the other half took Gemzar (the mildest form of chemotherapy with the least side-effects). After one year, the cancer returned in all but 9% of the 'no chemo' group. The percentage increased among those who took chemotherapy to a meager, but significant, 21%. Without a doubt, pancreatic cancer is the most resistant to treatment of all other forms of cancer. Radiation therapy has been deemed totally ineffective against pancreatic cancer. The oncologist himself eliminated the option of submitting to that. Gemzar, as it turns out, is the particular therapy that Debbie's brother Bill had used successfully some ten years ago and is still clinically "cancer free" today.

As we conclude our consultation with the oncologist who agreed to support any decision we make, he added, "Do you understand that you are in a very small minority of individuals who would have even been considered for this particular surgery?" The impact of this statement was only fully realized later that evening during more of my personal reading from other doctors about pancreatic cancer.

A consistent pattern emerges in the volumes of material I have consumed over the past several weeks. Pancreatic cancer is all but impossible to successfully treat, surgically, chemically, or naturally (humanly speaking, of course.) The oncologist's statement of how rare the surgery is even attempted, allowed me to better interpret what the surgeon had actually meant by his statement during the initial review of the CT scan. "I think I can help you." This simple sentence was, in my opinion now, his way of relaying the conclusion of the surgical staff at the hospital. I now believe the doctor's careful bedside manner prevented him from being more harsh and direct in the reality of what we were actually facing. Without putting words into his mouth, let me express my understanding of Debbie's condition prior to surgery. **Most cases like this – a metastasized pancreatic tumor in the tail of the pancreas – are, for the most part, inoperable and of little benefit. In spite of that, the surgical staff has agreed to perform this delicate surgery, because, without an IMMEDIATE successful distal pancreatectomy, you basically will have no more than a few months to live.**

The realization of this around midnight as all pieces seemed to 'come together' in my mind completely focused my attention in thanksgiving toward my God. He IS sovereign! He IS in control of all things. All the events of the past five weeks did not happen by coincidence. The coordination of people and places is no less miraculous than the healing touch of the Savior.

Even as I reflect on [the] several months prior to September, I see God's hand preparing us, financially, physically, emotionally, and spiritually. Early last spring Deb and I had begun more physical activity and had increased the nutrients in our *diet. Only three months before, we had become entirely debt-free other than the eight years remaining on our mortgage. One month before, I had replaced our adult choir Christmas Cantata with a piano concert, giving our ministry a needed 'break' for the end of this year. This past month a new, official "Assistant Police Chaplain" has come alongside to help with my ministry at the Westminster Police Department. I am reminded of more and more elements as each week passes – of interesting coincidences? No, these things have been carefully orchestrated by the One Who knows all things and controls all things.*

Is Debbie completely healed of her cancer today? Of that, I have no idea. But with no reservation, I acknowledge that we are completely in the hands of The Great Physician, Jesus Christ, Who not only created us but sustains us every day! I know we will have many more days of testing and struggle ahead of us. For that, we will continue to be completely dependent on Him.

Why would a loving God allow such things to happen? It is for the same two Biblical reasons I have always believed and sought to teach others. God allows difficult events to happen (1) for our learning – our edification – drawing us closer to Him, and (2) to ultimately provide a vehicle for Him to be magnified – His glory. "But, why me?" I believe the perspective here is two-fold. First of all, negatively stated, why would I be selected by

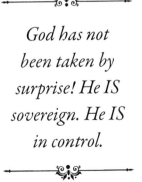

God has not been taken by surprise! He IS sovereign. He IS in control.

God to have to endure such a devastating life event? On the other hand, positively as a follower of Christ, why would I be selected by God to be a partaker of suffering, thereby receiving special grace and mercy that I would in no other way experience? The answer to both is: "Why NOT me?"

Ultimately, how this all plays out has not changed from the very beginning. God has not been taken by surprise! He IS sovereign. He IS in control. What He has demonstrated so completely to both of us is that he cares about Debbie. He cares about me and every member of our family. When we hurt, He hurts. Now we once again commit ourselves to that final goal of God the Father – that He receives all the glory, regardless of the outcome personally to us. It IS for our good and His glory!

In December 2011, Debbie continued to recover and had just completed her first cycle of chemotherapy before being "launched headlong into the most difficult and chaotic weekend of our lives!" Blood clots had developed with their many complications resulting in a "near death experience." Many questions had arose "overshadowed with the most obvious one, What if God wasn't in control?" Daniel 5:23, "The God in whose hand thy breath is, and whose are all thy ways." Job 12:10, "In whose hand is the soul of every living thing, and the breath of all mankind." Acts 17:24, 28, "God made the world and all things there in... For in Him we live, and move, and have our being."

After this traumatic week, Debbie continued her chemotherapy, and her cancer marker test revealed an unbelievable drop from twenty-one to fourteen. Meanwhile, Karen and I continued to pray for Debbie's healing through these ups and downs. We were both encouraged to see Debbie returning to her normal activities, particularly playing piano in church. It was exciting to know so many had prayed for her and to hear what God had done. Later we were saddened when we heard that cancer had returned, and Debbie was slipping away. Questions arose in my mind. Why had God seemed to allow a healing for a short time and then removed that healing? Some of God's people had asked for and trusted God to provide a longer-lasting healing.

This situation seemed so reminiscent of Mrs. Snyder and Bob Botkin from the church in Ross Corners. Wendy Wasey, Cinthy Midkiff, and Amy Bixby from Tri-City. We pray, see God provide temporarily, then seemingly see God remove His hand of healing provision. God causes or allows for an ailment, gives a one to three-year reprieve, then calls that person home; at least, this is what has happened in the examples I have shared. Why does God work that way? How can God be growing His children's trust in Him? Is God successful in testing the faith of His children and building the trust of others who witness these trials by having these types of outcomes? Can God's people joyfully thank Him after enduring the heartache and suffering from the trials God has allowed them to endure?

What should my future outlook be as I look at the examples of those who have endured the pain, sickness, and suffering God has allowed them to experience? What should my attitude be during times of disappointment? Finally, how should I pray? Should my expectation from God be of total and long-term healings? Or should my expectation be more closely aligned to what I have observed as God's working in the past?

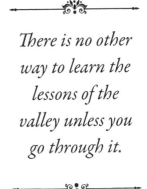

There is no other way to learn the lessons of the valley unless you go through it.

Pastor Larry's attitude concerning desiring God's will being accomplished above all else, even the lack of healing for his wife, is consistent with most if not all the other Christians previously cited.

The following is from Pastor Larry, written approximately twenty months after Debbie's death. His words and the example he has been answer many of my previously raised questions.

Through the process of the discovery of pancreatic cancer and subsequent surgeries, procedures, and treatment, there were certainly numerous prayers for healing. Having complete confidence in The Creator and Great Physician, Deb and I were completely aware of God's ability to have prevented the cancer, heal the cancer temporarily, partially, or completely if He so chose to do so. We also know He had the right to not bring healing at all. Unsure of exactly how God was to answer and direct our paths is documented in my journal through the first four months. Ultimately, God gave us a full year together before Deb died. The year was filled with discussions of how God was leading through every phase. We often stated how we could see "God fingerprints through every step" - even for the months leading up to the original discovery of the disease.

The only comfort and encouragement once you are in the valley is Jesus Christ holding your hand and guiding you through it.

There was a direct comfort and peace that came on a regular basis as we carefully studied medical options, physicians, and supplements. While we felt like (and am still confident) that we were neither negligent nor unconcerned about our part in making wise, healthy decisions, we never questioned God's goodness, His sovereignty, or His mercy in dealing with us. Ultimately we understand that our days are numbered. How and when God chooses to end this earthly life is His doing.

Once Debbie's cancer returned following her choice to suspend chemo treatments after three months, we were rejoicing that there was seemingly "no cancer present." Within a couple of months, it became evident that the cancer had returned. Prayers for healing continued, along with asking for wisdom and peace as to how we were to proceed. Our desire and expectations were for God to receive the glory; however best He chose to cause that to come about. There were certain days when Deb would say, 'I feel so good, I forget that I have cancer!' These days did not bring a false hope of healing but thankfulness in God's continued mercy and goodness.

Disappointments are a part of the losses that we experience before, during, and after the loss of a loved one. The melting away of future expectations of how we may have imagined or viewed our later years together brought much sorrow. A refocusing on the glories of heaven and reuniting there bring a measure of comfort. Am I truly thankful for having gone through this experience? There are certain parts for which I am grateful: the wonderful last year of fellowship and companionship we had together, the abilities to bring a little more understanding and empathy to others who have suffered great personal loss, and the increasing knowledge of the valley we sometimes must go through on our journey to the "promised land." (There is no other way to learn the lessons of the valley unless you go through it.)

The journey of grief is a long, arduous trek through a seemingly endless valley. The only comfort and encouragement once you are in the valley is Jesus Christ holding your hand

and guiding you through it. I trust because He knows the way and will faithfully comfort me through it. I cannot go around it. I cannot just "get over it," either. The valley will gradually lead me to a point of experiencing joy once again WHILE still having pain. I can only be thankful for the pain if I keep my eyes on the end result - coming out of the wilderness and entering into the promised land. Scripture verses that address having joy through trials are coming from an eternal perspective. I will not be, cannot be, completely thankful for the loss of a mate until I finally have that complete heavenly perspective. My objective now is to continue to grow and walk in His goodness, experiencing new joys along whatever days he has left for me to serve Him.

Chapter 6
GARY: HOW SHOULD I PRAY?

*I*n life, our confidence is built on the previous experiences we
have had. Those experiences, negative or positive, develop our
confidence, drive, and, ultimately, our actions. It is said that if you
want a young person to love the sport of fishing and continue to fish,
that young person will need to be successful - catch fish when they
first begin that sport. If they are not successful for whatever reason:
inadequate training, improper equipment, lack of fish in the fishing
hole, then likely they will not continue that activity and never be a
successful fisherman.

In the Bible story of "David and Goliath," we read that David
refused to wear King Saul's armor when going to fight the giant
Goliath. David had not "proved" or used that armor; he was not
familiar with the armor. Although Saul's armor was likely the best
armor in Israel's arsenal at that time, David was not confident in its
ability (or need) to protect him.

The question in my mind now is, how should I pray for my wife?
Karen is in a coma, somewhat stable for now, almost brain dead
(although she does not meet the technical/medical definition), and
if she does not gain consciousness in a few more days, her life support will be terminated, and she will die.

Based on my previous experiences praying for sick people, God
has sometimes granted temporary reprieves and sometimes not. I

recall having asked for full and total long-term physical healings, but I do not recall witnessing any. I have little or no confidence in my ability to appropriate (that is, receive) a total, long-term physical healing for someone else. Again, the question, "How should I pray for Karen?" Time truly is running out, and I am powerless in and of myself to do anything about my wife's health. Will my Heavenly Father, who is greater than all, perform this healing? I have interpreted Scripture that seems to indicate God is willing to grant longer-term healing if we ask in faith, but my personal experience conflicts with my personal interpretation of those Scriptures. I believe and am convinced that we should never place our personal experience above the actual meaning of God's Word. However, experience has to play a part in our understanding of God if nothing more than to show us we are incorrect in our own interpretations of God's Word. I do believe God's word to be totally trustworthy. If I remember my experiences of how God answered prayer in the past, then I should know with confidence how He will likely answer in the future and what my expectations should be. How then should I be praying for Karen, my wife?

I have asked God a question since day two of this experience, "Is this what You really want?" instead of asking, "Are You going to heal Karen immediately and for the long term?" The first question was more consistent with my experiences and was becoming more consistent with my understanding of God's working, particularly after Cinthy passed away. The latter question, concerning immediate and long-term healing, was and continues to be more consistent with my desires.

How should I pray for Karen now? I thank my Heavenly Father for what He has given to me: my very being, my existence, any and all my abilities, talents, and my proper understanding of Him. I recognize that I literally would be nothing and could do nothing without Him. God is my creative source, redemptive source, and my sustaining source. I thank Him for allowing me to have an ability to love and be loved by Him and others. I recognize that only God is qualified to run His universe, and I believe that His way of doing things is far better than we could do ourselves or expect from others. His ways are perfect or fully complete, lacking nothing. Further, He (God) created Karen and loves her far more and more perfectly than I do or could. He recognizes our feelings and infirmities and sympathizes with us. Karen's recent trauma and potential soon decease is not a surprise to Him. God has a pre-determined plan and is pleased when we, His creatures, joyfully and thankfully accept the revealing of that plan.

The tension in prayer for healing, from the human perspective, is that complete long-term physical healing is always considered a good thing and usually the best thing. Partial or short-term healing while being somewhat good and praiseworthy is still considered lacking. If there is little or no evidence of healing, often, it is assumed there is a problem somewhere: lack of faith and trust, or maybe sin. God's perspective likely is vastly different from ours and beyond our comprehension. While a lack of faith and trust and sins are possible reasons for lack of healing, those are probably in the minority. God commands us to pray for one another that we might be healed. In James 5:16, the word "healed," defined by Strong's concordance, means "to cure, heal, make whole, figuratively or literally." I recognize that although physical, long-term healing may not be God's desire or action, it is, however, still His will that we pray for one another so that we might be healed or made whole. This is why I continue to pray for Karen. I recognize that being made whole has spiritual implications for the sick person and those associated with the sick person. From God's perspective, healing may not be in the best interest of those involved. The quiet testimony of a dying person that is at peace with God and longs to be with Him in Heaven, I believe, is more powerful and longer remembered than even a miraculous physical long-term healing.

Survival Nugget: Psalm 23 is a very familiar psalm to many. "The Lord is my shepherd; I shall not want. He maketh me to lie down in green pastures: He leadeth me beside the still waters. He restoreth my soul: He leadeth me in the paths of righteousness for His name's sake. Yea, though I walk through the valley of the shadow of death, I will fear no evil: for Thou art with me; Thy rod and Thy staff they comfort me. Thou preparest a table before me in the presence of mine enemies: Thou anointest my head with oil; my cup runneth over. Surely goodness and mercy shall follow me all the days of my life: and I will dwell in the house of the Lord for ever." I was in the shadow of death, and God was there to comfort me.

Chapter 7
TERMINATE LIFE SUPPORT?

Debbie: Singing to a Friend

As the month of November moved forward, and Karen's progress seemed halted, I hit upon an idea: if familiar, favorite things could comfort and stimulate a comatose mind, why not bring some familiar, favorite music to Karen? I called my mom to see if she was in agreement and would like to visit Karen and sing Christmas carols to her. Not surprisingly, she agreed and was very excited about the idea. When I shared our plans with Janine, she was excited, as well, and asked to be included in the effort, and so we went November 19 to Karen's room in hopes of evoking a response from our "sleeping" friend. With the hymnals we borrowed from church and our list of carefully chosen selections, we began to sing to Karen. At one point, she slowly wriggled her body in position on her left side so she could hear us better. And then it came: my mom noticed a tear trickling down Karen's cheek...we all stopped singing for a moment, amazed. Then, after collecting ourselves and quietly offering our praise to the Lord, we resumed our songs, interjecting friendly introductions between each selection. Our mini-concert lasted a total of two hours.

Looking back on Karen's physical appearance, I remember becoming keenly aware of her complexion, the shape of her nose, her hands, fingers, and her hair. Because of the swelling in her face, Karen's lovely complexion and delicate nose were suddenly very noticeable. As for her hands, they were curled into what is commonly referred to as the "stroke position," which the medical staff would watch carefully over the next few months. Some of Karen's fingertips began to blacken slowly as the days turned into weeks, and my mother and I took turns massaging her hands and fingers during our visits in the hope of stimulating increased circulation and restoring their former color and function.

Pastor Senn: Let Her Go?

One of the most difficult visits was when Gary asked me to come when the neurologist had set up an appointment to talk with him and the boys. We met the doctor; she was very matter-of-fact and business-like. She pulled out her computer and showed us images of Karen's brain and pointed out markers that indicated that she likely had gone through severe brain damage and that her condition was irrecoverable. We were likely looking at someone, who if would live, would live life in very poor quality, perhaps even as a vegetable. The doctor was trying, as she fumbled around with her words, to explain that it would come to a decision the family would need to make about pulling the plug to all the systems that were sustaining Karen's life and to let her go. Just watching the family and listening to the report was very, very troublesome. It was overwhelming news to hear. The Lord had brought Karen through so much, and we all were hoping for a different outcome. But the reality was, from everything this doctor said and experienced, it would be best to let Karen go. Fortunately, Dr. Babu and the family wanted to wait longer and give the Lord more time to bring Karen out of the comatose state and show us where she was mentally.

Gary: A Hard Decision Soon
Tuesday, Day 11 – November 20, 2012

Doctors say Karen is not expected to wake up since it has now been five days since she has been off sedation and pain meds. However, should she become conscious, she will not have mental capabilities or be able to feed or dress herself. We needed to plan for "options" / "decisions."

The options/decisions meant terminating life support. It was not so much a question of **if** the life support should be terminated, as it was **when** the life support should be terminated. Karen's mom was flying in from New York the next evening to "say goodbye" to Karen. It is difficult for a parent to be predeceased by their child. Karen and her mom have always been quite close; Karen is her only daughter. This would be a sad time, just as it was four years earlier for my mother to lose her only daughter.

Church's Earlier Update 11/20/12

Karen's condition has not changed much, although her skin color looks better, and the body's swelling has gone down. Gracelyn said that Karen appeared to respond to her conversation. Timmy Price asked his mother to blink her eyes, and she did. She did this twice on command. These could be hopeful indications. We are praying that God heals her and that she will awake from her coma. Thanks for praying. We will see her today and post an update.

Church's Later Update 11/20/12

Yesterday the Price Family was given the results of the most recent CT scan. IT was not good news. The neurologist is not giving Karen any hope to return to a normal life. There is just too much brain damage. Karen's condition is also deteriorating. She continues to be kept alive by a number of machines.

Allissa and I visited and hoped to see some response. There was no outward response, although we thought she was trying to communicate with us. The doctor stated that the part of the brain that controls speech has been damaged and that she will not be able to talk. Karen's mother is flying in today from New York. Pray for the family; they are going to have some very difficult decisions to make in the near future.

Chapter 8
IS SHE FINALLY WAKING UP?

Gary: Karen's Mom Arrives

Wednesday, Day 12 – November 21, 2012

The phone call came early Wednesday morning from Karen's surgeon Dr. Babu. He stated there was some positive news; Karen had blinked her eyes on command and answered some questions by blinking. Because of her now somewhat conscious state, we needed to hold off on any (life support) decisions for at least a few days. This time was needed to determine her mental condition. This news was great, and we tried to remain hopeful; this news at this point in time was not expected. We could now at least delay any life-terminating decisions and once again focus on health improvement choices. Karen's mom had called just a short time later to review her travel plans.

Since I had not yet seen Karen, I felt it best not to share this news with her mom, thus avoiding a potential roller coaster ride for her mom. If Karen slipped back into a coma, we potentially would still need to make decisions concerning life support. If Karen remained in this semi-conscious state, this would be a pleasant surprise upon her mom's arrival.

Our first son Timmy and third son Andrew picked up their grandmother at the airport that evening and related the good news while en route to the hospital. This reunion was much happier for all than what was anticipated just twelve hours earlier. It brought a sense of comfort to me having her mom there, someone that was so close to Karen, with whom I could share this good news during this continued time of uncertainty. What was described many times over the phone could now be better understood, viewed in person.

For Karen's mom, there was no time wasted. She went immediately to ICU to see her daughter and was now also able to communicate to Karen in person. She told Karen who she was and asked her if she understood. She told Karen she loved her and that she was happy to be there with her little girl; it was a very touching moment. Once again, I was thankful that God has given us the ability to love, be loved, and share love.

Survival Nugget: I knew God wanted me to humble myself before Him, give Him everything I was concerned about, and believe that He cares for each of us. It was a time when, in my weakness, it was easy to succumb to Satan's temptations. God in His grace was there. I only suffer for a while, compared to eternity. His desire for me was to become more established, stronger, settled, and thus be more like Christ. I Peter 5:6-11 says, "Humble yourselves therefore under the mighty hand of God, that he may exalt you in due time: Casting all your care upon him; for he careth for you. Be sober, be vigilant; because your adversary the devil, as a roaring lion, walketh about, seeking whom he may devour: Whom resist steadfast in the faith, knowing that the same afflictions are accomplished in your brethren that are in the world. But the God of all grace, who hath called us unto his eternal glory by Christ Jesus, after that ye have suffered a while, make you perfect, stablish, strengthen, settle you. To him be glory and dominion for ever and ever. Amen."

Pastor Senn: A Highlight

Just a couple of days after that encounter with the neurologist, Karen would come out of her comatose state. We were all glad that she did. We learned very quickly that Karen had not had all the damage to her brain that the doctor had pointed out to us, or if she did, she had been healed. That was an amazing resurrection, in a sense, one of the highlights for all of us. Also, the doctors were shocked, as well as the nurses, that Karen did not suffer other physical issues while in her comatose state. One explanation could be attributed to Gary and his care for her toes and fingers and his gentleness with her. But even with that, they were still surprised that she did not have other life problems. Once she stabilized after coming out of the comatose state, she was hooked up and continued to be hooked up to various pieces of equipment to keep her heart going and blood flowing.

Allissa: Faithful

Those were ten long days of waiting for Karen to come out of her coma. What stands out in my mind the most is how their family pulled together to respond in the face of such a horrific situation. Gary was just steady each day and did what he needed to do. I do remember Ben, who had such a sad and somber look. He and his Mom were very close. I hurt each time I looked at him. It was great to see Matthew join the family. He stayed very close to his Mom through this ordeal. Timmy so ably helped his Dad field all of the phone calls and handled questions. Andrew was there too. All the boys were together and supported their mom and dad in a special way. Sometimes trials break families apart, but in this case, God used the situation for His honor and glory. It did not look good for Karen from an earthly perspective. We thought that she was going to pass from this life to her heavenly home.

When I saw Karen after she first woke up, I was at a loss for words. I have never done really well in hospitals. She was hooked up to so many machines, and every one of them was so particularly important to sustaining her very life. Karen looked afraid when I saw her. Her eyes and face told the story. It was hard to grasp and to understand. But, there she was, alive and able to sustain the treatments that she was receiving. Again, Gary and the family stuck close to wife and mother. Faithful is the word that I will always think of as I recall this difficult situation and how Gary and family handled it all. It was a wonderful thing when we realized that Karen was going to make it!! God in His precious care was deciding to give life – to Karen!!

Benjamin: Readjusting

It is now Wednesday, November 21. It has been ten days since mom's initial incident. It was this morning mom first showed signs of waking up. The doctors told us that what she was doing was common among people whose brains were not active, but their bodies were being controlled by their subconscious. Basically, they tried to nicely tell us that she was a vegetable and probably never going to get better than this.

A couple of days before this, my family and I were in a special meeting room in the ICU in the hospital with the head nurse, the surgeon, her main doctor, and some other people I didn't know. Through the course of this meeting, they showed us CAT scans of her brain. There were two massive spots that had occurred due to strokes. They said one spot was 1/4 the size of one that was big enough to kill or render a person brain dead. She had eight times as much as that; she had no brain activity at this point, her physical condition was improving, but it was slow. Like a tortoise trying to run a marathon, it would take so long; who knows if it would ever happen or what other issues would happen along the way. After a two-hour meeting, they advised us that pulling the plug on her life support would probably be the best option. That ultimately, it was our decision, but they didn't see her getting much better; they couldn't possibly see a way she would wake up. That was a hard meeting.

Up until the point of the meeting on the 20th, 90% of what I had heard was that my mom would not live, that she would not have any type of life if her body got better, that she would never talk, walk, understand anything, think, or be happy ever again. That her life would be a miserable struggle and painful until she died at a later date. However, I did hear that 10% of news that was good, that miraculous things were happening, that she was making steps towards getting better, that there was hope! Again, it was like trying to keep a candle lit in a hurricane. I was trying to be honest with myself, "How long can that really last?" I love my mother; I'm the baby of the family; I'm a mama's boy; we are best friends. I didn't want my mother to die, but I also didn't want her to suffer. I didn't want her to die (I still don't). I think it was in the first couple of days that I started making peace with my mom dying; I started preparing myself for that reality. That as a socially awkward, emotionally unprepared 15-year-old, I would no longer have my mom. She wouldn't be there for graduation, or my wedding, or be there for my children. I was a long way down that path when I was shown proof, in that meeting, that it was better for my mom to go to be with our Lord and Savior in Heaven. That proof was the final assurance I needed to let her go. Some would call it giving up on her, and looking back, it sure does look like that, but at the moment, I thought I was thinking about what was best for both of us.

Now I'll go back to the 21st. So when I got the news that morning that mom had shown signs of waking up, I was really confused. I had gotten peace about my thoughts from God, that I was making a justified reaction. But now God is changing? No, that can't be right. I could not reconcile the contradiction of what I knew to be true with what I thought was true. When we got to the hospital to see mom, we saw what was going on. Yes, she was "awake," she was "moving," but she was not cognizant, and she was not in control of her body. Like I said earlier, she was posturing her arms in a way that shows she has no higher brain function. She was moving her legs like she was uncomfortable and in pain. Her face was twisted in a grimace, with her eyes blankly moving from one side to the other. My mother was not awake. Her body was awake, but my mom was not there. This was another confirmation for me and my way of thinking; my mom was gone, and her body would be gone soon too.

She would continue posturing for another day or two, but eventually, she seemed to calm down. And it was the morning she calmed down that someone felt her ever so lightly squeeze their hand. Then she blinked in response to a question like, "Blink twice if you can hear me." Then a few minutes later, she was back to being out of it. When I heard about this, it was very hard for me because I had so many proofs that God was going to take her home to be with Him. So was I not listening, or was God changing? I had already made peace with her passing. I had already lost my mom. She was gone. My pain and my feeling had found their spot where they could be compressed, repressed, and ignored until I had the ability to deal with them. Now I was supposed to pull them out, deal with them, and make room for all the new feelings, new hopes, and life-altering new future of rehabilitating mom and taking care of her? I cannot communicate the magnitude of doing just one of those things, let alone all three. The reason all the feelings were all in "long-term storage" to begin with was because I could not handle them; now I have to grow them exponentially by a power of three? This is when I think most of the long-term damage was done to me. My heart broke, my brain died a little, and my emotions drowned me. It was years before I saw the light of day again. The worst part was I had brought it upon myself. God was not to blame; my mom was not to blame; no one told me to think this way; it was my fault. In my mind, that was reason enough to not talk to anyone about this until about five years later. There was guilt, pain, shame, grief, and just sadness. All of which were on such an extreme level that I have nothing to compare it to.

For the next few weeks, I had to come to terms with these feelings. I had to learn how to overcome them and how to heal from them. I mostly failed at doing this; instead, I just suppressed the negative emotions and just declared that I would do and be what people wanted me to. Figuring out who I was and what I felt about everything was too close to impossible, so I'd take the easier road by letting my family and a few close friends decide who I would be. I just chose to seek their approval. This also was a bad habit that took quite a long time to break and to figure out how to live properly. I needed to let that type of influence only come from God. Only my Lord and Savior can choose who I am and how I act, no one else.

At this point in the story, I think it was about the time my two weeks off from school were coming to an end. My next struggle was about to start, my schooling. Now I won't blame this entirely on the situation with my mom, but I will say the situation made it much worse. I was exhausted from a poor sleep schedule; I was stressed for obvious reasons; I was emotionally drained to the point of emptiness, and I am normally a "C student." With all of these things combined, I was on track for my second worst academic year of high school. (The worst would be the next year when I had a concussion and was suffering from those effects.) Needless to say, school was especially difficult for the rest of the year. My day would consist of a few things: I would wake up around 6 am to carpool to school, then try to stay awake all day and force myself to learn as much as I could to pass maybe; as soon as school was over, we rushed over to the hospital to spend as much time there as we could, and then get to bed between 11 pm and 1 am. It was grueling, and it wore me down.

There were a couple of things that kept me going. I was helped by the hope and progress my mom was making in her recovery. Also, I was helped by the friends I had at school and church and neighbors that all would offer encouragement the best they could, and I'm very thankful to all of them. The biggest thing that carried me through was the supernatural grace of God that He gave me. I've heard some people describe it similarly to an extremely effective pain reliever that just nullifies all of the pain. My experience was much different than that. From my experience, when I prayed and when others prayed for me, God looked at what I was going through and raised my "pain tolerance" so that I could handle it, but just barely handle it. I still had all the same struggles; I still felt the same pain; the suicide thoughts were just as real and potent. Everything was the same; just when it came down to the very edge where I was about to fall over the edge into the abyss below, God would keep me from falling and give me one step towards recovery. If God is trying to grow us, I do not believe He is going to give us a trial or test that we cannot handle with the amount of help He will give us. I believe the trials will be harder than what we can handle alone, but if we rely on God as we should, then it will work out how God wants. I also believe that God would not just take away the trial in the hardest point just because we cannot handle it. If we cannot handle it, it is either because we have not grown through Christ yet or because we are trying to do it alone. Neither of which would be beneficial to us if God removed us from the trial. All that to say, I think the grace of God is not a "highly effective pain medication," I think He chooses to grow our ability to face the pain and to tolerate it better; that is the true growth.

Gary: Very Happy Thanksgiving!

Thursday, Day 13 – November 22, 2012 ~ Thanksgiving Day ~ Kevin emailed, "*In everything give thanks: for this in the will of God in Christ Jesus concerning you*, I Thessalonians 5:18. Wednesday afternoon Mom flew out to Denver in the anticipation of saying her final goodbyes to Karen by this coming weekend. The doctors had expected her to wake up from her induced coma by last Sat. or Sun. after taking away the comma medication a week ago today. Although her blood flow, breathing, organs, skin color were all looking good, the Cat scans of her brain were showing limited activity. Each day after Sunday, the chances for recovery did not look good. A lot of prayers are being made across the country, but it seemed God was preparing to take her home with Him.

However, several hours before Mom arrived in Denver, Karen started opening her eyes on command and later hand movements on command. When Mom got to the hospital, she was keeping her eyes open for long periods and was showing response to pain. The doctors are amazed. She still has a long way to go as she is still on the heart pump and dialysis. We also need to see future progress in the coming days. The initial thought is that God still wants her here with us. Keeping praying."

Responses came back saying, "What an answer to prayer!" "This gives us a lot to be thankful for today." "Truly good news." "What completely, beautifully joyous news on this Thanksgiving Day! I just read the family your email, and we all were so filled with rejoicing in what God is doing for Karen! Thank you very, very much for this uplifting news today. We will be giving thanks for Karen's progress and 180-degree turnabout today! Hallelujah! Your mother must have been weeping with thanksgiving to see this with her own eyes during a trip when she thought it would be the last time she saw Karen. God bless your family." An Uncle wrote, "What Glorious news you send. I am so thrilled." Another person wrote, "Thank you for sharing the good news. I have been thinking of you, your family, and especially your mother all week." There were many people giving thanks with us for what God had done so far. They promised to continue to pray.

An excellent day of Thanksgiving! The youth pastor and his wife (Bart and Kasey) spent many hours and days waiting with us at the hospitals and had even made plans to bring Thanksgiving Dinner to the hospital. Due to Karen's recent improvement, they invited our family to their house. On Thanksgiving, they started a tradition of having everyone sign the tablecloth with a permanent marker and state something for which each person was thankful. Of course, this year, most thankful statements were about Karen and her recent return to consciousness. It was a wonderful day filled with new hope. What might the Lord be doing?

We visited Karen that evening. We tested her memory skills with yes or no type questions. She was able to respond now by nodding or shaking her head instead of only blinking her eyes as she did the previous day. She did well.

Survival Nuggets: Timmy went to China to teach English and to be a witness. We received a call in December 2010 that Timmy was in a taxi on his way to a hospital. He thought that his lung had developed a hole in it again and was deflating. We thought back to when Timmy was in college and had Spontaneous Pneumothorax causing his lung to rupture. We knew that if it burst again, he had only a short time to live without medical intervention. After this December call, all of life's activities stopped, and we prayed. We soon learned that he did again have a ruptured lung, but this time it was his other lung. He recovered slowly in the Chinese hospital. Psalm 33:20-21, "Our soul waiteth for the Lord: He is our help and our shield. For our heart shall rejoice in Him, because we have trusted in His holy name." We waited, and God strengthened our faith and trust in Him some more during this time. On Christmas Day, we had the best gift; Timmy was released from the hospital and back in his apartment! God took care of our son on the other side of the world.

Chapter 9
GOD'S MIRACLES ABOUND

Karen: Very Little Hope...But GOD,
part 2 written August 2013

*W*hat I remember is waking up after what I thought was just a few hours and having Timmy ask me, "Mom, do you know who I am?" I was vaguely aware of many tubes and wires hooked to me, and I was in a lot of pain, but I thought, "of course I know who you are; you are my son, my oldest." Due to the breathing tube, I couldn't speak, but I nodded my head.

People have often asked, but no, I never saw a light, nor felt like I went to Heaven. Earlier I had felt I was in one of Benjamin's video games, spinning around, falling through layers, unable to get out and find reality. Then I felt like I was in a desert; I was so thirsty and dry. I was not aware of anyone near me, and I felt so helpless and all alone. I thought I was in a hospital in China. I'm not sure why, except Timmy had been in one there and told us how they were much different from US hospitals. Maybe since I thought no one was around, my brain thought I must be somewhere away from my family. It was wonderful to see Gary and each of our sons that day.

Another thing I remember from that first day awake is that I was so thrilled when my mom came in. I didn't know it at the time, but she *had gotten on the plane to come tell me goodbye. Mommy was there comforting and encouraging, and all seemed a little better. I appreciated Timmy asking if I wanted to know what had happened, saying that if he were in my condition, he would want to know. When I nodded my head, he briefly and, in general terms, explained some things to me. I remember hearing Matthew's voice and trying to turn to see if he was really there. Pastor Senn came to visit and said something like, "I see the family is here." And the first thing I said to him, the first since the incident, was "All four boys!"*

I don't understand it, but I trust You.

Before this all happened, I knew I could trust God, but that was put to the test. I woke up thinking I was just having a simple procedure, so why am I in so much pain, and what are all these things hooked to me. Even in my foggy state, God was there and prompted me to pray, "This is happening, so it must be Your will, I don't understand it, but I trust You. Please help me to endure this, and take care of my family." I had mentioned to my ladies Bible study group the week before I went to the hospital that we need to trust God in the little things and not just the big crises. What I did not think about at the time was that if we make it a habit to trust God in the everyday little things, it will be an automatic response to trust God when the big things come.

I wanted to quote Scripture but could not recall any verses. Over and over, right when I needed one, a verse I had memorized would pop into my head. They were such a help to me; God used them to direct my thinking. I remember many doctors and medical personnel coming into talk to me as well as many visitors. Dan and Mary Becker prayed out loud for me, and that meant so much; I really missed hearing prayers. I knew my Ladies Sunday school class was especially praying for me; that was a comforting thought. I did not know at the time, but many people were praying all around the country, including many I did not even know.

Timmy brought in some music CDs and a player; they were a great blessing over the next several months, for a while, the only devotions I was able to have. I was so scared and anxious much of the time; when Timmy was ending his visits, he would often turn on one of the CDs, and they would calm me and help me to better handle being alone. Timmy came almost every day to visit me. Andrew would come for longer visits when he could and spent a couple of nights in the hospital with me. Matthew came often to see me and talk, mostly on the weekends. Gary came every day except when he was sick for a few days. Benjamin came when not at school and a few other activities.

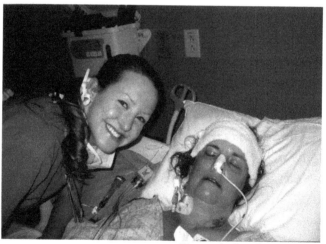

Karen and a Special Nurse, Lindsey

After a few days, whenever I fell asleep, I would wake a short while later, feeling that my body was unmovable, and I was very fearful and panicky. God gave me Lindsey, a special nurse that took the time to help me immensely. She would say, "Karen, you are doing well; your numbers look good, breathe deeply, and relax; you have much to be thankful for." Much of what the nurses did or said scared me, as did all the machines beeping in my room. One time another nurse, Bob, was silencing an alarm, and I asked him to talk to me. He said, "Ok, about what?" I replied that I wanted him to tell me what he was doing and what the beeping meant. He usually did that with patients, but as many did, he thought I was sleeping since my eyes were closed. It helped to calm me to know what was happening. It did concern me that I could not hold my eyes open for very long and could not focus to read. That eventually cleared up when I was no longer taking narcotics.

Another time I heard a nurse about to give me blood, verifying my blood type. What she said was not mine, and I thought that if they kept giving me the wrong type, they would kill me. When Timmy came in, I motioned that I wanted to write something. He put a marker in my hand and held a small whiteboard. I wrote a shaky "O" and then tried to write a negative, but my hand dropped, and it was just a squiggly line. Obviously, no one could understand. I just had to pray and tell the Lord I had done all I could and that He would have to take care of it however He chose. Later I found out that I had received so much blood, over 100 units, that my "O-" blood type had changed to "O+." Timmy was very patient with me several times, pointing to pictures or phrases on a card so I could communicate a little. All the boys and Gracelyn waited on me and tried the best they knew to help.

Almost everyone told me I was looking great and doing well. I remember seeing a scared look in Benjamin's eyes and thinking that I may not be doing as well as I think they are telling me. When Ben could laugh and joke with me again, I knew I was much better. He told me that when I asked him if he remembered to feed his tortoise, he knew I was back being a mom. Gracelyn noticed things that others did not and cared for me tenderly. She wrote out some Bible verses and put them on my wall. They encouraged me and also gave me chances to witness when others read them and commented.

Gary is my biggest hero, and from him, I drew much strength. He was with me most of each day in the beginning and spent at least one night in the hospital. After he returned to work, Gary would work a *full day and then come and spend five or six hours with me. He took such good care of me: rubbing my fingers and toes to restore the circulation, helping me exercise in bed, feeding me, brushing my teeth, reading to me Bible verses, talking, and encouraging me. I have never felt so loved.*

It meant much to me when Pastor Robbins came to visit. I didn't know then that he had been there often, but I knew it was hard for him to be in a hospital so soon after his wife Debbie had gone to Heaven. He came as a pastor and friend and talked with me several more times in the hospitals and after I was home. I had a reality check when a couple of friends came for the first time to the intensive care and had to leave abruptly, not able to handle what they were seeing. They didn't realize how much I had improved. So many came to visit me.

God always provided the encouragement I needed, sometimes in ways that surprised me. Two janitors came in one each day to sweep and mop my floor at the convalescent hospital. One day something had happened, and I was discouraged but praying for help. The janitors normally did not speak to me beyond a polite greeting. One day, one of the janitors saw that I was sad, came over by the bed, and said something like, "You are going to get better. The race is not to the swift but to those that persevere. You don't give up; God will help you make it through." He told me that he understood my situation because he had almost died and had spent an extended time in a hospital. He said that he prayed for me each day while he was cleaning my floor!

Some nurses were good; some were excellent. One took the time to teach me about my medications; some were bubbly and encouraging. One of the best was Alex; she treated me like a person and not just a patient. She left the stress of her job and what was bothering her about other patients outside my room. The man that often emptied my trash and linens each day was a kind black man named Melvin. One never knew what he would say, but he often made me laugh; I needed something to laugh about. One day he said to a nurse in the room that I was his mama and that he would visit me when I left the hospital. Neither the nurse nor I knew what to say. He lowered his voice and said," She's my mama, you know; I was just the black sheep of the family." I laughed every time I thought about Melvin.

One day when I was still in intensive care, a lady from church came in the evening after my family went home. I still had the breathing tube down my throat and could not communicate with the medical staff or my family what I wanted or about what I was concerned. In her typical style, she said what she thought and asked me several questions. It made me so grateful that someone understood and could voice what I was thinking. It surprised me that within a few days, all the items she talked about were addressed. She told me later that the head nurse was listening at the doorway.

Survival Nugget: I came to know Jesus as my Savior at the age of seven when I realized that it was not enough to go to church and be relatively good. John 3:15 says, "That whosoever believeth in Him should not perish, but have eternal life." To become a child of God, there needed to be a point in time when I admitted my sins, believed that Jesus died on the cross to pay for all of my sins, and rose again. I asked Him to take over my life and be my personal Savior. Jeremiah 31:3 says, "I have loved thee with an everlasting love: therefore with lovingkindness have I drawn thee." I John 4:10 says, "Herein is love, not that we loved God, but that He loved us, and sent His Son to be the propitiation for our sins." The stabilizing truth, God's Love for me is Unchanging, is shown by Jesus' death on the cross as the atoning sacrifice for sin. It is wonderful always to know that whatever happens, I will be in Heaven right after I die, whenever that day is.

Gary: All Four Boys
Friday, Day 14 – November 23, 2012

Today there were problems with the chest tube and a collapsed lung. Dr. Babu developed a plan, successfully addressing the issue. Dr. Babu stated that since there is continued progress, he would like to connect two external heart pumps: one for the left side (LVAD) of the heart and one for the right side (RVAD). This surgery would take place Sunday and is needed because both sides of her heart were damaged. This is a longer-term life support option. Her current life support equipment (ECMO) had already exceeded the seven to ten-day maximum time limitation. Karen was now much more susceptible to internal and external clotting if remaining on the current life support equipment. Pastor Matt Von prayed in the waiting area. Many people still visited the waiting area daily - several bringing food. These are continued blessings.

Saturday, Day 15 – November 24, 2012

Dr. Babu states further testing has revealed that the right side of the heart is pumping. While its ability is impaired, he feels it is adequate and will try to connect only one external pump for the left side of the heart instead of the two previously planned external pumps. I was excited to hear this good news!

Church's Update 11/24/12

Karen Price is still defying all odds. The doctor told the family that they have never seen anyone come back with the complications that Karen has. Karen is now communicating with family and friends through eye contact, blinks, and the squeezing of one's hand. She knew Allissa and me yesterday when we were with her, and when I said, "Let's pray," she closed her eyes, and when I said, "Amen." she opened her eyes. Karen is definitely processing more than the neurologists ever

122

imagined. Her kidneys are still shut down, and with her recent communication with family and friends, [Karen] is putting herself in a position for another heart surgery.

This surgery will likely be in the next few days. The doctors told the family that her chances for survival from this surgery are poor, but there are no other options at this point if they want to give her a chance to live. Karen's mother is here from New York. Keep praying for the family.

Sunday, Day 16 – November 25, 2012

We met in Karen's ICU room to pray for her prior to her leaving for surgery. Pastor Dean Hendrix and his wife Brenda, Tyson Schrecengost (Karen's boss at church), and our family followed her as she was wheeled into surgery, well in advance of her scheduled surgery time, perhaps to start surgery early. Bart and Kasey waited with us in the surgical waiting room. Our sons' Taekwondo instructor Patty Lorenz and her husband Dave brought us breakfast.

The 7 1/2 hour surgery was scheduled to start at 8 a.m. and finish at approximately 3:30 p.m. At approximately 8:45 a.m., Dr. Babu and some other hospital staff approached us. Dr. Babu had a somber look on his face. My heart sunk; this indicated to me that they had lost Karen shortly after the scheduled start time for surgery. They had said her chances for surviving this surgery were poor, and now perhaps that prognosis was our reality. I think Dr. Babu sensed our anxiety and immediately said, "Everything is ok. We have not started surgery yet. I have been talking to my colleagues, and we feel that since your wife continues to improve that it would be in her best interest if we go ahead and implant her with an internal heart pump called a Left Ventricular Assist Device (LVAD). I will personally hear about this from the insurance company because normally, patients are in a much healthier condition when implanted with this type of device, but it is the right decision to make." Doing this now will prevent at least one additional surgery, and if she recovers, she can go home with this device. If she receives an external LVAD pump, then she is confined to the ICU until she either gets an internally implanted LVAD or receives a heart transplant.

I breathed a sigh of relief and concurred with Dr. Babu. Later Alyson, an LVAD coordinator, brought a non-working model of the LVAD equipment to the waiting area. She described where the pump would be located in the chest cavity underneath the heart, where this pump would be fitted to draw blood from the bottom of the left ventricle and pump that blood into the Aortic Artery (the main blood supply artery for the entire body). This pump will be powered by two sources: batteries, which allow for mobility or plugged into an electrical outlet for home use. The surgery went well, and Karen came out from sedation that night.

Church's Morning Update 11/25/12
3 ½ hours into Karen's surgery, could last up to 6 hours, so please keep praying. Called for the S.S. classes to spend extra time in prayer for the Price Family. Services starting now.

Evening Update 11/25/12
Karen made it through the surgery, some issues addressed, doctors pleased - they will wake her in 12-24 hours if all looks good. Thanks for praying for her and the entire Price family.

More responses to Kevin's emails include the following statements. "Thank God for the wonderful progress." "Thank you for letting us know this continued miraculous news!" "It does sound so hopeful!" "What amazing progress Karen is having. God is hearing our prayers. I'm so happy to hear the wonderful updates." "These reports are so amazing–just like our God!" "We all thank God for his generous gift of Karen's new life. Truly a marvelous miracle that only He could give!" "We are still praying. So happy to hear some positive news, although recognizing the long road ahead." "Thanks for the good news about Karen." "God certainly is good. I have had my church praying for her also."

Tuesday, Day 18 – November 27, 2012

Karen spent nine hours off the ventilator. We are told she is doing well. She may have the ventilator removed tomorrow.

Church's Update

Karen Price survived the installation of a permanent pump on Sunday morning. She was in surgery most of the day. Yesterday they worked her pump very hard. The doctor is pleased with the surgery and the performance of the pump. Karen is not in a position to take visitors this week due to her need to recover from the last two weeks of surgeries. The family has asked that just the pastors and her family and any invited friends should go by to see her. We will continue to have daily updates and will let others know when a visit could be made. Still, she is very, very vulnerable. Thus far, we are looking at a miracle!

Wednesday, Day 19 – November 28, 2012
Church's Update

Today was a big day for Karen. She is doing majority of breathing on her own and had multiple tubes removed from her body today. With all the positive changes, it has increased her exhaustion. Continue to pray for her strength and recovery. Family continues to do well.

Thursday, Day 20 – November 29, 2012

Doctors removed the chest tube, a throat tube, and another tube. Karen said/whispered her first word, "Hi." She could not talk but started eating ice-chips. She is able to lift a suction tube to her mouth only with one hand and with much effort. Her other arm and hand do not exhibit motion. Uncertain of the exact day, but medical staff told us that Karen would lose (have amputated) a minimum of three fingers and several toes. The need for amputation is due to the high dosage of meds called pressors. It was stated that these meds were used as a last resort to keep Karen's blood pressure from dropping to zero during those first few days. The pressors work by pooling blood in the core organs, which pulls the blood from the extremities, thus starving the fingers and toes. The tissue dies then requires removal (amputation). Soon after this time, we were given approval to start massaging Karen's feet and hands then later her fingers and toes in an attempt to improve circulation.

Kevin emailed, "Monday was mainly a day of rest – waking up some and answering a few yes and no questions. Monday afternoon, they started turning off the ventilator for 4 hours at a time so she could breathe on her own. Tuesday, they started removing some of the drains and wires to her heart for possible shocking (never needed), raising her bed, and turning off the ventilator for 6 hour periods. Today around noon, they removed the ventilator all together. She is now breathing on her own and talking with a whisper. The doctor indicated that each day she should be a little stronger with her voice. Gary had forgotten a password for their computer. Karen remembered it right away. This afternoon they removed a temporary pic from her neck and installed a long-term one in her arm. She is sucking on ice chips and taking some medication orally. They will work on some therapy tomorrow, including evaluating her swallowing. They are working very hard to prevent infection. Still very weak, but making significant progress." "Gary is able to stay off from work so far. He and Mom go to the hospital mid-morning, eat lunch, and leave in the afternoon to get Benjamin [from school]. They eat supper at home or eat out, and then they go back to the hospital for several hours in the evening. Again thanks for praying. God is so good." Many responded; one said, "If one didn't have faith before Karen's incident, they would now. So exciting to see God working." "Amen...God is so good! Great to see answers to prayer!" "Wow! The Lord is able! Glad to hear the good news." "It is astounding that she can remember their password... We will continue to pray for God's amazing grace." "What amazing news!" "This whole situation must be a HUGE testimony to the Drs. and hospital staff." "God's hand is on her. What a miraculous recovery. I will continue to pray."

Saturday, Day 22 – December 1, 2012

Matthew visited and told his mom that he loves her. Also, he gave her a hug, further recognition of God's reconciliation in this family. All four boys had a group picture taken in Karen's ICU room, and all had sincere smiles. This picture is the first taken of all four of them together in approximately five years. Again, I saw another

Our Four Sons with Karen's Mom

127

affirmation that God is at work, turning the hearts, thoughts, feelings, and minds of His children back to loving each other.

Church's Update 12/1/12

Karen Price has had her breathing tube removed and is breathing on her own. Amazing! Yesterday, she talked for the first time in nearly three weeks. Again, amazing! I can still see the computer picture of her brain and the concern that the neurologist had that it was quite possible that the damage to her brain would not permit her to talk again. Again amazing, she is talking. Her voice is weak, barely a whisper, but tonight she could not wait to tell me her four boys were there earlier in the day and that they were all laughing together. Laughter is a great medicine, so is family! We still need to pray that her kidneys begin to function. She is still very, very weak. The family has asked that there not be visits in to see her for a few more days. She needs the rest, and every motion requires much energy, of which she has little. The physical therapy that will be needed will be extensive.

Kevin sent out, "Karen continues to progress each day. She is now talking almost regular, but a little horse. Still very weak. They have her sitting up an hour at a time, several times a day. They continue to work on swallowing. Today they ran a camera down to see the swallowing progress. The technician said he thought it looked good, but the doctor would make the final call to remove the feeding tube. However, she did have apple sauce and graham crackers today. They also took her off the constant dialysis and now only have her on dialysis for four hours a day. She also had her hair washed tonight. She is worn out by the end of the day and doing better at sleeping at night." A cousin responded, "All truly great news of Karen's recovery progress. It seems a miracle has saved her from dropping into oblivion. Certainly, this has had a genuine influence on everyone's outlook. And if they were not close to God in the outset, they must surely have drawn closer to him thru their prayers." "It is God's way of bringing the family together and making them stronger to be prepared for a more severe "next step" in the lives of the Lilyea clan. My sincere commendation to you and to all those who are near to you, more so now than at the start of this deep dark episode in their lives."

"When we hear the expression: 'Truth is stranger than fiction,' we have seen that proven in this documentation of one family's true life experience, played out in cold, scary episodes, day by day, hour by hour. We can say 'Thank you, Dear Heavenly Father, for looking down on us this day and smiling on your children one more time. Please continue to give us the strength to endure.'" "Karen is truly blessed to have the love and devotion of so many, as well as her care and keeping from God." "It is going to be a long road." "Isn't it wonderful to watch God at work?" "This is fantastic news! Praise the Lord for his goodness and grace."

Survival Nugget: During his college years, our second son, Matthew, decided to leave our family, change his name, and asked us not to contact him. I continued to pray for him many times a day, loving him, and weeping over him. I cannot describe the agony and heartache this was for us. We did not know if we would ever have a close relationship with Matthew again on earth. Yet, God was with us, helping us to continue with daily life activities, proving that His love was unchanging and that His grace was sufficient. We knew that God continues to love us and does not give up on any of us. Only God knew when and how our family would be whole again.

Matthew: Forgiven

I am Gary and Karen's second son. My story is probably different from many of the others in this book. My path was not nearly as straight or easy as I would have liked or envisioned as a child, but I am thankful to God for what He's brought me through and taught me in spite of myself.

To begin, I think I should give some background on the person that I have been. I was raised in a Christian home and was taught all the truths in the Bible from the time I was very small. When I was four years old, I prayed a prayer to get saved. My parents had me in church every Sunday and Wednesday night, and sometimes other days if there was anything going on. I learned the Bible stories, knew all the songs and many of the Bible verses. I learned to obey and be respectful and, for the most part, was thought of as a pretty well-behaved kid. As I moved into my younger teenage years, I grew into the role that was expected of me and began serving in the church we went to. I'd teach young children's Sunday school, go to nursing homes, pick up chairs, play an instrument in church, sing in the choir, etc. I remember, about that time (I think I was 13), I went to a Christian camp with the church youth group. At one of the nightly services, the speaker was preaching hard from John 3:14-16, which talks about looking to Jesus to be saved. I realized that I had been looking to my upbringing and the way that I lived to be saved from sin. I walked the aisle at that camp, was talked to by a counselor, and prayed again. Unfortunately, that realization alone was not enough to bring me to Christ.

I came back home after that trip and settled into very much the same life. While I looked clean on the outside, I had a secret side to me that harbored lust, deceit, and selfishness. These three would play an ever-increasing role in shaping my life and my future. My awareness of all these things began to build. I went to a Christian college out of state to study Bible. I thought with my knowledge of the

Bible that I would make a good pastor. My sin continued through college. Once again, I was able to cover up my sin by playing the role of being spiritually mature. [Matthew and Christine left that college and were married.]

I determined to do better, get therapy, make changes, and be different. I felt so guilty and decided to confess and was forgiven the first few times. Soon though, my wife became convinced that I would never change. I did everything I could to fix and mend the marriage at that point, but it was too late. I still remember the conversation we had one Sunday afternoon when she told me she just couldn't take it anymore. As we were in the middle of that conversation, my phone rang, and it was my brother Timmy. I ignored the call because I hadn't spoken to him in months, or maybe even years, and whatever he had to say could wait. Christine and I finished our conversation, and I called Timmy back; he informed me of the medical incident with my mom. Given that I hadn't seen any of my family in a long time, and I didn't really understand the situation, I didn't even plan on going to the hospital to see my mom. Christine's mom had been a nurse though, and told me how serious the situation was and that I was probably just going to say goodbye. So after much prodding, I decided to go down to the hospital, and Christine came with me.

It was definitely interesting seeing my family all together again for the first time in almost six years. I hadn't seen either of my younger brothers for probably close to three years, and even then, it was for just a couple of minutes. The first thing my dad did when we walked in was, give me a hug and tell me he was glad we were there. I was very much out of my element, not only dealing with everything that was happening with my mom, but also trying to talk to people from the church I grew up in, who came out to support my mom, many of whom I hadn't seen in years. I survived that night, as did my mom, but she was barely clinging onto life. I remember when they transferred her into ICU at the conclusion of her surgery, I saw her for the first time in a very long time: bloated and comatose. I stayed that night at the hospital, returned home the next morning for a shower and a change of clothes, and spent the entire next day and night at the hospital. I must confess that most of the time I was there was spent grieving, not so much the loss of my mom, for I had spent the last five years dealing with that pain, but instead the imminent loss of my marriage. I knew that I had a small window and that nothing would happen with the marriage while my mom was critical. It was hard to put up the facade of a good, loving marriage when it was on the brink of being over, but I thought I might have a chance of pulling it from the edge. My mom's life was teetering on the edge as well, but I knew there was nothing I could do to affect that. I will not go into the details because I'm sure they're discussed in other parts of this book, and I do not trust my memory to get them all correct.

I do remember that a few days later, my mom was transferred to University Hospital, and she began to stabilize, at least physically. Soon the focus shifted from her physical health to her mental cognition. Day after day, the doctors were getting no response from her brain. Before long, they told us that soon it would be time for us to decide how much longer we would wait for her to come out of the coma. I remember that after that meeting, Christine and I stayed in the conference room, and I told my dad that whatever he decided, I would support, and I knew he would make the right decision. He thanked me, but what he said next shocked me. He apologized to both of us for his part in the falling out between my parents and me, and he said he was determined to build a relationship with both of us if we'd let him. We did forgive him and said we'd like that very much. A few days went by, and my mom started to wake up and become more aware. Soon she was moved to a rehab hospital. God had begun to heal my mom, performing a miracle, and pulling her back from the edge of death. I was elated and hoped he would do the same thing to my marriage. In his perfect wisdom, He decided not to heal my marriage, and just a few weeks after my mom began to recover, Christine and I filed for divorce.

I was devastated. I vividly remember spending that Christmas in an empty, unfurnished apartment, with nothing but a pillow and blanket, a laptop, and a few boxes of my clothes. I was soon able to get more furniture and put my apartment together, but I was unable to pick up the pieces of my shattered life. I felt totally alone, with no friends, no church, no social group, and no hope. I reasoned that through my choices, I had made this bed; now it was time to lie in it. No matter what I'd done or how much I'd tried to change, nothing had worked. My "good boy" persona had been completely stripped away, and the only thing I felt I was left with was my sin. So I dove back into it headfirst, partly in an attempt to numb the pain, and partly because I felt I had nothing else. On weekends I would spend time with my family and got to know them better. One night, one of my brothers told me that their church played volleyball on Sunday nights, and I decided to go. I enjoyed the games, but when we weren't playing, I mostly kept to myself for a long time. Soon I started going to the evening service with them, then staying for volleyball after. I was able to meet a few people and have a good time. I was still incredibly empty, though.

At the beginning of May, I received an email from an organization called Pure Life Ministries regarding a conference they were having in Colorado Springs that next weekend. For whatever reason, I decided to go. I had already embraced my sin and known just how bad I was. That weekend though, God showed me another side of the situation that I hadn't considered. He showed me He loved me. Even though I had steeped myself in sin, been unfaithful to my wife, and gotten divorced, He still loved me. Even though He knew I'd do all those things, He had still sent His Son to live the perfect life I could never live and be killed in my place, paying for all the sin that I deserved death for. In addition, even though I'd rejected Him for over 23 years, He was still calling to me, pleading with me to accept His gift of salvation. When I finally saw all that, I broke. I began to cry and couldn't stop. I didn't talk to anyone but God that day, but He was the only one I needed. I had finally come to the place where I was ready to completely trust Him for the payment for my sin instead of taking it for myself.

Since that time, my life has been different. I'm not perfect, but God has changed my heart and filled it with His love. I am thankful for what He's brought me through, and looking back I can see a few ways that God has used my mom's trauma in my life. First, he used it in part to bring me to the end of myself. He also used it to bring my family and me closer together and restore the relationships there. In addition, He used that closeness with my family to bring me to a church with a group of believers to fellowship with and to have a positive influence on me at a very tenuous time in my life. I can't say that I ever would have chosen the things God has used in my life, but I am so thankful for what He's done and what He's able to accomplish.

Chapter 10
SAINTS GONE TO HEAVEN BEFORE US

Gary: Further Maturing

It was during this time I became aware of two other people with health crisis events starting within a few days of each other and simultaneous to Karen's crisis. These events were a clear demonstration to me that God was at work, further maturing His children's trust in Him. The stories also serve as a further affirmation to me that God does not always heal, but He does allow "bad" things to happen to His children: my cousin Phil and his wife Diana from Iowa and Byron and Ahna from a sister church in Colorado. Byron provided his reflections, which he wrote specifically for this book. Excerpts from Diana's story are used with cousin Phil's permission and also appear in Caringbridges.org, written by Phil Price and daughter Danielle Price. Also included are email updates from Phil's sister Mary Price Morgan.

Diana Price
Diana had flu-like symptoms. The symptoms began approximately November 24, 2012, and included a sore throat and trouble catching her breath. Her "flu" then presented itself as bronchitis,

then as pneumonia. She was admitted to the Creston Hospital on December 3, 2012, for approximately one week, then discharged to home with oxygen and nine different medications.

Per Cousin Mary:

Good afternoon Price family: 2:15 pm:

Some of you have heard about my brother, Phil's wife, Di, who had pneumonia and bronchitis and was in their local hospital in Creston, IA, last week. Some of you haven't, so I'm sending around a mass email for prayer.

She has asthma, so struggles with her health somewhat. After being in the hospital for the majority of last week, she was released on Saturday. Didn't do much over the weekend, but on Monday, her right foot felt cold and funny, so she took a shower, and it was still cold. Phil noticed her toes turning blue, so took her pulse in her foot. None there. He rushed her to the hospital. They put her on oxygen and did tests, and concluded she needed to be in Des Moines Methodist Hospital as she had two blood clots that had to be removed in order to save her foot. They had such dense fog; they couldn't medevac her by helicopter, so an ambulance left immediately. My brother followed right behind. It was dark, and he could hardly see. I talked to him a bit as he drove, and as he arrived at the hospital, he found he had caught up to the ambulance. By then, it was nearing 11 pm. They had a vascular team on hand to take her right into surgery. They let Phil have a minute with her and rushed her off. In the middle of things, they pulled in a heart team, and when they ran more tests, they discovered she had a massive bacterial infection in her heart, which was sending out fragments around her body. They came out at 1:15 to tell my brother she might not make it through surgery if, they felt, they had to amputate her foot. That sent around a bunch of phone calls and prayers. At 3, I woke up with a start and began praying. At 3:15 am the phone rang, it was Phil to further explain. They found a 4" and a 2" mass in her right leg, plus they did a lot of suctioning out of blood clots and infection pockets. They did not guarantee her survival, especially if a big chunk of infection broke off. More calls around the country.

After clearing out her veins, they were able to get a tiny pulse in her right toes, so did not amputate the foot. She survived the night, but they put her in a coma and will bring her out of it in two days. She is on a ventilator, which is keeping her going. Her pneumonia is worse than ever. The doctor asked my brother how he knew to check for a pulse, and he said it was reliving the experience of our mother 10 years ago when she had both legs removed, section by section, going under 7 times in 2 weeks. The doctor was amazed at his knowledge, but it helped as he understood what the doctor was saying.

Since then, it has been up and down, with the pneumonia filling her lungs. Always the threat of amputation and then a glimmer of hope with a tiny pulse in her leg and foot. Phil just called asking for major prayer – they were venting a lung to prevent brain damage, she was going into septic shock, her body appears to be rejecting any help, and her blood pressure and heart rate are dropping. Would you please pray for God's will for her life at this time, and if it is in His gracious will, we might have a Christmas miracle. Sadly, it was 10 years ago we had my mother's funeral, and we know septic shock all too well.

Thank you - Mary Morgan

Septic Shock is life-threatening and occurs when blood pressure drops to a dangerously low level after an infection. The infection will first cause a response from the body known as sepsis. If left untreated, it can lead to something worse - septic shock. Complications include respiratory failure, heart failure, kidney injury or failure, or abnormal blood clotting.

Typically, 50% of all sepsis cases start as an infection in the lungs. The mortality rate for sepsis is 40% in adults, 25% in children, and is significantly greater when left untreated for more than seven days. Septic shock is the thirteenth leading cause of death in the United States and the number one cause of death in intensive care units, as stated in NHS choices and Wikipedia.

Per Danielle:

There were multiple clots removed from her calf, knee, ankle, foot, and groin. Diana was "very unstable" after the 4-hour surgery and still had no pulse in her foot. The doctors sent the clots, they referred to as "organized grey matter." to the lab and stated, everything isn't happening as it should be. Her condition was listed as critical. She was placed on a ventilator and given a generic antibiotic because the medical staff did not know what they were treating.

Per Cousin Mary:

Miracles never cease! Just got a call that the pathologist's report came thru and they learned what antibiotic will work on her infection, and the doctor started barking out orders for everyone to get this and that and pour it into her system. Saving her leg is on the back burner – saving her life is paramount. Since the 2:15 call, they got her a bit more stabilized and are focusing on getting oxygen to her heart and lungs. Keep praying for the family who are there, those who are 90 miles removed in a snowstorm (12" of snow in Des Moines)

– no one is going in or out. Everyone's lives are flipped upside down, and they need prayer for strength to bear it all.

At this point, December 23, 2012, Diana or "Di" has been sick for approximately twenty-three days. Di does not have full circulation in her right leg, does have pneumonia, but her heart is both strong and now free of infection. It was during this time that my wife, Karen, was able to speak. Karen was apprised of her own condition, including the failed angioplasty, double bypass surgery, the coma, and transfers to three different hospitals, potential life support termination, current prognosis, potential future heart transplant, associated risk factors, and life expectancy outcomes. Initially, we were hesitant to share this information, but Karen was insistent and wanted to know.

She was doing her own mental analysis of her potential outcome. Karen had stated to me that since God had taken Cinthy home followed by Amy, then Debbie, the latter two being pastors' wives and having had so much prayer for each, that she (Karen) did not "stand a chance." If God had taken these three women and her own condition was now so tenuous, there was no reason for God not to take her as well. Karen was receiving narcotics, which can cause anxiety and fear, and she displayed both of these emotions.

She was, at that time, extremely fearful of dying and expressed that numerous times. I do thank the Lord that one of the graces He provides is comfort. God gives comfort and peace to some of His children that are close to death. As I stated earlier, my remembrance was that Ken Fagin was at peace with God. Ken quietly accepted that if God was going to take him to Heaven, then he was ok with that and ready to go. Ken Fagan was not fearful of his own imminent death. My wife, Karen, however, was fearful. Perhaps this could have been an indication God was not ready to take her at this point.

Approximately four weeks later, Cousin Phil would pen these words referring to his wife, Diana.

She is starting to understand a little of what is going on around her. We need to be cautious of what is said so [that] she has clarity of mind to comprehend and not panic. Not everything she needs to know is necessary at this time.

We do have to be careful not to cause panic, anxiety, or unnecessary fears to allow time for "clarity of mind" to be present. We need to provide the truthful information the ill person is requesting and hopefully lessen their anxiety. It is a tough call. We also had to make those same types of decisions with Karen.

Cousin Phil and Danielle provide these updates to family, friends, and the church members he pastors:

12/23 Continue to believe that God is healing as He sees fit.

12/24 We still pray that she may still be able to keep her foot because if it is His will, He will provide us with another miracle...it is unbelievable what is happening through God's healing hands.

12/25 Merry Christmas Everyone...Sleeping really well today... Fever has come down quite a bit...trouble finding...pulse in [foot]...sure wish she was awake to celebrate this blessed day with us, but having her alive and getting better is a great blessing in itself. Thank you all for your words of encouragement. It's so wonderful for us to see how special Mom is to so many people. Once again, our faith holds firm, and we know who is in control of Di's health and wellness. This...really proves that our prayers are working...We will still trust that God does have her and our best interest at heart, and if we continue to talk with Him, He will hold us up and carry us through this.

12/26 Found pulse in her right heel...no decision about amputation...lungs slowly clearing...still critical...vent tube may be leaking. We realize that her condition affects so many lives as well as ours...our hope is in God and that He is truly taking care of her...slowly, our prayers will be answered...receive a peace that only God grants to those who have faith in Him.

12/27 Dr...may be able to try to put a bypass in her foot...no origin or reason that she developed these blood clots and that her health did not warrant them.

12/28 From Jeanne, Foot...able to get a pulse on top and on the side which means there is still hope of saving the foot.

12/29 Opened her eyes and began to nod her head, and tried to talk. What an overwhelming experience. She hasn't really responded to my voice or anyone like this for 13 days. What a joy...prayers are answered. Moving her left foot and toes and squeezing her...hands. Thank God for such healing power when we need it most...tonight we have elation. Little by little, He is still answering our prayers. Still hope to save foot.

12/30 Uplifting moment with her [Di] last night. God granted us just what we all needed. That boost that helps propel us to trust whatever may come, we will succeed. Had a wonderful sleep in our [own] beds.

Di started to show emotion. As everyone left, I reminded her that I was there and wouldn't leave. Relax and remember

God is still caring for us all. I reminded her also that 28 years ago that I took a vow through richer or poorer, in sickness and in health. Told her this is the sickness [part], and we will go through this together and walk out of this hospital.

God gave to me...one special blessing that I never expected, Di. [Even though] we are here, it is still precious when we share time with [those] who matter [to us].

12/31 Foot has maintained even if not good...lungs...small improvement. I looked at DI and said we were ok. I then thought of the 23ʳᵈ Psalm and that the Lord is our shepherd, and He will lead us through this. Because of this, our days will be full, our cup will run over, and His goodness and mercy will follow all the days of our lives.

1/2/13 Foot...pulse...easily found our answer to prayer...first pulse in 2 days' great news. I told Dr, "I still believe we are going to walk out of this hospital." Dr. is very pleased with her white blood count. Antibiotics started yesterday were working. First morning... hadn't had a high fever. Another answer to prayer. Heart was looking good and ready for surgery...pulmonary...most crucial - very little improvement.

1/4/13 Foot showed another sign of improvement. "Slowly God is showing His healing hand in Di's life...faith and trust... blood gases and numbers good. 3ʳᵈ day without high grade fever, and that is great news. Once again, we are blessed beyond our measures.

1/5 Another day of small improvements.

1/7 Each day, we can keep improving, the better chances are for saving more of her foot. God is still touching her foot and healing it slowly.

1/8 Blood gases good, white count down...red cell better hemo-globin good, and rested really well...night nurse...surprised at Di's progress...thought she didn't have much chance. I told her Di's a fighter, many people are praying, and (we have) a God greater than us.

1/10 Off vent...agitation

1/11 Back on vent...heart rate...up...has a fever.

1/12 Fever yesterday and today. Another bacterial infection in her lungs. Lungs showed little improvement, blood gases... better heart rate normal...blood pressure [normal]. Nurses have been wonderful and very caring. We still see God's hand in her healing and know and trust He still has control of the situation. We...are truly blessed by...those whose faith sees the need to lift up prayers on behalf of another person in need.

1/13 Found another bacteria growing in...lungs, start another antibiotic to fight it. Keeping a positive outlook and trusting God once again. Our next obstacle now is one we have prayed and hoped that we would never have to face. Di will have to have her right foot removed [somewhere] below the knee. Our prayers are to have her lungs heal and that her odds are better facing this surgery. They.... are watching her general health as to when is the best time. Our window of opportunity with minimal risk is fading due to her foot's health changing. Pray that her health increases and that God grants in all of us the strength we need this next week. We may not understand any of this as to why or how, but trust God, and He promises us that our rewards will be great and only the best. From day one, the surgeons and I have had an understanding, life over limb. This surgery will bring along another set of issues, but I know all things are conquerable to them that love and trust in God. I have all the faith in the world Di will succeed in this situation. She has beat so many odds, and she will continue to recover knowing so many hold her dear to their hearts and continue to pray for her.

1/14 Surgeons and I today talked, and we agree it is time to do what we need to do, but survey all aspects, make a knowledgeable assessment, and do what is in the total and best interest of Di.

I was reading in Psalms 145 today and found that we need to understand that God created man and everything else and that we still have a finite mind, and His is infinite. In verses 8 and 9 David describes God as merciful, gracious, slow to anger, good to all, and His tender mercies are over all His works. Comfort comes from trusting in Him when we truly do not comprehend what we are surrounded with.

This week Di has gone through many health issues unknowingly, and for us here, it has been difficult and tiresome. Reading this passage truly enlightens the heart about the preciousness of life and loved ones. Still see God's hand in all things, and trusting Him will lead us to promised blessings.

1/16 Mom just got out of surgery. Dr...said everything went very well. The anesthesiologist said all went very smoothly.

There is only a little swelling. The muscle looked good. With amputation, they wrap the muscle in the leg around the bone for a cushion when they use a prosthesis. Everything went just as planned. Thank you for all your prayers - Danielle.

> *Comfort comes from trusting in Him when we truly do not comprehend what we are surrounded with.*

1/17 No signs of any problems. When Di is able to have visitors...I will let everyone know. Thank you for your prayers because they really are working.

1/18 She is starting to understand a little of what is going on. Reassured her that she will be going home someday when she is ready. I thought of a passage once again in Psalm 91, David tells us, "He who dwells in the secret place of the Most High, shall abide under the shadow of the almighty. I will say of the Lord, He is my refuge and my Fortress, My God in Him I will trust." "For He shall give His angels charge over you, to keep you in all thy ways." NKJV

Truly through all of the events of the last 32 days at Methodist, we can truly say this is true. God has given us strength, perseverance, comfort, wisdom, and, most of all, the ability to trust. That is one of the hardest things to do. Humbling yourself to the abilities of others and admitting you are incapable of making your loved one be healed. God has blessed us with such a wonderful set of doctors, nurses, support staff, and a place to stay close by.

1/19 Today's been a good day for Mom. Able to sleep ... gaining her strength...off ventilator all morning...leg ...everything looking good - Danielle.

1/20 Limb...healing nicely...no fever...resting well...blood gases and other counts...good.

1/21 "Leg...is healing and think she is on the mend...last night off ventilator for...two and a half hours." 'panic attack...starting to figure out the differences between her two legs. Reassuring her she is healing...focus on...lungs...I was reading yesterday in Psalms 90 when I was reminded when David encouraged us to be glad in our afflictions. Kind of hard at times to see those words of wisdom. So many times we question WHY, but God then reminds him that I have known you before the earth and heavens were created. The comfort then comes from developing a relationship with our maker.

1/22 Today was a day of rest for Di. After a hard and tiresome day, yesterday realizing that she has lost part of her right leg. She was very anxious and restless. Sedatives and pain meds really wouldn't work because of her anxiety. Finally started to calm down...and rest. This morning...removed bandages. Found no concern. Limb looked good. No redness anywhere.

God has given us... the ability to trust. That is one of the hardest things to do.

1/23 Resting well. Heart safe, blood pressure, and respirations have been good.

1/24 Another quiet day. Saw a fever again. Got results from new infection and started to treat it. Not much more news than that, so once again, thank you for your prayers. - Phil

1/26 Today God called another angel home. He opened up His arms and welcomed Di to His heavenly home. I am sure that Gram and my mom walked her through those pearly gates. We all have lost an adorned and loved person in our lives. We have all been blessed with the time we have shared together. Her warm smile let you into her accepting heart. I truly have been loved in my life by this sweet, charming, forgiving adorable woman. When I first met Di, I had no realization how she would change my life. She was fun, beautiful, and desirable. She melted my heart away. We have known each other for almost 29 years and come July 20ᵗʰ been married 28 years. She has brought such delight to not only my life, but also to our two daughters and our families.

Many memories I carry in my heart from the time we shared together, and I know so many of you will dwell on yours [memories of] Di. She has touched so many lives, and we can all say, what a friend. We all are thinking that she has departed from this earth way [too] fast, and we ask why? Life is life. It has its uncertainties and mystery. As I said in one of my earlier updates, how blessed I am to have been loved by her and to love her. It was easy to do when she was so warming and caring.

The pain we all share is for the loss of someone special that melted our hearts away. She loved to enjoy time with family, and yes, going to work. She served at Bunn for nearly 30 years, taking time off to have Erica and Danielle, and then making sure she provided the best she could. God gave me someone special to share this time with, and I will thank Him for it.

One of the pleasures in life we've enjoyed is this woman who was always about her family. She made sure her two daughters were provided for, loved, encouraged, guided, strengthened, and supported with their endeavors. Di received much enjoyment witnessing the achievements they had accomplished, and if they fell short, she embraced them with a loving hug and kisses and always said, "Next time." She was certainly a role model to have and to become. Di was the same mother to others' children as she was to her own.

I could have never dreamed to have had a more endearing, loving, supportive wife as the one God gave me. Stopping one day to give her a ride home from her broken-down car was the start of what some may deem a chance meeting. The almost 29 years we've had together have been such a pleasure through all circumstances in life; I was blessed to have been supported by her. Our time together on earth may be no more, but in my heart, she will never be gone. Because of the kind of woman she has been, she had to have left an impression on all. Her tenderness and kindness embraced our life together to expectations I have never thought [possible]. I love you, Di.

A little piece in all of us is missing, and I pray that God will grant in us the peace that only we can find in Him.

I would like to thank especially Di's family for all of the love and support through the years and [during] this time of her illness, as it has not been easy for anyone. My family, through all the miles apart, I know where your hearts have been, and

I love you all. I would like to thank our church family for reaching out, wanting so badly to comfort, support, and assist in any way. Once again, a big warm hug from the bottom of my heart for your love, prayers, cards, calls, visits, and notes you have sent our way. I truly have meant it when I said, without you, this time in our lives would have been so hard. I gained strength from all of the love you have shown.

THANK YOU, From Phil.

May 16, 2014, almost sixteen months later, Cousin Phil shares the following note with Karen and me.

I hope your days are going fine and that you may enjoy the spring days. God does give us so much to appreciate and see. As you both have come to realize, we as believers aren't guaranteed special treatment from God from adversity, but what He has given to us, is a spirit ... to accept all things are for His glory and praise, and we need to have faith that His ways are for a greater good. We at first may not see it due to the adversity, but in my case with Di's passing, my suffering is deep and heartfelt, but where she resides is with her Heavenly Father, and there is nothing here on earth that I could give her like what she is enjoying. I also know because of our faith, others have been reached to examine their lives and come to accept Christ. I am reminded of what Paul says, "For me to live is Christ, and to die is gain."

Prayers for you both, Phil

Ahna Pollock

During the time we were receiving updates concerning cousin Phil's wife Diana, we also were being updated about Byron's wife, Ahna. Ahna and Karen were patients on the same floor at UCH at the same time. Some of the same people came to visit them both. Karen and I had never met Ahna, although our family knew Byron during his high school years. During mid-December 2012, I met Ahna and Byron's parents. They were in a surgical waiting area at UCH during one of Ahna's rough times. Although Ahna's prognosis was bleak, the family's demeanor impressed me. Ahna's mom and Byron's parents, while greatly concerned, exhibited a quiet acceptance, a trust in the Lord. They conveyed a strong desire for Ahna's healing, although I sensed a quiet resolve from them that God was in control. They did not know how God was going to work this out, but they were patiently trusting Him for whatever outcome God had planned. Ahna's dad was also trusting God. He appeared more excitable and expressed more vocally that God could heal his daughter, and God would heal Ahna if asked. It was clear to me that Ahna's dad was expressing the type of faith needed to move God's healing hand and perform a healing in Ahna's body. This type of faith is what I had heard from the radio preachers while Karen and I lived in California, and I had believed when praying for Cinthy. I felt encouraged when I heard these words of "faith." It was this type of understanding, belief, and verbal acknowledgment I had been taught was needed to move God's hand to perform a healing. Several years earlier, I would have been excited and hopeful. Now, however, I felt empathy for this man. His child was physically in poor condition and not likely to survive. Ahna soon needed another surgery in addition to a liver transplant. Due to her current condition, she could not have the necessary surgeries. Ahna's dad seemed to be hoping and trusting God to ultimately allow Ahna's recovery. I did not feel hopeful since I had exercised this type of "faith" with

Cinthy and others. I had remained hopeful with Amy and Debbie. In all cases, much prayer had been raised to God for physical healings. God had not caused, performed, nor allowed long-term healings for any of the Christians I've mentioned. Maybe God would restore Ahna's long-term physical health. We would all rejoice with that outcome!

Byron provides the following testimony written in July 2014 and used with his permission.

In 2005 Ahna was diagnosed with a liver disease known as PSC, or primary sclerosing cholangitis, and Ulcerative Colitis. PSC affects the bile ducts, and because of scarring, does not allow them to function properly. At that time, she was placed on the liver transplant list in Kansas City. That April, she received a transplant. All this took place before I met her, and when I did meet her in 2007, she was relatively healthy.

In the summer of 2008, Ahna and I began dating, and we were married in 2010. During this time, Ahna ended up in the hospital on several occasions, mostly related to bleeding in the GI tract. I believe there were three times we took her to the emergency room, and she ended up in the ICU for several days. After we were married, this happened three different times. It normally started the same way each time; Ahna would catch a common cold, and because she was on immune-suppressive drugs, her body would have a hard time fighting off the cold. Generally, a cold would last 1½-2 months. Due to the coughing caused by the cold, she would start bleeding internally. She would lose so much blood that she would require several units of blood through a transfusion. During our marriage, she got to the point in her health that it became apparent that she would need a second liver transplant. Her liver was in chronic rejection, which basically means her body would ultimately reject the liver. Common side effects of the liver problems were jaundice, fatigue, forgetfulness, and generally feeling awful. But combined with the UC (ulcerative colitis), she also had severe stomach aches, upper and lower GI bleeding, and several other problems. During this time, I was amazed because Ahna never once complained. She was focused on others and did not seek attention for herself. She could be feeling terrible, and nobody would know. As I got to know her better, it became evident how much her health affected every aspect of her life and how she struggled with simple daily tasks, but she kept on going. Ahna was an incredible testimony to me with her sweet and accepting spirit. I rarely ever heard her complain.

During the summer of 2012, Ahna and I were working for Camp Eden. During that time, Ahna was struggling health wise. She had been to her liver doctors as well as her PCP and GI doctor. Although she was doing what was needed to take care of herself, something was wrong. None of the doctors could figure it out. She spent the majority of that summer in bed resting; she was extremely weak. By the end of the summer, she was doing much better. In October, Ahna caught a cold. We had seen the pattern and were determined to do everything in our power to avoid the hospital. Ahna had to quit working and basically was in bed. Finally, despite all our efforts, Ahna needed to go to the hospital. We went to St. Joseph in Denver. In the emergency room, she received multiple units of blood, then was finally moved to the ICU. She was there just over a week, receiving blood and fluids to get her blood count back where it needed to be. Because of the fluids, she gained close to 100 lbs. Finally, she was stable enough, and the doctors gave her the option to stay and receive diuretics to help lose the *water weight or go home and let it take care of itself. Despite her heart showing some strange rhythms, she opted to go home. Those three days at home were extremely painful and hard on her; however, she kept a good attitude. The next Monday, she went to her GI doctor. He immediately sent her back to the hospital. She spent one day in St. Joe's, then was transferred to University of Colorado Hospital (UCH), where her liver doctors were. During this time, she was on the cardiac floor, ICU, and transplant floor. Throughout the first couple of weeks, the doctors were just trying to figure out what was happening in her body. The bleeding seemed to have stopped, but her white blood count (infections) was high, and her liver numbers were not good either. She was starting to feel better, and we would go for walks around the hospital. Honestly, it was a very sweet time enjoying each other's company. Her mother had come out during the first stay at St. Joe's and continued to stay. I was able to go to work, and Ahna's mom stayed with Ahna during the day. I had never really gotten to know my mother-in-law very well before that time, but during those several months, I came to realize where Ahna got her sweet and quiet spirit, her laugh, and even some of her mischievousness. Because of the time I spent with Shirley Carbon and was able to see how she responded and lived, I now have a very high level of respect for her.*

Ahna started on the cardiac floor but was soon moved to the transplant floor. Things seemed to be going smoothly; there was even talk of her going home before getting a transplant. Her heart still had strange rhythms, but the doctors and nurses did not seem worried about it. After a few days on the cardiac floor, she was moved to the transplant floor. This floor is typically for people who have received transplants, but they thought it was good for her to be there. Things were looking much better for Ahna, and the talk of her going home was happening a little more frequently. She still had much of the water weight but was slowly losing that weight and was able to walk up and down the hall. On our many walks, Ahna and I talked about everything, from what we would do when she got out, to how crazy we looked with her family walking with us. Her father, Don Carbon, was generally talking to everyone, handing out candy, laughing, and making people smile. We probably looked like a Thanksgiving parade. On Thanksgiving Day, we had a feast of the typical Thanksgiving Day food that was prepared by Ahna's mom as well as my mom. We invited the nurse taking care of Ahna to have turkey and pie. It was a good thing Ahna had a private room because it was a pretty loud and exciting event. Friday was another typical day with walks and talks. Saturday night Ahna and I were taking a walk by ourselves, just enjoying each other's company. Her family was planning on going back to Kansas the next day. I remember asking Ahna what she was thinking or feeling, and she said, "I don't know, but I feel like I am on the edge of something big." I asked what she meant, but she wasn't sure, just something didn't seem right. I went home that night, and the plan was for me to take Ahna's brother Asa to church, then go back to the hospital where Ahna's parents would be spending the morning with Ahna, then Mr. Carbon, Amanda, and Asa would go home.

While sitting in church, my phone vibrated. I saw that it was Mr. Carbon, so I quickly left the service. Mr. Carbon told me that Ahna woke up Sunday morning vomiting blood, a pretty big setback. The doctors wanted to see what was happening, so they scheduled her for an upper GI scope. Since she was *vomiting blood, they wanted to intubate her. By the time I got to the hospital, she was heavily sedated and intubated and stayed intubated through Tuesday. The attitude of the doctors and what they were saying didn't sound like things were really that bad. They saw bleeding ulcers in her GI tract, but there didn't seem to be any real worry about it. The hope was that medication could take care of the problem. Later that night, all but Mrs. Carbon went back to Kansas. I continued to go to work, sleep at the hospital, go home, and shower, then back to the hospital. I don't remember what day it was, but I remember Mrs. Carbon calling me while I was at work. I did not really understand what was going on but realized that I needed to get to the hospital. I can't really tell this story without mentioning the incredible blessing I received from my employer, The Deck Superstore. During this time, they constantly let me off work with little or no notice. The employees even gave Ahna and me, Christmas money. The Mitchells, owners of The Deck Superstore, were overwhelmingly gracious and understanding during this time, as was Paul, my direct boss at the time.*

As I rushed to the hospital, my mind was flying through the possibilities of what was happening. I didn't understand much of the phone call but did hear that they wanted to intubate Ahna again. I really wanted to talk to Ahna before that happened. I made it, but she had to be sedated quickly, so I got to say hi and tell her that I loved her. When I got to the hospital, Mrs. Carbon told me that she had called Don, and he was on his way back to Colorado. This was serious. Soon the attending ICU doctor came in along with various other doctors and nurses. He proceeded to tell me that Ahna had a perforation in her bowel, meaning that anything Ahna had eaten recently or drank was basically being dumped into her stomach cavity, producing a big problem since it wasn't sterile. We asked what options we had, and we were told that there was a surgery the doctors could do. I thought, "Ok! Let's do the surgery." But then they explained that because of the ulcers, her intestines were too weak, and the surgery would probably just make things worse, and she would die. So, what are the other options? Well, we could do nothing, but most likely, she would die. We questioned the doctors, but those were the only two options, and both of them ended with Ahna dying. I remember just slumping to the floor in that ICU, crying and praying, questioning God about why this would happen. My mind was flying through every possible thing I could think of having to do with Ahna's health and what I could have done differently. One of the hardest parts of this was mentioned somewhat in passing; the possible cause of the perforation was the scope she had a few days prior. As we talked to the doctors, it became clear that surgery was not an option at all. The surgeons refused to do it, and the other doctors supported that decision. So we waited.

Later that night, Don, Amanda, and Asa arrived; Ahna's other sister Abi was scheduled to arrive later. The same shock of what the doctors told us earlier that day hit again. There were so many tears and questions. The poor doctors and nurses really were patient with us. That night, we all slept in the ICU room. I remember holding Ahna's hand in a chair pulled as close as I could be, crying and praying and talking with her siblings until, one by one, we fell asleep. I woke up to find a blanket had been laid across me as I slept. The nurses did a wonderful job of taking care of not only Ahna but also all of the family; Ahna had nearly 100 different nurses and CNAs.

I had a lot of respect for nurses before this time. After the stay in the hospital, watching them, getting to know them, crying, and praying with them, I felt like they were some of my best friends when it was all over. Four of them even came to Ahna's funeral. I believe that God was able to use us during that time. I had several nurses tell me that they have had other "Christian" families stay in the ICU, but the peace they felt in Ahna's room and the way we lived and responded to the situation was

God is in control.

totally different and refreshing. I know that was not because of us but was God working through us. I have prayed several times that God will use us to plant a seed. I got to share what I believe with several of those nurses, and I am excited to see if that was used in any of their lives. Ahna and I had talked at one point, and we decided that if even one of those doctors or nurses were saved because of our testimony, it would all be worth it. I still believe that to this day.

The next day, the story was the same. She will probably die soon, so we needed to be ready for that. I didn't find this out until later, but the attending doctor had left the night before, expecting her to die during the night. That second night he felt the same way and even said that if she made it through the night, it would be a miracle. Little did he know that we serve the God who can and does work in miracles. Ahna survived the next night, and the next, and for the next two and half months, God proved that He could work miracles.

During this time, even though the nurses said we exhibited such peace, I was going through a battle. My heart hurt, my mind was constantly going through possibilities, and so many different times I questioned, demanded, yelled at, and pounded God with questions. I wanted to trust Him, I wanted to let Him do what He thought best, but I was convinced He was doing it wrong. Every little procedure or changing of the IV solution, my heart worried. I was able to keep a calm demeanor, but it was not indicative of my heart. I was not at peace. I prayed, telling God I trusted in Him and His ways, but still, I hurt. During this time, the first attending doctor left, and a new one came in. Something was now going on with Ahna's lungs, and they wanted to do a bronchoscope. I struggled with this because I was still thinking of the last procedure, the GI scope, and the possibility that it caused the perforation. As they were getting ready for us to leave the room and start the procedure, I asked the doctor if I could watch. She looked surprised but said yes. I was able to see the screen as they looked into Ahna's lungs. The attending doctor, Dr. Abigal Laura, explained what we were seeing and the different parts of the lung. About halfway through the procedure, I was hit with an indescribable peace. I don't know why God used that moment to cover me with that peace, but He did; from that point on and even through Ahna's last moments on earth, I felt that peace.

The reality is, so many of the procedures and tests run together. For the last two weeks of Ahna's life, she usually had two chest x-rays a day. More blood tests happened throughout her stay than most of us will have in our entire lives. She had several Interventional Radiology procedures, which I was allowed to observe.

I remember riding with my pastor from the church to the hospital. He mentioned to me that God is in control. I knew this, or at least I had heard this, and I would tell people that I believed it. After several weeks in the hospital, I had to decide if I really believed that. There were times of prayer, crying, arguing, and trying to convince God that I knew what was best. I knew that I needed to let God have control, but for me, this was a hard step. I wanted control, and I thought that I had control, but the reality was, I never had control. I went from praying that God would heal her, to praying that He would give me peace and that I would accept whatever His will was. I did still pray that she would be healed, but my outlook on the entire situation changed. Resting in the complete confidence that God really was in control and that He knew best was a wonderful place to be.

I have thought many times about God's grace and how it is really shown to us. In some ways, it is unexplainable. I think that if we really lived in light of the fact that God's "grace is sufficient" for us, that it would totally change our outlook and the way we live our lives. God's grace did not become available the second I decided to acknowledge His control and sovereignty in Ahna's situation, that grace was already active and moving. I was unable to see it because I was so blinded by worry, anger, heartache, and resisting God's plan. The grace of God really is so overwhelming, so powerful, but I just could not see it. However, once I acknowledged that His control and His plan, whatever that was, was the absolute best thing to bring Him glory and to bring a change of Christ-likeness to the lives of Ahna, myself, and so many people affected by this situation. Then I could see just a sliver of the magnitude of His grace. That small sampling

> I have thought many times about God's grace and how it is really shown to us.

was a taste, just a tiny portion of the grace God has and is always giving. There was the thought that if God loved Ahna and me as much as He says He does, and if He gives the grace needed, or above and beyond what is needed, then why would He not heal Ahna? But through prayer and seeking Him, I came to realize what I had always been told is true. We don't realize that the life we have, the friends, the family, the jobs, and anything else we have here on earth are not the best thing. Though they are a corrupt, twisted illusion of happiness, they are ironically still an example of God's grace. The Life that God offers, the ability to have a relationship with Him, the absolute joy found in Him, and the chance to know and be with Him is what everything is really about. There was nothing wrong with wanting Ahna healed, but in wanting that, I was trying to pull her away from the opportunity for her to be completely healed and in the presence of God. I know that Ahna is not suffering and that she is living with God; I, too, have that opportunity coming to me someday.

I truly did expect God to heal Ahna. I expected the doctors to come up with some solution, some answer that would end it all. But as I look back, I can honestly say that the only thing I would have changed is how soon I let God have complete control. Because of that situation, I was able to: witness to people I would have never known, develop a strong relationship with God, see a glimpse of the grace of God, and experience His love. It is a blessing to serve our amazing God, who loves me no matter what I do.

---Byron Pollock

Chapter 11
WHICH ROAD WILL I CHOOSE?

Gary: The Road of Skepticism or the Road of Faith

As I mentioned earlier, Byron, his parents, and Ahna's mom exhibited a quiet patience. I sensed they definitely wanted God's intervention for Ahna, which was desperately needed at that time for her to live. Instead, they seemed more willing to trust God for whatever outcome He had planned. They were not making demands on God for Ahna's healing. The attitude they displayed was more consistent with my attitude during this trial period with Karen and her need for healing. I will pray for healings. I will hope God grants healing. I will try to continue to trust God to accomplish His plan even if no healing is granted. I will try to be joyful with any outcome; this is easier said than done. I do recognize that God permits times of trials in His children's lives. God uses trials or times of adversity to grow His children's faith, to help them learn to trust Him more. In this life, we experience pain, sickness, and suffering. Our promise from God is that in Heaven, we no longer will experience the pain, sickness, and suffering that we currently endure in our mortal bodies. These are temporary afflictions used by God to draw us closer to God. How then do I learn to trust God joyfully in the midst of trials? In one sense, I have the easy part. I just have to go along for the ride; God already has a plan to mature me. I do not have to make a plan, and I do not have to execute a plan either; I just need to be faithful doing what He desires of me. God is not taken by surprise with any event that occurs in my life. God works all things for my good. Not only for my good but also for the good of all who love Him and are called according to his purpose, Romans 8:28. God will use all events to conform me (Romans 8:29) to the image of His Son. Good and bad things happen in my life. I cannot control them, but God can and will use them. Even the things that are considered <u>bad</u> things, God allows, to be able to mold me to be more like Christ. Saying this is much easier than thinking this way and acting on this belief. We still see <u>bad</u> or horrible things happening to people. Husbands abandon their wives; mothers lose their husbands due to health issues like heart failure or cancer and are left to raise their children on their own; parents lose their children; children lose their parents; husbands lose their wives. Each diligently sought human intervention and prayed for healing. All of these examples I have witnessed; most were stated previously in this narrative.

What options do we have? Ideally, we joyfully trust God in <u>good</u> circumstances and in <u>bad</u> circumstances. We can have a growing confidence or trust that God is working His will on our behalf to mature and to conform us to His image. The end goal is that God will be pleased with us, and we will be happy people filled with the joy of the Lord. As God's people, we could say, "It does not get any better than that."

Conversely, we could fail to trust God. We could choose to become suspicious of what God is doing or question whether or not God is even concerned with us or if He even exists. If God does exist, does He really care about us since He is allowing all of these "bad" or horrible things to occur? Does God really have a good plan for our lives? The skeptic would state, "There must not be a god? God, if there is a god, whoever he or she is, would not allow these horrible things to happen. Also, if this god is trustworthy and gave us written promises that do not come true, then this god is at least a liar, but more accurately, not a god at all." There is no hope of anything better than what this life has to offer. One is born, lives, and dies; there is no more to one's existence. After death, each person ceases to exist. It is an empty, hopeless existence. The previous statements are the belief system of the skeptic filled with doubt; the skeptic is a faithless person.

In contrast, the person living by faith has a different belief system; it is based on a hope in God. The basis of this hope is a belief that God has revealed Himself through a written word, which He, the Creator of the universe, has kept, pure or free from error. Through this word, we learn to trust Him even if difficult times come. God says that He has a plan to give us a hope. Jeremiah 29:11 NASB, "'For I know the plans that I have for you,' declares the LORD, 'for welfare and not for calamity to give you a future and a hope,'" While this promise was given to Israel, I believe it has a general application to all Gods' people.

The skeptic calls this faith system a "pie in the sky" mentality. He may say, "You can't see your god; you can't touch your god. All your rewards are supposedly received after you die. The words that supposedly come from your god were just written by men in an effort to control the population and allow the elite in societies to retain control over the masses or the simple people." The person of faith recognizes that the hope they possess is based on something trustworthy and that prophesies given years, decades, and centuries in advance have become a reality. If God is able to either predict or direct events in human history to cause prophecies to be fulfilled, then this God is both worthy of our trust and demanding of that trust. When the person of faith experiences <u>bad</u> things, he continues to trust God despite negative outcomes. The person of faith recognizes that they may not understand the reason for suffering until they gain the "eternal perspective," meaning they are able to see the big picture from God's point of view. This understanding, however, is not gained until they are in Heaven with God. Both systems are, in fact, belief systems. Adherents to either system have made a choice to put their own personal belief or faith in something that is more consistent with their own worldview.

What then do I choose? Do I start down the road towards skepticism because I am not able to appropriate what I have perceived as the healing promises from God's Word? This road leads to the continued denial of Christ, no hope, and eventually bitterness of soul. We, as believers in Christ, have a hope in the salvation promises from God and are content with those promises. If Christ weren't true, then we as believers would become discontented and miserable. I Corinthians 15:19, "If in this life only we have hope in Christ, we are of all men most miserable." The road of faith leads to hope and contentment. Since the road of faith is preferable to me, how then should I now pray for Karen?

Mrs. Snyder, Bob Botkin, Ken Fagan, Wendy Wasey, Cinthy Midkiff, Amy Bixby, Debbie Robbins, Diana Price, and Ahna Pollock traveled the road of faith, and now all of them are with God in Heaven. Likely, all these people had hoped for physical healing in their bodies, but to my knowledge, none had demanded healing from God. The earlier examples of Mrs. Snyder and Bob Botkin helped me to initially form my expectations of God's working regarding physical healing. However, now all of these examples together are what God is using to reform my expectations to more accurately show me how God works regarding physical healings and what my future expectations concerning physical healings should be.

I should pray for Karen scripturally and use as my examples the lives of the people of faith God has literally placed before me. Yes, I will ask God for Karen's physical healing. I recognize that God can easily perform the physical healing and also that God is working a greater good in my life and the lives of others. The healing or the lack of healing may not be related to my personal needs and desires, but perhaps someone else's need. I do not possess that knowledge; God does. I just have to trust that God is working out that greater good; I can then rest and be content with that knowledge. This, I believe, is the essence of faith. I do not have to worry, fret, or have anxiety; I can leave it all to God to work things out.

Another excellent example of leaving something totally for God to deal with was happening at this time. God was working out the relational healing of my absent son. As mentioned earlier, it had been approximately four years since Karen had seen him and five years since we had enjoyed a good relationship. I had tried to involve others in helping to restore that relationship. I felt I had performed as much as I could to allow restoration of this fractured relationship. Finally, I just turned it all over to God. I was still hoping for restoration, but I was no longer demanding restoration from all that were involved. I was available should restoration occur, but I was no longer actively pursuing restoration. I had given this over to God to perform in His way and in His time, and God did! The restoration process did happen!

Survival Nugget: God's PURPOSE for Me is Christlikeness. Jeremiah 29:11-13, "'For I know the thoughts that I think toward you,' saith the Lord, 'thoughts of peace, and not of evil, to give you an expected end. Then shall ye call upon Me, and ye shall go and pray unto Me, and I will harken unto you. And ye shall seek Me, and find Me, when ye shall search for Me with all your heart.'" I had plans: to keep working in the church office, to have our new dining room furniture delivered, to continue selling textbooks to homeschoolers, to go to NY at Christmas, and to order the new couch I had picked out. More generally, I planned to be a supportive wife and mom and serve God in other ways. My plans were not bad things; they were things I felt God wanted, but He did not want them for me at that time. I often do not understand why things happen as they do or when they do, but I can rest in the truth of this verse and let God be God. He knows all, He is all-powerful, and He loves me. I seek to know Him and trust Him completely.

Chapter 12
THE GREAT PHYSICIAN

Sunday, Day 30 – December 9, 2012
Church's Update

We are very encouraged to learn that Karen Price's kidneys are beginning to function. This was a major concern. We will know more in the next few days, but this was a big one!!! The next steps will be for her to start the long road of physical therapy. Karen had been moved out of ICU to a step-down room. She still required dialysis, had nausea, still needed NG feeding tube, and started very preliminary physical therapy.

Survival Nugget: When I woke up from the coma, and during the first few months, things did not make much sense. I did not have to understand; I just had to trust. I was totally dependent on others, and sometimes those people did not do their job the way they should. God's grace was sufficient for me. In 2017 I read in a book *When Trouble Comes* of a college guy who was in a car accident and became a quadriplegic. Some quotes from him resonate deep within me, putting words to some thoughts and feelings I had.

I didn't need to progress through the five stages of grief: shock, denial, anger, guilt, and depression. Why? In part because I had a competent medical staff attending to my physical needs and dedicated parents [family], who daily provided me with support, but most importantly because my relationship with God's Son had not been altered in any way through this unanticipated incident.

Practically speaking, this meant that when everyone had left my bedside, there was still someone there – Christ – the one who promised that He by no means would desert or abandon me (Hebrews 13:5). When my body became spent, my emotions spongy, and my thoughts shaken, I could rest on Christ, the everlasting Rock, as the prophet Isaiah describes Him (Isaiah 26:4), who provides lasting stability.[1]

God was working through me. Left to my own self-centered ways, I could have become bitter and discouraged. I, like this young man, prayed the following: not to be fearful, discouraged, and lack hope, knowing that what I wanted was not the most important. When I was first trying to communicate with my family, they thought I was trying to tell them I was afraid to die. Instead, when I said, "I don't want to die," I was telling Gary that I chose to live. Gary said that when I was in a coma, he told me that if I chose to go to Heaven, it would be okay. I wanted him to know that if I died, it was not because I chose to leave him. If I had a choice, I would choose to live, not to die. But I could not accurately express my thoughts, and therefore, he did not understand what I was trying to say. Often, during that time, my voice was weak, and I could barely get out a few words. I did not try to communicate much since I could not figure out how to communicate in a way that they would understand. So, I would listen, try to think, and wait on God. God's

---

[1]   Jim Berg, *When Trouble Comes* (Greenville, SC: BJU Press, 2002), pp. 33-34.

purpose for me was Christlikeness, and during that time, He taught me more about waiting and about Himself.

Gary: Out of ICU!

Tuesday, Day 32 – December 11, 2012

Kevin emailed out, "Karen has now been in the hospital for over four weeks. Last Thursday, she was moved out of ICU and into a private room on another floor. This meant a new set of nurses. The other significant progress that past week is that, as of Saturday, her kidneys have started working again. They have been giving her apple sauce, crackers, broth, jello, and similar type foods. Although her swallowing seems to be working okay, her stomach is having a challenge in keeping the food down. They are working with medication and giving her food through the feeding tube for 24 hours rather than just 12 hours. Same amount of food, just over a longer period. They are working with her each day with therapy and trying to push her a little farther each day. Still quite weak. Once she can start eating regular food, that should help with the energy level. They are also continuing with every-other-day dialysis until she starts eating and drinking regular food and making sure all the levels are okay.

Tuesday, Day 39 – December 18, 2012

On December 17, we learned she has been off dialysis for seven days! She was transferred today to a rehabilitation hospital.

Part of Kevin's email says, "Gary says he sees improvement in her each day." "As they were leaving the Univ. of Colorado hospital, the main doctor for Karen told Timmy and their pastor that he had never had someone come into the hospital in as bad a shape as Karen and been able to make it. He also thanked the family for all they did in helping her."

Wednesday, Day 40 – December 19, 2012
Church's Update

Update on Karen Price. She has been moved to a rehabilita-
tion hospital. Her doctor stated that she will be in rehab for a
minimum of four months.

Thursday, Day 41 – December 20, 2012

Karen sat in a chair for the first time. A hoist was required to move her from her bed to her chair. It was used to get her back and forth from bed to chair daily for several weeks.

Tuesday, Day 46 – December 25, 2012 ~ Christmas Day ~

The family visited Karen on Christmas. Andrew was sick but was able to visit Karen via Skype. A few days before, Pastor Whitcomb came to sing Christmas carols to her, a cappella solos. Karen was very pleased by that and stated that the singing helped it feel more like Christmas. Nurses enjoyed him singing as well.

Benjamin: Doing Our Best

It was around Christmas 2012 when my mom finally was well enough to go to a "rehabilitation hospital;" it is better described as a "where they stick people to take advantage of their insurance company hospital." This "hospital" was supposed to help her get better, teach her to walk, eat food, dress herself, and help her fine motor skills in general. In the end, they did get the job done, but only because we did a lot of things the nurses were supposed to do, and also because my mom was a fighter. She never gave up; she took it upon herself to do many things herself. Many of the staff was not qualified and did not care about the patients. They were rough with my mom, left her alone for hours, and sometimes took hours to answer the call button. I could go into the ugly details, but just know it was very rough and not conducive to recovery. My family and I did our best to encourage my mom. We would each spend 25+ hours a week at the hospital with her. It wasn't long before she had her feeding tube out, and she was able to speak and start learning how to have conversations with us again. Mostly, she would just sleep. Healing is exhausting.

This time was very difficult for me for a few reasons. First off, my whole family was having an extremely tough time, just like I was. It led to everyone being more inwardly focused, trying to deal with themselves. I do not blame anyone for this. It just worked out where everyone had deep support from someone, and for whatever reason, I got mostly overlooked. Maybe it was because I was young, or because I am a lot better at hiding things than I thought, or maybe people just didn't know how to help me; I'm not sure. I just know that I felt very alone during this time, except for one friend and a relationship I was in at the time.

Another reason it was difficult for me was because of my mom. Don't get me wrong; it was not anything that she was doing wrong. She was focused on healing. She was learning to think, walk, talk, eat, sleep, hold a spoon, tie shoes - all the basic things we take for granted. She was taken back to ground zero as a person. She was not who I remembered from my life. For one, the coma and strokes had messed with her memory; she did not remember things for a long time. We still joke about it when she cannot remember something, or if something is confusing, we say, "that was before the coma," or she says, "I don't remember because I was in a coma." Also, she had experienced so much physical, emotional, and mental trauma in a short time that for a long time and a little bit still to this day, her personality was altered. The second thing that was hard for me was that it felt like I was getting to know a second mom. Obviously, this was the same physical person that had always been my mom, but she was not who I had left in the hospital that first Saturday evening. I now know that I just didn't know my mom to the extent I thought

I did, and I was just seeing who she was at her very core. But it was a long time before I was able to connect the two personalities I saw and realize that she was not a different person, just altered. Now I see and better know her on a deeper level than I ever would have, or at least could have for many, many years.

One special memory I have of this time was in February of 2013 when I had my birthday. My sister-in-law made a point to make it special for me. It was one of the first times my mom was well enough to leave her room and make her way down to the cafeteria in a wheelchair; granted, it took four of us to make that happen. It was very special to have a birthday party with my mom and the whole family with me.

Gary: Not *A* Healer, *The* Healer
Wednesday, Day 54 – January 2, 2013

Karen was able to take her first steps in a very controlled environment. She uses handrails with one therapist in front of her and one behind her. Seeing her relearning to walk was an emotional time for me. I was in tears to see my wife taking her first steps. She literally had to relearn <u>how</u> to walk. Parents are joyful when they see their children walk for the first time. This was different. Six weeks earlier, Karen's prognosis stated her recovery, if she were to have a recovery, would not include the ability to ever walk again. Her inability to walk would be due to the strokes and the brain damage she had sustained during the heart attack, inadequate life support, and the prolonged coma. Thankfully the Lord was allowing her to walk again!

Kevin sent out, "This afternoon when answering my cell phone, the voice on the other end said, 'This is Karen.' We then proceeded to talk for about 10 minutes. This was the first time I had heard her talk since she went into the hospital the first half of November. My mom had talked with her on the phone a couple of times in the last two weeks, but she indicated it was only with short sentences and a lot of yes and no. Her voice sounded a little weak but clear. We carried on a regular conversation, with her talking about half the time. She is not yet able to manipulate the phone herself, but Tim dialed the number and put the phone on speaker for the conversation. She indicated that they put her into a standing position yesterday, and she stood between two bars for about 30 sec. Today they did it again, today three times for about 90 seconds each time. She was happy with the progress. The eating is improving, but slowly. She will go two days without nausea, then a day when it comes back. Yesterday she had a small amount of mashed potatoes successfully, still on the feeding tube. They are now having her sitting up in a chair for much of the day. (between 4 - 10 hours each day). She realized about 3-4 days ago she had her smell back; she did not even realize that she had lost it. She is getting more feeling in her hands and feet."

Thursday, Day 55 – January 3, 2013
Church's Update
Karen continues to do well in recovery. She is doing physical therapy daily and working hard in recovery. Please pray for her nausea; she is unable to keep solid food in her stomach. Doctors are hoping the nausea subsides soon for a quicker recovery with nutrition from solid foods. Family is doing well. Karen and family appreciate your continued prayers.

Karen was transported via ambulance to UCH for her first routine monthly clinic visit at the heart failure clinic. Two things surprise the clinic staff. First, the staff did not know why Karen's surgeon Dr. Babu requested to see Karen while she was in clinic. Surgeons are welcome at clinic, but they do not come to clinic. Dr. Babu had previously stated that Karen had been the most ill patient he had ever had that survived. He had heard about Karen's speedy recovery, and he particularly wanted to see her fingers and toes. As stated earlier, Karen would lose (have amputated) a minimum of three fingers and several toes. However, it now appeared that all fingers and toes were recovering. Second, the doctors were very surprised and encouraged by her progress; this was faster than they had seen before. When Dr. Babu said, "You're a healer." Karen said, "No, but I know <u>the</u> Healer!" This provided yet another opportunity for Karen to give God praise. She knew God was in control, doing miracles, and taking care of her. We were told sternum restrictions were in place for a few more weeks; the scar was healing nicely; doctors discussed the continued nausea. Karen happily shared with the doctors about taking her first steps.

As a family, we thank God for His watch care. Approximately seven weeks earlier, we had hoped that Karen would survive: first the failed angioplasty, then the transport to the second hospital, and then the emergency bypass surgery, followed by a transport to the third hospital. Then we longed for her to emerge from the coma, and for God to reverse the reported brain damage. The negative results of the CT scan and EEG test presented us with a very possible, soon termination of life support decision. This was followed by a discussion of amputation of at least three fingers and several toes. God sustained Karen's life, and she is improving in many ways: the brain damage was not as severe as reported, she still has all her fingers and toes, her kidneys and lungs recovered. Karen is able to walk, communicate, and display previous cognitive levels despite the "dismal" neurological prognosis.

While God took care of Karen's physical health, I believe He also showed His concern for her medical care. We prayed for Karen to be in the facility God wanted. It was planned that Karen would be sent to a rehabilitation hospital and then returned to UCH for some specialized rehab prior to being discharged to go home. We were pleased with that plan and looking forward to her returning to UCH. However, we were very disappointed when we kept hearing conflicting reports from the rehab hospital's social workers. They stated that the insurance company did not want to have Karen sent back to UCH but rather discharged to home from this rehab hospital. Then, it was stated that Karen would be transferred to UCH, then the transfer was postponed for unknown reasons, and then eventually, they said that she was beyond the rehab UCH could offer Karen. All these statements were found to be either false or misleading. One of the social workers was let go very unexpectedly while Karen was still a patient at the rehab hospital. The other social worker was let go a few months later. These dismissals are confirmation to me that God is concerned about the disappointment caused by those who are entrusted with the care of His children.

Saturday, Day 64 – January 12, 2013

Karen is able to walk from her bed to the hallway. Three days later, she walked twenty feet. After six more days, she walked 140 feet. Eight days later, with much assistance, Karen walked up a flight of stairs.

Survival Nugget: I am thankful for the opportunity to serve Him here longer. A short time before going into the hospital, I prayed, telling God I was still willing to go to the mission field. This time He did send me to the mission field – the mission field of the hospital, medical personnel, and other disabled people. Because of my experiences, I am in contact with people that I would never have been; God has used me in ways I could not have been used before. I have compassion, with an understanding that I did not have previously. "And of some have compassion, making a difference," is a verse, Jude 22, that I learned as a teenager, but one I understand better now. I learned the hard way that most people in wheelchairs especially, or with a walker or with other noticeable medical devices (such as but not limited to oxygen or LVAD's), are treated by many like they are mentally disabled. People often stood above me and talked or spoke near me, thinking I could not understand. People often speak louder to some in a hospital bed or a wheelchair. I am more compassionate now, and I am careful not to be the one to avoid a disabled person or turn away from them. I now go over and speak to them, telling them that I had a walker just like that or that I was in a wheelchair for a while and did not expect to ever get out of it. Sometimes, I thank the caregiver saying that I'm sure they are appreciated. Usually, I see a head nod and a smile from the person in a wheelchair who cannot speak. These simple ways of connecting to others initiate conversations in which I try to point people to the one true God. I plan to continue to minister to people this way.

Wednesday, Day 68 – January 16, 2013

Kevin emailed, "About 10 days ago, the physical therapists put Karen in a standing position. The first time she stood on her own for about 30 seconds between two bars. Two days later, she was standing for 90 seconds three different times. She has continued to improve, and about a week ago was taking several steps on her own between two parallel bars and then several steps on her own between her chair and her bed. The end of last week, she talked to mom on the phone and told her that she had walked about 70 feet down the hallway with a walker. She was quite excited with that progress. Although she can read, it is still too exhausting to hold a book and turn the pages. Karen is still struggling with nausea. The plan last week was to limit the food in the feeding tube to only at night. Not significant improvement. The plan for this week is to take her back to the University Hospital where they will remove the feeding tube from her throat and install a new one directly into her side. Without the tube in the throat, they hope the nausea will go away. It has now been over two months since Karen first went to the hospital with chest pains."

Fortunately, the University cardiologist did not agree with the convalescent hospital's plans. Although that new tube might deliver better nutrition and help with the nausea, it had its own set of potential side effects. It also could potentially interfere with the LVAD and its driveline. It was not worth the risk. This stomach tube was not inserted. Another medication was prescribed, and Karen was finally able to eat more.

Karen: More Energy Please

In November, when I was taken from St. Joseph's Hospital to University the first time, the two ambulance paramedics did not think there was any chance that I would live. I was already maxed out on everything, so there would have been nothing more they could have given me if I struggled in the ambulance. Their main focus was to get me from the ambulance and into the hospital without any further trauma. Over the following few days after the transport, they were puzzled as to why they were never interviewed about me or the ride. That would have happened as a standard procedure if I had died soon after arriving at UCH. I learned this from separate conversations they each had with me. The first conversation was when one of these paramedics came to get me for my ride from the convalescent hospital back to University Hospital for my first clinic visit. He came into my room, looked at me, and smiling broadly said, "It **IS** you!" as he was literally jumping up and down around my room. He told me who he was and that he recognized my name but thought it could not be me, as I surely had not survived. On the next trip, I got to meet the other original ambulance paramedic. He was also very happy to see me; he and many other paramedics heard from the first paramedic that I was alive. He told me that it was very rewarding for them as paramedics to see me alive since they do not usually get to find out what happens to people after they deliver them to the hospital – they do not hear the success stories. I am grateful for the part they played in keeping me alive and for how we could encourage each other.

Each time I went to a clinic visit, my LVAD nurse Will would hook one of my controller cords to a computer. By doing this, he and the doctor could see on the computer if there had been any incidents and how my machine and heart were doing. During one of these clinic visits, I told my LVAD cardiologist, Dr. Brieke, that I was feeling much better and doing more, but I was tired most of the time and wished for more energy. He said that he could take care of that – no surgery, no procedure was required. The doctor simply asked Will to turn up the speed of the machine. With just a few clicks on a computer, my LVAD was running faster, and I had more energy! How many times over the years, as a mom of four sons, had I craved more energy? Having the heart pump provided the doctor with the remarkable ability to increase my energy so easily, which was unlike anything I had experienced before.

My internal LVAD was hooked to an external controller that hung on a belt I wore. In the hospital room or at home, it was connected to a machine that was plugged into the wall with a seventeen-foot cord. When I had to leave, I would transfer from the wall power to batteries. These batteries were also attached to the belt and later a vest. Before I left the convalescent hospital, I had to learn how to switch from the cord to the batteries on my own. This awkward and arduous process was very difficult for me since I was so weak, and my fingers were stiff and sensitive. My LVAD coordinators came over from University Hospital to teach me (and the convalescent hospital staff) how to do this. Gary and Gracelyn learned how to care for the equipment and had to practice sterile dressing changes. The site where the driveline exited my body that connected the internal pump to the external controller required dressing changes to prevent infection. These several-step processes were done every day in the beginning, then eventually twice a week. Following my transplant, dressing changes continued for several months until the site healed. My site took longer to heal than most; it was not until later that we would learn the reason.

Survival Nugget: In the convalescent hospital, I remembered the words on a plaque given to me when I was in elementary school. It is a small piece of blue glass with a silver chain around the edges. It has a few tiny pink flowers painted in a corner, and the center has the words from a Bible verse, "Hope thou in God." It hung above my bed for years. The verse is from Psalm 42:11, "Why art thou cast down, O my soul? And why art thou disquieted within me? Hope thou in God: for I shall yet praise him, who is the health of my countenance, and my God." A couple of years ago, I found that plaque and put it out again, so it could serve as a reminder of the encouragement I had received in the hospital from this admonition the psalmist repeats often. This truth continues to sustain and encourage me today. The hope mentioned in this psalm is not the hope with a slim chance of happening. It is a word for a sure thing, something I can trust in because God said it. Instead of worrying or being discouraged, I tell myself, "Hope thou in God."

Gary: Continued Improvements
Wednesday, Day 82 – January 30, 2013

Karen had to relearn the steps of how to get out of and back into bed. She can now sit on the side of the bed, pull her legs on to the bed, lie on her back, and also pull herself upright and swing legs off the bed. During therapy, she was able to slowly walk up a flight of stairs and then turn and very carefully walk back down a flight of stairs without resting. "Her smile was so big!"

Friday, Day 92 – February 8, 2013

She is now able to walk up and down two flights of stairs. She also walked down the hallway to the physical therapy room, opened the door, walked in, and sat down.

Thursday, Day 98 – February 14, 2013

Karen walked slowly on the treadmill for three minutes, took a sponge bath, and dressed herself. She continues to use the walker. The biggest excitement of the day was that after three months, the NG feeding tube was finally removed!

Saturday, Day 100 – February 16, 2013

Kevin emailed, "It has now been three months since Karen went into the hospital. She had been doing two-plus hours of therapy each day for the last several weeks. Her therapy includes: walking with and without a walker, going slowly up and down steps, and picking up cones. With the bed in a sitting position, she can now slide off the bed into a standing position. All of her movements still require someone close by to make sure she does not fall. She has made a couple of calls with the hospital phone. She is now eating all of her breakfast and about half to two-thirds of lunch and supper. Still not able to take medications orally. Still on the feeding tube and still some nausea. About a week ago after a major evaluation, the lead doctor felt that physically she was about three weeks ahead of schedule. The doctor that performed the surgery indicated that all the wounds were completely healed. New skin has now grown on each of her toes and fingers, with feeling in each."

Tuesday, Day 103 – February 19, 2013

Karen continues with physical therapy. She practices sitting up in bed, getting out of bed without using a rail, and dressing herself.

She had a controlled fall today and then learned how to stand up from the floor.

Thursday, Day 112 – February 28, 2013 ~ Timmy's Birthday
Church's Update

Update on Karen: After her doctor's appointment Tuesday, she got a new medication and is expected to be released Friday to return home. PTL! Please contact Gracelyn before visiting.

Friday, Day 113 – March 1, 2013

Karen was discharged to home! She walked around the downstairs with her new walker. She viewed the new furniture that she had ordered prior to going into the hospital but had not yet seen it in our home. She ate at the kitchen table with the family – the first time in almost four months!

Survival Nugget: I needed to have a humble dependence on Him, and He provided inner strength. As I needed things, He would bring another memory or nugget of truth to my mind, or send someone with just the words I needed then or a phrase from a Bible verse. God's Word is my final right answer. It was a long time before I could hold a Bible and read it. My oldest son Timmy made long-playing CDs of Christian songs filled with Scripture and God's truths. Many mentioned Heaven. One I remember in particular was, *Before the Throne of God Above* by Charitie Bancroft. The words especially spoke to me about God being a High Priest, Love, and the King of Glory, that my name is graven on His hands, written on His heart, and that He is unchangeable. These helped calm me and helped ease my hunger for Scripture, prayer, and Christian fellowship. Especially when I needed it most, God sent friends and family members to pray with me, read the Bible, and encourage me.

Benjamin: The Real Work Started

March 1, 2013 was the big day! My mom was finally well enough to come home. The day was a happy day but also a scary day as well. At this point, my mom was not fully human. She only had half of an operational heart. The left side of her heart was an artificial pump that was installed months earlier. This pump needed electricity to run 24/7. This means she was either plugged into a machine that was plugged into a dedicated circuit my dad set up in the house or that she had to wear a ten-pound battery pack that could sustain her for about 8 hours. At any given time, if the power went out, she was only 48 hours away from the pump stopping and her dying (we had three sets of batteries). We got a backup electricity generator and made sure to keep all the batteries fully charged at all times. It was very stressful. We also had to take care of the logistics of all the other things a human needs to stay alive. It was nearly overwhelming for us, and sometimes I wonder how my mom ever made it through.

Over the next month and a half, my mom slowly got better. She practiced walking and eventually was able to walk with a walker to the bathroom across the hall. Every little victory was a big "step" for her. Her first outing outside the house was at the end of April to my school play. I was very excited to have her there for one of the performances. I did not have a flattering role, and no one in the school could act, but it was special to have her there nonetheless. They say that laughter is like medicine, and if that is literally true, I would like to take credit for a substantial part of the healing my mom and my whole family underwent while at the play. I mentioned that my role wasn't flattering, I was a 6' 2" 146 pound Father Christmas in Narnia, and my costume was made for someone three times my size. The moment I walked out on stage, it was absolute silence for about one second, then a small corner, in the handicap section where my family was, erupted in laughter. The laughter lasted through the whole two-minute scene. It is still a source of laughter until this day.

If this story were a Hollywood movie, it would end right about the time mom came home from the hospital. That is the end of the story, right? The answer is no, surprisingly. When she got home, the real work started for us, and it was a different kind of struggle for everyone. It was full of ups and downs.

Andrew: Thinking Back

Late one Friday night after work in November 2012, I arrived home to see my mother sitting on the floor. She said that she had been having some chest pains and just needed to rest. The next day I went up to the mountains with some friends for the weekend. Before I left, I asked my mother how she was feeling, and she said that her chest was feeling tired but that she was fine. I then advised her to go make an appointment with the doctor, and I made sure she promised before I left. I remembered feeling nervous for her that weekend and not being able to wait to get back home to check on her. I had lost cell phone reception, and then I got just enough to receive a text message from my dad that said that she was ok but had to stay the night in the hospital. I was still worried. When I finally got home, I remember walking into the house, seeing my brother and sister-in-law, and trying to get a response as to how my mother was doing. They said she was fine, but that's when my younger brother came into the room with the phone in hand and a serious look on his face. My mother was in the middle of an angioplasty when one of the doctors messed up and ruptured one of her arteries in her heart. It was supposed to be a simple and routine procedure. No one was prepared for this to happen. I remember arriving at the hospital, and the nurses and doctors were confused and were not sure what to tell us. The hospital she was at did not have the personnel or equipment to support her, so they decided to send her to St. Joseph's but told us that she would not even survive the transport. I remember rushing out to my car with my family and watching the ambulance pull out into the parking lot and then stop. I had one of the worst feelings I have ever felt. I found out later that they stopped because they lost her in the ambulance right then. They continued to do CPR all the way down and lost her four more times after that. I actually got to meet the man that saved my mother's life five times.

We arrived at St. Joes and met with the caseworker and surgeon. They both told us that she is very sick and that they have to perform a bypass surgery but that there is no hope of her making it. Tons of friends and people my mother had reached out to came over and waited with us. She made it through the surgery, but everyone involved with her care constantly reminded us of how sick she was. I remember going in and seeing her while she was in a coma. I remember seeing everything swelled up and seeing that her chest was still open from the surgery due to the swelling. Her room was filled with machines that she was hooked up to. None of her organs were working. Her fingers and toes started to turn purple due to the inadequate machines there.

A few days later, the surgeon that was in charge left on a hunting trip, and the new one advised us to transport her to University of Colorado Hospital. It was a hard decision; our choices were to either leave her where she was and let her slowly weaken or transport her with a high risk of the ride being fatal. We decided to give her a fighting chance. Every person involved in the transport did an outstanding job, and she arrived still holding on.

The new surgeon was very confident in what he could do and went into surgery right away even though he was pretty sure she would not make it through the first surgery. Within two days of her being there, her chest was closed up, and her condition started to improve. But they said that she had no brain activity and that we should start considering our options, meaning we were going to have to decide when to pull the plug because she was brain-dead. The next day she woke up and quit all the posturing that they said would never go away. After three and a half months and four separate hospitals, my mother returned home. She is very much alive. All of her organs, except for the left side of her heart, have started working again. She is very sharp mentally. She can walk. She has kept all of her digits. She is recovering faster than anyone would have thought.

Pastor: Learning to Walk Again

It came to a point with her improvements that she would be transferred to Kindred Rehab in downtown Denver. That was a monumental move. We knew it was hopefully the last step between the hospitals and home. I remember several times Allissa and I visiting there and watching her agonize to take literally one step, or five steps, or ten steps, or to get to the end of the hall, and then eventually to add steps to her routine. It was a very tedious, draining process to watch, and yet she would celebrate, and so would Gary, her progress.

Finally, on March 1, she would come home to a very happy household and see all the things the boys did to make her return home special. It was great to see; it was neat to see again the care of the family, knowing it was going to be an ongoing process of coverage needed to help mom finally get on her feet.

Chapter 13

WELL ENOUGH TO LEAVE THE HOSPITAL?

Karen: HOME!

I had much uncertainty in many areas, including the level of care I could do for myself and if I would even be able to walk again. Many times I wondered why God had allowed me to be in this condition. Over the previous few years, He had taken three of my friends: Cinthy (wife, mother of junior high children, full of virtue), Amy (wife, mother of seven children, one who had a very godly testimony that influenced many), and more recently Debbie (pastor's wife, mother of two grown children, consistently God-fearing). Each had taught me through their daily living to trust God and rely on Him. God had taken them to Heaven but left me here despite my poor condition. Pastor Robbins shared with me, during one of his visits, that it was normal to feel like I did. It was similar to how a soldier feels coming home from the war when so many died in battle. God always has a plan. It is an honor to be the conduit whom God chose to channel His power and miracles.

One doctor told me that it was good that I was stubborn because many would have given up when it was so hard, but he said, "You never do." I had never thought of stubbornness as a positive trait, but stubbornly refusing to quit trying helped me stay alive. Shale, a physical therapist at the convalescent hospital (one of the people in that hospital who made the most significant difference for me), taught me to never say, "I can't" (even when we all thought I could not) but to say instead, "I'll try." I tried again and again, desiring to exceed my projected potential.

The convalescent hospital was hugely different from University Hospital in the type and amount of care, as well as the staff's demeanor. Despite this, I can still remember four wonderful nurses that stood in stark contrast to the rest of the convalescent staff. They treated me like a person in contrast to others' indifference who just gave me pills and then turned their back and typed into the computer. One of the things I disliked most was the Hoyer Lift. It was used to transport me from my bed to a recliner and later back again. It was frightening to be in a harness dangling from the lift while a nurse tried to figure out how to use the machine. I was very grateful when someone taught me how to put a foot on the floor and use one toe to pivot to a wheelchair or bedside commode. It was a simple thing but difficult for me. It made my existence so much better after I learned and was allowed to do that simple act. As I relearned to walk, my therapist added more and more steps until I learned all fifteen actions we all do while walking. I was astounded that so much was involved; babies learn these, and most do them without thinking. The slow, laborious process took me months. I kept trying, doing the best I could.

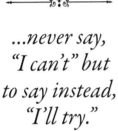

...never say, "I can't" but to say instead, "I'll try."

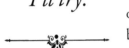

One humorous event was when a nurse from another unit was temporarily assigned to my floor. She had been a nurse for a long time and did not think there was more for her to learn. She started to take my blood pressure using the standard procedure. I told her it would not work because of my LVAD, but another machine across the room would work. She did not believe me, so I told her she could ask the other nurse who had worked with me before. The substitute nurse did not know what an LVAD was, so she proceeded to try to take my blood pressure. When there was no lower diastolic number (usually that means the patient needs reviving), she hurried out of the room to get the other nurse. He came in a short time later, the substitute nurse listening at the door, and he patiently and calmly explained to me that my situation was unique. My LVAD machine constantly whirred blood through my body instead of the left side of my heart pumping, making it impossible to obtain a standard type of blood pressure. He explained that the other machine was a Doppler and could instead get a MAP (Mean Arterial Pressure). He told me as though I was hearing it for the first time. It was a clever and respectful way to teach the older, "experienced" nurse something new and not get her more riled.

I was improving in little ways regularly in the hospital, but I was shocked at how much energy it took to go home. I realized that I still had a very long way to go to get stronger. Upon arriving home, I saw a sign on the front door, posters inside, cards displayed, flowers, a tree with leaves of notes from our Taekwondo friends, and new furniture that we had ordered just before I went into the hospital almost four months earlier. Timmy and Gracelyn had a soft purple (my favorite color) fuzzy robe waiting for me in the downstairs bathroom. Gary had gotten a hospital bed delivered for me to sleep in the downstairs, and the quilt from the Heavenly Quilters was displayed on top. I took a walk using my walker around the downstairs level of our home and then took a nap on the bed. One of the best parts of being home was seeing my family more frequently, not simply when they had at least two hours in which to drive and visit me. Each one was happy to have me home. Andrew showed it by exuberantly shouting one drawn-out word, "MOTHER!" each time he came in the door while rushing to see how I was. I enjoyed having each son come talk to me when they arrived every day.

Survival Nugget: Right after high school, I went away to college (about a fifteen-hour drive from home). I had to rely on God not only for wisdom but also to overcome loneliness, and to persevere in pursuing what I knew God wanted me to do - a difficult Mathematics degree at the college He led me to attend. I Thessalonians 5:24, "Faithful is He that calleth you, who also will do it." This verse often came to my mind in college, especially during very tough Physics and higher-level Math classes. I learned to do my best with the time and ability He gave me. Using these experiences from college helped me heal and navigate the various therapies in which I was involved.

Monday, Day 115 – March 4, 2013

Kevin's email said, "I just had a phone call with Karen. She had the feeding tube removed about 3 weeks ago. At the beginning of last week, she had a major evaluation, and the doctors determined that she had progressed enough to go home. She came home last Friday after spending 16 weeks at various hospitals. She is sleeping in a hospital bed in their family room. She has to be plugged into her power supply for her heart pump, and the cord is long enough to reach to the kitchen. She can now get out of bed, and a chair by herself and is eating most kinds of food. The [nausea] is all gone. She still gets tired of holding her head up after about two hours and is still working on fine motor skills with her hands. She moves slowly but is seeing progress each week. She used the battery pack to go outside for a little while yesterday. She will be having someone come to the house for physical and occupational therapy and eventually go visit a facility for [cardiac] therapy. She is thrilled to be home. She was surprised how weak she was but is happy with the progress. Still a ways to go."

Sunday, Day 121 – March 10, 2013 ~ Andrew's Birthday
Church's Final Update
*Karen Price is home watching the services today over Skype
thanks to her sons Timmy and Andrew.*

Survivor Nugget: God's Word to me is the final, right answer. II
Peter 1:3-4, "According as His divine power hath given unto us all
things that pertain unto life and godliness, through the knowledge
of Him that hath called us to glory and virtue. Whereby are given
us exceeding great and precious promises: that by these ye might be
partakers of the divine nature." God is with me all the time; He is
good. Even when all seemed hopeless, He met all my needs. I found
that His promises are true, and I can rely on them!

Karen: Very Little Hope...But God, part 3 written August 2013

*I appreciate immensely all those who supported my family during
this difficult time. Some came to visit, sent gifts, brought food, or sent
a card. One of the gifts that helped me especially was a small LED
Christmas tree. Four-year-old Titus was praying with his family for
me daily. He told his parents that I needed a Christmas tree to help
me get better, so they went to the store and bought one. Many a night,
I would wake up and watch it turning colors, and it would help me not
to be lonely and sad knowing that a little boy was so thoughtful and
praying for me. I had my family leave it in my hospital room long after
Christmas. I missed the Christmas events at church, Christmas songs,
baking, and sending cards and notes. My family came on Christmas
Day, but I was not having a good day and don't remember much of
it. I was thrilled when Pastor Whitcomb came a couple of times and
sang, using his talent to minister to me. One of the times was a short
time before Christmas. He sang Christmas songs, including "O, Holy*

Night!" and told me of the plans for the services at church. It was excellent and made me so happy.

Another very special gift was from the Heavenly Quilters, who sew quilts at church a couple of times a month. I regularly visited them when I worked at church, never thinking I would be the recipient of one. My beautiful quilt is mostly pinks and blues; it continues to bring me much joy whenever I use it or even just see it.

When I first sat up, my neck muscles were so weak that my chin hit my chest. I was surprised by how weak I had become and how much effort it took to do simple things. It was months before I could stand up straight. I also was not aware, but I was often frowning. I think it was because I had been in so much pain; I forgot to smile. I did not want to be unhappy or complaining, so I worked at remembering to smile.

One time Matthew made spaghetti for me; another time, Gary made me homemade chicken noodle soup. Both were much better than hospital food and encouraged me to eat. I had an NG tube from my nose to my stomach, which kept me nauseous for three months. I had to be able to eat enough on my own and swallow pills before it could stay out. It didn't come out until we were sure I was ready to have it stay out. It had clogged and had to be reinserted a couple of times, and I did not want to go through that trauma and pain again.

Doctors thought that I would probably lose several toes and at least three fingers and be on kidney dialysis and oxygen for the rest of my life, but none of these are true! After several weeks at the third hospital, I went to a 4th hospital to get stronger and then home March first - 3 1/2 months total in the four hospitals. Some are surprised that I didn't get pneumonia since I lay flat for so long. Doctors usually put a defibrillator into people with my device; since I was so weak and had not had a history of arrhythmia, they didn't during my surgeries. I don't need one, at least for now. Doctors, nurses, and others have no explanation of why I am alive, except that there were several miracles. God answered so many prayers!

I was not able to attend church for six months. Although we listened to the sermons on the Internet, I missed church services and the people tremendously. On Mother's Day, my family rolled me into church in a wheelchair just after the service began; we all sat together. I used to sing in the choir, and I looked up to the loft and watched huge smiles spread through the choir as different friends noticed me. When Pastor stood behind the pulpit, he said that it was good to see me back at church; there was a collective gasp (One friend likened it to when Cinderella arrived at the ball.), and then people began to clap! It was wonderful for us all to see how far God had brought me. I appreciate so much more than I ever have the privilege of going to church, hearing the music, and worshiping God.

Today, I remain plugged into a wall or on batteries to keep my internal pump working (LVAD); I am slowly getting stronger; my toes still tingle and in some places are numb (nerve damage); my head wound is healing; my pinkies are still sensitive. I have been cleared to have a heart transplant when I am stronger, and my head heals, and I finish some immunizations; we are praying for peace, whether to proceed or not. There are huge risks either way. I have had many opportunities to witness to people I would never have met and encourage believers. I am thankful I am alive to be a wife, mom, and friend and to serve God longer. God has used my events to work in the lives of those around me. I am slowly getting stronger and beginning to do more things again that I used to do easily without thinking. Gracelyn comes during the day to care for me and to do much of what I used to do around the house. It has been a huge blessing to have her with me and get to know her better.

Whatever the future holds, I want God to get the glory.

Survival Nugget: My dark days were opportunities to demonstrate Christlikeness and provided events we used to turn people's thoughts to God. I am grateful that God counted me worthy to suffer so that He could receive glory. I am thankful for the miracles that He performed in my body. I am grateful that God answered the prayers that people were praying on my behalf. But even if He hadn't answered the way they wanted, I would still praise Him for His love, His Word, and His grace. What were the alternatives?

1. Being in Heaven! I agreed with Job 13:15, "Though He slay me, yet will I trust in Him." I knew that I was a sinner, and that Jesus had died for my sins, and that I had put my faith and trust in the Lord Jesus Christ as the only way to Heaven. Going to Heaven was not an unwelcome thought to me. "Who died for us, that, whether we wake or sleep, we should live together with him," I Thessalonians 5:10. I do look forward to going to Heaven when I die; for now, whether I woke or slept, I knew I would live with Him.

2. Left here in a much different state – Tests showed that I would never be coordinated enough to dress or feed myself and that I would remain on kidney dialysis, on oxygen, in a wheelchair, and mentally slow. Proverbs 3:5 says that I should trust the Lord with all my heart and mind. I had to trust Him, to come to a place where I accepted as okay if He did not give me back full use of my mind, my kidneys, my lungs, or my heart. I grew to trust Him with all my heart: my physical heart and the LVAD. We prayed for God to heal my heart miraculously, but He chose not to do that. I then had to trust Him for my new heart and <u>if</u> He would choose to give me one.

Wednesday, Day 159 – April 17, 2013

Kevin emailed, "Karen continues to improve steadily each week. Other than trips out in her yard and to the mailbox, her only trips so far have been to doctor appointments. The doctor wants to make sure she does not get any illness or infections from other people.

They have run a number of tests to make sure she can be a candidate for a heart transplant sometime in the future. All have come back fine. She is not yet strong enough, but hopefully, with a physical therapy program that she will be starting in the next month or two, she might be ready to get on the list by the end of summer or fall. She could be on the list for a number of months, depending on how many candidates are in her category and their level of need.

Her fingers continue to heal. They are still sensitive. She can turn pages in a magazine but not a regular book. She now can use the cell phone but cannot yet use the computer keyboard. She had some low blood pressure issues a couple of weeks ago, but none recently. She is still having some issues with a bed sore on the back of her head from her stay in the hospital and went to a wound specialist last week. She continues to do all kinds of physical and occupational therapy.

I had a good talk with Karen Sunday afternoon - about 45 minutes about all sorts of topics. She is in good spirits and very happy to be at home. Although she can get up and walk on her own, someone is always home with her in case there is a need."

Karen: Cardiac Rehabilitation

I went through a series of tests, starting right after I got home from the hospital. Since I was still so weak, I was genuinely surprised when the results were good enough for me to get on the heart transplant list. Then I went for a series of shots. During all this time, I did in-home physical and occupational therapy, and then I went to cardiac rehabilitation at Good Samaritan.

On the way to rehab, I enjoyed noticing the mountains again! I remember thinking, "They are still there; they have not changed!" Most of my world had drastically changed, but it was nice to look up at them and think of what the Psalmist said, "I will lift up mine eyes unto the hills, from whence cometh my help. My help cometh from the Lord, which made heaven and earth."

I'm grateful the cardiac rehab was in a separate building from the hospital (for that hospital was the one where I started this journey, the one where the failed angioplasty happened). For years it was hard for me to even look at that hospital; I think it is similar to the feeling one gets when going past the place of their near-fatal car accident. The nurse and therapists at cardiac rehab were very patient with me and helped me get on and off the machines, reminding me what to do next, encouraging me, cheering me on, and adjusting my program when I was able. After just a few sessions, a therapist asked me to use my hands on the stationary bike poles as they moved back and forth. It was more than my weak muscles could handle, and I began to ache intensely. I had to stop going to cardiac rehab for many weeks. I tried not to take the narcotic pain pills; I did not want to go back to the side effects of those. I had a shoulder massage, but it only helped for a few hours. Then I did something I never thought I would do. At Kaiser, I had acupuncture treatments. These treatments and the massages helped the pain diminish and my atrophied muscles heal; then, I was able to go back to rehab.

One day a nurse came over from the hospital to substitute in the cardiac rehab department. I think this was in August, and she remembered me from caring for me in the Emergency Department nine months before. She was so excited to see that I was recovering, for she knew how grave I was when I left Good Samaritan Hospital.

Repetitively, I felt dizzy and like I was going to pass out. A few times, I did not just feel like I was going to; I did; fortunately, someone was with me each time to keep me from hurting myself as I fell. It happened one time when a therapist was at the house. She had us call my doctor, and off we went to the brand new Emergency Department at University Hospital. The doctors ordered many tests; they were concerned that my LVAD cord had moved up near my lung. Other than that, I was okay; drink more water was the remedy given, and I would continue to be watched and monitored. As I left the room in a wheelchair, I saw two ambulance workers coming down the hall with an empty stretcher. I asked Gary to pause, hoping it was the paramedics I would recognize. It was the two ambulance drivers that had first brought me to this hospital the previous fall! We chatted briefly; they were pleased to see how well I looked. A nurse near us said, "Who is friends with ambulance drivers?" We all smiled; I truly did think of them as my friends. Once, I became dizzy and almost passed out during cardiac rehab exercises. I was hooked up to a heart monitor, and it showed I was having arrhythmia; I asked the nurse to send the readout to my doctor.

The doctor ordered an ECHO and made an appointment for me to see him. He came into the exam room and said, "I know why you are passing out. You are dehydrated; even your heart is smaller from not enough fluid!" I asked, "How much should I drink," telling him that I was drinking 150 ounces of water a day. He then realized that I was not eating enough salt. The nutritionist had said that all heart patients should cut down on salt, and I had. Now we learned that people with an LVAD need more salt than other heart patients, and I needed more than I was getting. It was a simple change; we were thankful that I did not need to undergo another surgery to have a heart defibrillator installed. Eating a salty snack before I go to bed helps me to retain enough water.

Survival Nugget: God gave me such peace, even though the future was unknown. Psalm 18:30, "As for God, his way is perfect: the Word of the Lord is tried: He is a buckler to all those that trust in Him." God was definitely a buckler and a protector to me during the beginning of my recovery. I did not comprehend all His ways, nor did I anticipate this change of pathways, but as I have trusted,

He has shown me some of the reasons for this way He chose for me. I have peace knowing God is in control of my way, and His way is the best way for me.

Karen: Ten Steps of Preparation

Practical preparation happened right before my sudden hospitalization due to the failed angioplasty. Some of these have been mentioned before in this book, but thinking of all ten steps at once shows some of what God was doing to prepare us for the event of our lives. We did as God prompted, not knowing for what we were preparing. When struggling with some disappointments, I sometimes would try to remember all ten as a way to get my mind to focus on the goodness of God.

1. During the year before my "incident," I did a Bible Study on the attributes of God to learn more about Him. My desire was what the Bible says in Philippians 4:10, "That I may know Him, and the power of His resurrection, and the fellowship of His sufferings, being made conformable unto His death." At various times, I had studied that verse focusing on one aspect or another, always desiring to become more like Christ. This time it was "that I may know Him," but soon, it would be "the fellowship of His sufferings." Not long before going into the hospital, I made a notebook of God's characteristics and wrote out verses for each, getting to know God better. When I got home from the hospital and was strong enough to hold a book and able to read again, I asked someone to bring this treasured notebook to me. It continues to be a source of teaching and encouragement.

2. Benjamin began attending Beth Eden Baptist School. If he had not have been there, he would probably have gotten behind on an entire school year of work.

3. I thank God for providing for us financially. At the time of my incident, we had higher insurance coverage than at any time in our lives. Not long after my transplant, it decreased, but most of my bills were during the window of higher coverage. This change means that the plan United Airlines and our insurance carrier, Kaiser Permanente, paid for a substantial portion of my medical bills; without the insurance, the out-of-pocket would have been over three million dollars. During the prior year, God also provided more hours for me to work in our church office. I had increased income throughout the previous couple of years while training and selling textbooks to homeschoolers through HomeWorks by Precepts. Because of these jobs, I receive a slightly larger disability check to help pay for my care and medical bills. We used a company by the name of Allsup, and they were able to get the approval for me to be on social security disability faster than most people get it on their own and without any hassle on our part. We had prayed about this, and it was a welcome relief when the Social Security Administration approved my disability before the first possible time that I could have received a check!

4. Within the year before I went into the hospital, all our sons came back to Colorado. Timmy married Gracelyn, but due to medical issues, they did not return to China, where they were teaching English. At Matthew's request, we went to lunch with him in August, establishing contact again. Andrew decided not to return to the out-of-state college he was attending. They were all here locally when I went into the hospital.

5. I was a consultant selling textbooks and helped homeschooling families in a five-state region. I had tried for years to find someone to help. The summer before I went into

the hospital, I began training three new consultants to help. They were able to minister to the homeschool families after I could not.

6. God moved two medical people to CO to be there for me:
    - Dr. Babu came to the University of Colorado Hospital in July of 2012 shortly, before my being there in November. He was my champion, willing to take a chance with me when most thought I was too far gone. [He told me later that ideas came into his head of what he could do for me. He tried medical things on me that he had never done for a heart patient. Many were specifically praying for wisdom for Dr. Babu. We know that God was putting His desires into the doctor's head. Dr. Babu said that he wrote in medical journals what had helped me and was able to save, during the next couple of years, at least two people's lives because of what he learned from my situation. He was only in Colorado for a few years before leaving to go to Tennessee to restart a heart transplant program at a hospital there.
    - Will was my LVAD coordinator nurse. Usually, before an LVAD is placed in someone, training is done to familiarize patients and their families with the device. I could not understand what was to be done. I just knew I did not like the idea of being run by several machines: LVAD (pumping one side of my heart), a kidney machine, an oxygen machine, and the feeding tube. Will would talk to me, and I would relax and feel safe. Months later, I learned that Will was from near my home in New York State. He sounded like my uncles or cousins. God took care of even that little detail to relax and comfort me by sending Will

to Colorado, arriving at University Hospital several months before I came as a patient.

7. I purchased a few longer blouses the previous fall, not knowing that I would need them to cover the LVAD controller. They were already in my closet, waiting for when I arrived home and needed them.

8. In September, I did not renew my Curves membership. I wanted to continue to go, but I felt I should wait until a later date to have a membership again, maybe in January.

9. Gary had put on the market the apartment building he owned and managed. It sold right before I went into the hospital, and we paid off our home.

10. God prompted me to study for months "Trusting Him." I taught ladies at a Bible study on this topic a few days before going into the hospital. God wanted to be at the forefront of my mind to trust Him every moment for all things, little and big.

God used all of these things during the biggest crisis in my life.

Survival Nugget: God's WORD to me is the final, right answer, John 16:13, "Howbeit when He, the Spirit of Truth, is come, He will guide you into all truth." He guides us every day, but in the months leading up to my incident, we can look back and see Him guiding very clearly. God's Word, the Bible, has been a source of strength, encouragement, and a stabilizing presence in my life.

Karen: Lingering Effects of the First Few Days

Everything in my body was affected by the initial incident, the heart attack, the strokes, the days without enough oxygen and blood flow, and the laying so very still for days. Each time I went back to one of my former doctors, they could tell something had happened to me. At the dentist, I learned that the enamel on my teeth was much thinner. I remember the first time back to see an eye doctor. She asked me if there had ever been a time that I had extremely low blood pressure or not enough blood flow. I was surprised, but she could tell that by looking into my eyes. My optic nerve had sustained some damage, but my eyesight was not affected for now. I have become much more sensitive to light. To me, lights seem brighter than before, especially fluorescent, halogens, and LED lights, to the point that I would sometimes get sick to my stomach and be dizzy if I had to be under them very long. I prayed for help with this. One day I saw a sign at an Irlin booth and was able to get information from the representative and set up an appointment to get filter lenses made especially for me. They helped so much with my visual issues. When I was allowed to return to my chiropractor, he eliminated, during the first treatment, a pain I had for almost two years (since waking up from the coma). His advice and treatments helped my muscles immensely. Some great massage therapists also aided in helping my muscles recover.

Due to the use of drugs called pressers (that pooled my blood to my core organs) to keep me alive during the first few days after the incident, my fingers and toes turned black. They looked like totally burnt hotdogs. They were scanned to see if any life was present and how much of them could be preserved. Three fingers and parts of others and most of my toes were slated to be removed when I was well enough for the surgery. A doctor told me they would keep as much of each finger as possible. As I remember it, he was telling me that they would only do what was needed to prevent gangrene from affecting other parts of my body. At least two of my friends, Debbie and Diane, prayed daily for my fingers and toes. Others, including my family, were also praying. Gary started massaging my arms, hands, legs, and feet daily to help with circulation. Job 38:11 comes to my mind, "This far you may come, but no farther." As we compared stories, in cardiac rehab, I learned that I did not experience some health challenges that others did.

God chose to let me keep all of my fingers and toes. When I first arrived home, my fingers were very tender from the healing since several layers of skin died when I was not getting enough blood flow to them. They had been black, like gangrene. Slowly, the black plastic-like pieces came off, and feeling came back into them. I remember thinking that the fluffy soft bath towel felt like it was made of sharp pins. Over the next few years, whenever I was discouraged, I would look down and see my hands, thank God for letting me keep each finger, and I felt better. They are a constant reminder of His goodness to me. It was interesting to me that when they started to grow again, my fingernails grew very quickly. First, they had dents in them, then ridges one way, then ridges in the other direction. They are thicker and harder than they ever have been before. The toenails are not very pretty, and I developed neuropathy in my feet, similar to what a diabetic person may experience. But each toe and finger is entirely intact.

At first, all of each foot was numb. Then the feeling started to come back as the nerves began to regrow. It eventually felt like I had sat on my foot, and it "went to sleep," except it has stayed like that for years. Sometimes, usually at night, it feels like a needle is being poked up through a toe. I was on gabapentin while in the hospital, and the feeling started to come back into my feet, but I did not like how that medication made me feel. Some have said that while taking gabapentin, they had suicidal thoughts; it was just anxiousness and sadness for me. When it no longer seemed to be making any difference, my doctor helped me wean off it. Through my chiropractor, I learned of a ReBuilder machine. I used it many times in his office and experienced more feeling coming back into my feet. The insurance company wanted me to use a tens unit, but using it did not produce any benefit. Even though the insurance would not cover the cost, we purchased the ReBuilder unit, and I used it twice a day. Only my toes are tingly now, with pain shooting up them occasionally, and numb at the ends. I have gotten used to the prickly feeling and do not notice it most of the time. I think of it as my reminder of how far I have come, similar to Jacob in the Bible, walking with a limp for the rest of his life.

When I first came home from the hospital, I had four main things on which to focus, besides keeping my batteries charged. The first was remembering to take my pills at the appropriate time each day. The second was eating and drinking enough of the right things. The third was doing my cardiac, physical, and occupational therapy exercises, including learning to do more and more for myself. And the last was exercising my brain. I remembered things that I had worked hard to memorize: the password to the computer or how to tie my shoes. But I had to relearn how to roll over in bed, walk, feed myself, and even what a fork was. By the time I came home, I had relearned much. The brain is a muscle, so I thought if I exercise it, maybe I can think more clearly again and have it function closer to the way it used to work. I exercised it by doing thinking puzzles and craft projects, increasing in difficulty, as I was able.

I began to type on the computer with just a few fingers, mainly to look at email. I am thankful that I had previously purchased a lighter laptop. As I was able to write, I did logic books and easy Sudoku puzzle books, and when I was able to concentrate, I began again to read books. Then I took over doing the thank you notes and eventually paying the bills. My first craft project was a latch hook rug of a dog. It hung in Matthew's bedroom for years. Then I began to cut and sew quilt squares together by hand. It was just a basic quilt design. Every other square was light blue, and every other one was a memory from our life as a family. Gary took me shopping to get more fabric to complete this quilt that I call *Memory Quilt*. There were many squares to cut out and sew together. I also finished my *Hexagon Quilt* for our bed, that I had begun years before, but I only had worked on it while I waited for the boys at ball games, practices, Taekwondo, orthodontist, etc. After these, I made Andrew the *Falcons Quilt*, Benjamin the *T-Shirt Quilt*, and a *Star Quilt* for Matthew and Bethany.

When I could sit in a straight-backed chair, I did a puzzle on the dining room table, a fun, relaxing thing I periodically enjoyed BC. We coined this new time marker phrase in our family, "BC," meaning "Before Coma." Cross stitch used to be a common hobby, and I worked on a Thomas Kincaid picture I had started years before. All of these things made my fingers less stiff, prompted me to exercise my brain, and gave me some things to do when I could do little more than sit in the beginning. My family brought me boxes from the garage to sort. I was excited to find the Veteran's Day church bulletin, the last

> *God used the re-memorization of verses to unlock sections of my mind.*

bulletin I helped make and printed the day before I went into the hospital. It was a link to my past. Then, less than a year after I had almost died, it was very fulfilling to go back to church and begin to volunteer in small ways for a short time. Each of these milestones was huge for me.

I wanted to relearn the Scripture; I felt empty without verses that I memorized. I did not remember how to lead someone to the Lord. I did not remember most of my past. That gave me an unsettling feeling. I exercised my brain muscles more. God used the re-memorization of verses to unlock sections of my mind. As I memorized, many memories of things that had been said or happened around the time I first memorized that verse came flooding back. I found my memories, like old friends; they were mostly all there waiting to be found! My damaged brain had to make new pathways back to the stored information. During my time in the coma, the memories of what happened before 2012 were blocked to me, but now, almost all have been found! The brain God created is amazing.

During the first several days of the coma, the medical staff could not move me, nor even turn my head to the side, for the movement, I was told, made my blood pressure drop to zero. As a result of this and the fact that I was not getting enough oxygen flowing through my body, I developed a few big pressure sores on the back of my head. The hair follicles died, and scar tissue formed as healing happened over the months; they became bald spots. I was taken by ambulance from the convalescent hospital back to University Hospital for my doctor appointments – clinic visits. My hair began to fall out rapidly in February. I really did not want to be completely bald. I learned to submit to God in this, telling Him it was okay if He chose to take all my hair. His way is best, and I again exercised my trust in

Living with an LVAD was a unique, challenging experience.

Him. I shared my concerns with the doctor at my next visit. He simply asked if it had been about three months from the initial incident. We verified that it had been three and a half months. He said that often between the third and fourth months after a major trauma to the body, the body will be healed enough to address the hair and the scalp and that in about two weeks, the hair fall would stop. It did, and then new hair started to grow! We thought about how amazing God made our bodies. The bald spots remain; some are covered by hair. I just wear hats when I leave the house. I have been cautioned about not getting my head sunburned. It has been fun accumulating several hats and coordinating them with my outfits.

Living with an LVAD was a unique, challenging experience. I had to be plugged into a machine that was plugged into the wall at night. When I left my home, I was plugged into the batteries that I wore in a nylon mesh vest. I always had to remember to wear fresh batteries and take a spare charged pair with me along with an extra controller and cord in a roll-around bag. I took all of these, so if something ever went wrong with the ones I was wearing, they could be exchanged. I knew that at any time, the LVAD inside of me, pumping the blood for the left side of my heart, could malfunction. I forgot to switch to fully charged batteries before going to church on one occasion. Just as the church service was concluding, the loud, low battery alarm went off. From four places in the building, my family came to my aid, knowing the sound of that alarm. Others also came over to see if they could assist. We quickly changed to the spare batteries from my bag. It was an excellent drill for a potential crisis, and all went smoothly. I never forgot again to start with fully charged batteries.

I knew one lady who had a blood clot go through hers, causing her LVAD to quit. Fortunately, she was still in the hospital and had another one implanted. I wondered each day if something would happen to my machine or if there was a power outage, would I be able to get knowledgeable help in time. I tried to complete each task I was working on and not leave anything in the house untidy at the end of the day. I kept in the front of my mind that this may be my last day on earth. We should live like this all the time, waiting for the Lord Jesus Christ's return to earth, asking, "Am I ready?" I learned to trust God more.

Survival Nugget: Months later, I remember thinking like that college young man, "God is truly sufficient for whatever happens to me." II Timothy 2:1, "Thou therefore my son, be strong in the grace that is in Christ Jesus." Hebrews 4:15-16, "For we have not an high

Gary and Karen with Her Walker, Wearing Her Batteries in Her Vest

priest that cannot be touched with the feeling of our infirmities; but was in all points tempted like as we are, yet with out sin. Let us therefore come boldly unto the throne of grace, that we may obtain mercy, and find grace to help in time of need." God bestowed on me grace, mercy, and help as I needed them. God is more than enough.

Gary: More Mobility

Karen continued to receive in-home nursing care and physical therapy. She attended church first in a wheelchair and later used a walker. Now she can walk unassisted. Several months after her discharge to home, she began cardiac rehabilitation. Karen had passed all the numerous tests required to determine if she could be a heart transplant candidate. Her health and strength continued to improve.

Survival Nugget: I had a "routine" medical procedure and woke up from a coma ten days later in much pain; I could not move, I heard many machines, I could hardly see, I could not talk, and I could scarcely think. I knew who I was and knew my immediate family members' names and that I was in a hospital, but little else.

One of my first conscious thoughts was, "God, I do not know what is happening, but I know I can trust You. Help me know what to do and take care of my family." I was on total life support – making my heart work, lungs work, and kidney dialysis; my muscles had atrophied, and my brain was damaged. But my God had taught me in much smaller events, and it was ingrained into my heart and mind that I could trust Him. I was not aware of much, but I was confident that God was with me and that He loves me. Nurses later told me (when I witnessed to them) that they knew something was different about me. There was not the same attitude in my room as there was in most all others – my family's and my demeanor or responses were different even when my condition was critical or grave. We had something others could not describe helping us. God showed Himself to others through my family and me (even when I could not communicate)! Later, because of my responses and attitude, I had many more opportunities to witness for Christ and encourage others. As of 2016, at least four people have come to know the Savior because of my incident – there is no greater joy!

Janine: She's Back!

One of my most vivid memories was when Diane Huff, Debbie Fleming, and I went to sing to Karen in the hospital during a very low point. She was in a coma, and the doctors were concerned that Karen's brain had been severely damaged and that there was discussion about taking her off life support. The moment we started to sing, Karen tried to move her body toward the sound. We were all crying and saying that we think Karen is still there!

One funny story happened sometime weeks later when Karen went down to the rehab room. Gracelyn and I went to Karen's hospital room, and the nurse told us that she was downstairs with therapy. We went to find her and pushed the elevator button to go downstairs. The door opened; I saw someone in a wheelchair with a big smile on her face getting off with a nurse. My first thought was that this woman looks really nice. I started to get on the elevator, but Gracelyn stopped me and said, "That was Karen!" We all got a good laugh out of that.

I went one day in January to visit Karen. I was telling her about a wedding at church; then, Karen looked at me and asked if I remembered to combine them in Shelby. (Shelby is the software program that kept records for those who attend Tri-City.) It was a process that only Karen knew how to do at church. I asked how I would do it, partly as a test to see how much Karen would remember. She went through a very detailed explanation, and I thought to myself, "She's back!"

I have been able to share Karen's story with many people. It has shown me once again the power of prayer, even when we do not understand God's ways. Just to have Karen back in the office has far surpassed any expectations any of us had. It has made it a lot more fun to come to work!

Karen: We Prayed, and Prayed, and Prayed

I remember when I would attend church still in my wheelchair. Many hung back, probably not knowing what to say or do. I was very frail and looked poorly; some who knew me did not even recognize me. Gary said that when I was in the hospital, I looked like I had aged forty years almost overnight; by the time I went back to church, I looked only thirty years older than I was. One Sunday, I heard someone above my head ask Gary if I was his mother. (They knew me before the coma but now did not discern who I was.) Among the many children who were a big encouragement to me was Lucas, a boy I had known and whom I had tried to befriend. He was young and on my level as I sat in the wheelchair. He rushed by and simply said, "Hi, Mrs. Price." I was thrilled and encouraged since he recognized me and was not repulsed by my appearance. Two brothers,

David and Timothy, came up to me one Sunday and asked how they could pray for me; they said they were praying for me at every meal. Two years later, they were still praying for me every day. I thought, "Who have I ever prayed for consistently every day for two years?" Two other elementary-aged children, a brother and sister, Seth and Rianne, many times caught my eye from a short distance away and smiled and waved. These actions never ceased to make me smile.

A man named Greg had been visiting the church for a few months before I went into the hospital. Like many other new people, I had greeted him and chatted with him in the lobby several times. Greg came up to us after one of my first services back to church. He asked if he could talk with us and that it might take a while. Gary wheeled me in the wheelchair back into the auditorium, and they sat down in pews. Greg told us that he had sunk to a low in his life and decided it was time to go back to church. He said that when seven months prior I went into the hospital, he thought that if this is what happens to nice ladies that love God, "I am done." He did not plan to ever return to church, but something (or Someone) kept drawing him back. He listened to people pray and learned about my progress over the next couple of months. He thought about the God who could perform such miracles; then he wanted to know that God. He read Lamentations 3:21-25, "This I recall to my mind, therefore have I hope. It is of the Lord's mercies that we are not consumed, because his compassions fail not. They are new every morning: great is thy faithfulness. The Lord is my portion, saith my soul; therefore will I hope in him. The Lord is good unto them that wait for him, to the soul that seeketh him." Greg then humbled himself and trusted Christ as his Savior! We all had tears by the time his story finished. I thought that this makes the whole journey more worth it. Greg, his care for other people, his service for God, and his godly response to his own challenges are a continual blessing to me.

Gary and Karen – Late Fall 2013

For the following Thanksgiving, we received an invitation to the McNaughton's home for dinner. It was a much different Thanksgiving than the previous one; this time, I was able to go. It was the first time since the hospital that I had been in another home; it was a big step for me. Another family was also invited. Their youngest, Elijah, was a hugging little boy. He came to the couch where I was sitting and surprised me with a big hug, not knowing how fragile I was. I asked him if he knew who I was, and he said. "No." When I told him that I am Mrs. Price, he stepped back with big eyes and said, "We prayed for you! We prayed and prayed and prayed!" Elijah made me so happy that day. I was able to thank him and tell him that God had answered his prayers - I was doing much better. I deeply appreciate all who prayed for me. Jeremiah 33:3 says, "Call unto me, and I will answer thee, and show thee great and mighty things, which thou knowest not." Truly God did many things no one knew or expected.

Survival Nugget: Christ taught me about Himself through other dark times and built my trust. Proverbs 3:5-6, "Trust in the Lord with all thine heart; and lean not unto thine own understanding. In all thy ways acknowledge Him, and He shall direct thy paths." My little brother Johnny had to go to the hospital at eighteen months old; his kidney was about to burst, and he had to have it removed. We saw God answer prayer, and he quickly recovered. Then almost two years later, I went into my second-grade class and asked for prayer for three-year-old Johnny because his stomach was hurting. We thought his other kidney might be failing, but it was Mesenteric Adenitis. He was treated successfully, spending just a week in the hospital. Praying and seeing God answer prayers for my little brother helped me learn about God answering our prayers in both of these incidences. God grew my faith, trust, and confidence in Him and His power. He knew I would need a strong faith and trust many years later.

Chapter 14
TRANSPLANT DECISION

Karen: To Get a Transplant or Not

Now that I passed the tests and could get on the transplant list when I was strong enough, we still had to decide if I would get a heart transplant or not. We asked Pastor Senn if the pastors could get together and pray with us. Pastor decided it would be better if each came individually; he asked each pastor to pray for two weeks and then visit and pray with us. Many of our pastors came, listened compassionately, gave us some godly advice, and prayed with us. Gary was looking at statistics: the percentage of people who live through a heart transplant, the average life span of a heart recipient, etc. Some people questioned whether it was ethical to pray for a heart, knowing that it would require someone's death so I could live. I prayed that the person, who was going to die, would trust in Christ first and then that this person would have signed up to be an organ donor. I also prayed for comfort for their family.

The biggest thing we thought about was: If an angioplasty, a routine test, caused all this damage, what could/would happen during a heart transplant. Some talked to us about "quality of life," discussing how much improvement there would be to my "quality of life." I grew to despise that term. If people were thinking about "quality of life" when I was in the coma (as was suggested), the plug would have been pulled too soon, and I would not have had a chance to wake up and live longer and progress to this point. I was reliant on a machine to live, and that posed lots of restrictions, but I was alive. God had done many miracles (things unexplained by any medical personnel, things for which people prayed, things that only God could do); He left me here for a reason. Even though my family wanted me to make the decision of whether or not to get a heart transplant, I refused, telling them I would be content either way; I knew God was ultimately in charge. If I did not live, I knew <u>I</u> would be in Heaven, but <u>they</u> would be the ones to suffer and grieve until God called them home. After much prayer and discussion with family and friends, Gary decided that I should get on the transplant list. I prayed that when the time was right, God would allow me to get a heart that was a great match for my body – the one He chose for me to have. At the next appointment, we told the doctor our decision.

Survival Nugget: Both of the following two verses speak of God completing the work He began. Philippians 1:6, "Being confident of this very thing, that He which hath begun a good work in you will perform it until the day of Jesus Christ:" I Thessalonians 5:23-24, "And the very God of peace sanctify you wholly; and I pray God your whole spirit and soul and body be preserved blameless unto the coming of our Lord Jesus Christ. Faithful is He that calleth you, Who also will do it." He would finish in His way the work that He had begun. I was ready for whatever lay ahead.

Benjamin: Reminders of God's Love

Later, when Mom got on the heart transplant list, we lived every minute of every day on edge, waiting for the call to come in - the call where we would drop everything and mom would go back under the anesthesia and potentially never come back out. Heart transplants are much riskier than her initial procedure that set the whole chain of events in motion. If that ended up so poorly, then what could happen with the transplant procedure? Needless to say, it was a very stressful year. In total, we had three calls, and the first two we declined due to issues with the heart. One had a major STD, which would have greatly tormented my mom's everyday life and potentially killed her if not treated properly. The other one's blood was not a close enough match and would have caused other potentially life-threatening issues. I do not think anyone is prepared for the decision of whether or not to go through with a heart transplant. It felt like we were gambling with my mom's life. The only way we were able to go through with it was because of our faith in God. If I did not have God on my side, I do not know how I ever would have been ok with the transplant.

A year before the events of this story, I was a completely different person. If these events had happened to that person, I can only imagine where I would be, and honestly, it is a thought I do not care to foster. Who I was before was very self-centered, rebellious, and just on my own path with no concern for God. However, this all changed the summer before my mom's incident. For three weeks in July and August, I went to a Christian camp in Arizona. It was while I was working and attending this camp that I learned a few important lessons.

One was a lesson about God's will. I used to think that "God's Will" was some unattainable level of spiritual enlightenment that was only reserved for God's favorites. This is wrong for many reasons. God does not have favorites; "spiritual enlightenment" is not actually a thing, and God's will is not reserved for anyone - it is available for all. I was taught about the difference between God's sovereignty and God's plan for us. God is always sovereign, but we are not always following God's plan. When we follow His plan, we live our best possible life, following "God's Perfect Will," so to speak. Think of a Venn Diagram where one circle is "God's Sovereign Will" and the other is "God's Moral Will," and the overlap is "God's Perfect Will." We are always in God's Sovereign Will, but it is our choice to follow His moral will. When we obey God in the ways spelled out by Scripture and what we know to be true through reading the Bible and prayer, we will be living how God wants and with His blessing. Long lesson short: obey God, and things will ultimately work out in the end.

Another lesson I learned was the necessity of regular prayer and Bible reading. Sure, I knew it was a good idea, but it was boring, and I thought I had better things to do. I was so very wrong. Bible reading and prayer are the foundation of a Christian's walk and relationship with God. If we do not ever talk or listen to God, how are we supposed to follow him? If I had a friendship where I would ignore the person for weeks or months on end and then show up asking for help in the middle of the night, how strong do you think that friendship is? Thankfully God isn't shallow like humans; He will always love us and allow us to come back to Him.

While I was at camp and through all the lessons I learned, the main result that happened was that I gave my life to God. I started on the path towards giving up my selfishness, my anger, and my rebellion. God got ahold of my heart, and I will never try to go my own way again. That summer at camp gave me just enough of a foundation, so I wasn't swept away by the trials of life. I could have very easily started a downward spiral that could have ended in drugs, crime, or a life of pleasing myself in any desire I had. I had opportunities for each path, and God protected me, giving me the strength to withhold from each sin and keep myself pure. Through the trial of my faith that happened while my mom was in the hospital, God grew me and set me on the right path. There are many hardships, even now, that I deal with because of the pain and trauma; however, I like to view them as opportunities to do right and reminders of God's love towards me and mercy for the entire situation.

Gary and Karen at a 2013 Christmas Party

Gary: Steps closer to Transplant
Wednesday – December 25, 2013 ~ Christmas Day ~

Karen was placed on the heart transplant list on December 7, 2013. On Christmas Day, she received her first call for a potential heart transplant. We were told the heart was a high-risk one. We prayed, talked, and did not feel comfortable with the details the doctor shared about this donor. We were convinced that God did not want us to accept this heart, so we declined it.

Tuesday – January 28, 2014

Karen continued to get stronger; she was able to do more for herself and around the house. She began volunteering for a few hours a week in the church office, where she used to work. She received her second call saying a heart was available. This time it was not a high risk. We all went to the hospital. When Karen arrived in ICU as a "walk-in," the nurse was very surprised. She had never done an ICU admission for a person who <u>walked</u> into the ICU. We spent the night while additional tests and preparations were made for the transplant surgery. Even though it looked like a match on paper, the donor's blood antibodies did not closely match Karen's. Since there was a higher probability that Karen's body would reject that heart, the doctors decided to cancel this heart transplant. We went home later that morning.

Survival Nugget: Not long after we moved to Colorado, I received a call that my brother John had fallen off a ladder. We were thankful that he did not land on his only kidney! However, he was bleeding internally; we knew he might not survive. We prayed continually. When I heard of how God answered our prayers - John was doing much better and healing quickly, I cried. My three-year-old Timmy said, "Mommy, why are you crying? We prayed!" The faith of a child helped increase my faith. While I was in University Hospital, I thought about John, his hospital experience, and what I had learned from that time. I remember that he despised the NG tube and knew he understood my struggle with it. I was also motivated to do well in therapy, even though I could not walk out of the hospital after only a month, as John did.

Karen: Three Hospital Visits, But One Was Not for Karen

I was placed on the transplant list at the beginning of December 2013. To use when I got a call about a potential heart, we had a bag packed and ready (with a note in it for what else should be added, a map with directions to the hospital, and whom to call on the way). When making plans with others, my new most common phrase was, "If I do not get the call." I was taking a nap on Christmas afternoon when the first call came. I was excited, scared, stunned, and could barely grasp what the doctor was saying. I asked a few questions to comprehend all he was saying and understand the details. I asked for time, and reluctantly he gave me two hours. I called Gary at work and talked to our sons that were at the house. The story was that the person had syphilis, and although there was no detection of HIV or Hepatitis, if there had been contact within the last five days, those could still be present. There was no medical history of this person that could readily be obtained. I thought, however, "What if this was the only heart offer I would get?" Or "What if something happened to my LVAD, and this heart could have sustained my life?" We prayed, and Gary decided that since there had been no trouble with my LVAD for over a year, and since this heart was a high risk, that I should refuse. The whole family agreed, and I called the doctor back and rejected the offer.

The next offer came just over a month later. Gary and I and all our children came from where they were and went to the hospital. The nurses greeted me and started some preparation. My family was with me in the room. After many hours it was determined that my blood's antibodies were not a close enough match with the donor's antibodies, so the offer was withdrawn, and we all left. It was like practicing for a drama play, making the next time smoother. Before that next time, though, there were many months of waiting.

It was hard for the next seven months to make definite plans; I was always thinking, "What if my heart comes available?" And yet, life went on. I was living each day as if it might be my last. In June, Gary started to have chest pains. He did not want to go through what I did, so he put off going to the hospital. A few days later, he agreed that I could call and make a doctor's appointment. They told me to have him go directly to the closest hospital. We were both glad to learn that the closest hospital was University Hospital - our first choice for a heart hospital! He left work and went there. I got a ride and met him there. It was very strange for me to see my big, strong, capable husband (who had been my rock, encouraging me and caring for me, the decision-maker) in a hospital bed. He had back and shoulder surgeries before due to work injuries. But this was different. We did not schedule and plan ahead of time for this hospitalization; we were geared up and waiting for me to be in this hospital for my heart transplant. <u>He was in **my** bed</u>! He was, at least, in the same hospital and on the same floor, where I was going to be if and when I had my heart transplant. We did enjoy seeing some of my nurses from nineteen months before; they were thrilled to see how well I was doing.

The doctor decided that Gary needed to have an angiogram done. Everything in me screamed against him having one, for this was the procedure that propelled me to the near-death experience. I knew that compared to the hospital where I started my heart procedure, this was a more equipped hospital, and here he would be more effectively taken care of if something went wrong. However, it still was extremely hard watching him being rolled away for that procedure. It was an opportunity to put into practice the trust in God that I had learned. I prayed for his safety, for the doctors, and my calmness. I then decided to walk the halls, and God gave me what I needed. I saw Dr. Babu walking quickly down the hall and said, "Hi." He did not know who I was. He had not seen me in over a year and never out of bed. I told him my name, and he stopped midstep with a big smile on his face. He told me that he never thought I would get as good as I looked. Then he said, "I'm in a big hurry, but I have one question. I read your chart, but did you really get to keep all your fingers and toes?" I told him that I had and showed him my hands. He said, "And all your toes?" I nodded. Continuing, he said that he did not know how since he had scanned them himself, and "dead tissue never comes back to life!" I told him that people were praying for me, and God answered their prayers. He replied, "Someone up there is sure looking out for you." The crossing of paths was very brief but very encouraging for both of us and the distraction I needed.

After observation and many tests, Gary was put on medication to help delay and correct the effects of hereditary heart disease. Dr.

Babu was not Gary's doctor, but he came to his room later and said he had looked at the tests' results and agreed with his other doctor's decisions. It was reassuring to us and so kind of him. We were surprised and pleased when some of my LVAD and Transplant nurses and doctors came in to check on Gary and me in Gary's hospital room. Following a few days in the hospital, we brought Gary home, and I was pleased to be his caregiver, but it was a switch for us. He had been caring for me for the last nineteen months, and he would care for me again in the near future.

Andrew, Karen, Gary, and Benjamin - 2014

Survival Nugget: My dad was always very healthy. Mom said that he had two colds and one minor surgery in the fifty-two years they were married. But one day, Daddy abruptly became sick, and about a month later, the autoimmune disease we had not previously known he had, took his life. God called him home to Heaven. It felt like the world tilted on its axis. My constant rock of a godly father was no longer here. Things he taught and the lessons he lived before me have stayed with me. But, I had to learn to lean more on my Heavenly Father. This lesson helped when I was faced with the possibility of losing my husband. I learned many things about hospitals and medical procedures during Daddy's time in the hospital and my two years as a candy striper (teenage hospital volunteer). This medical knowledge and the added knowledge I had gained when others were in hospitals later helped me better understand what was happening around me in the hospital. I was also more intensely learning not just to <u>say</u>, "Trust in the Lord," but to trust God completely in all circumstances.

Gary: The Transplant

Sunday – September 7, 2014

Gracelyn was no longer Karen's caregiver. Karen was well enough and strong enough to do most household chores as long as she paced herself. Nine months after being activated on the heart transplant list, Karen received a call from a UCH doctor, her third offer for a heart. She was taking a nap that Sunday afternoon when the call came. There was a good heart with matching antibodies. Due to the donor having some type of trauma, there was still a possibility the transplant would not happen. Despite much prayer, God had not healed Karen's own heart, and we felt confident that God was leading us to move forward with this transplant; off we went to UCH. As a family, we all prayed with her before she was wheeled away. We asked God to grant a successful transplant while asking for God's will to be done. It was still difficult for me emotionally, and more tears came. I was reminded once again of how frail our mortal bodies are. The seemingly routine angioplasty that changed our lives is a constant reminder of this. The almighty, all-powerful, all-knowing, loving God was not surprised by any of these events; He was in control all the time. God has a plan and will bring comfort as we place our trust in Him. We would have to wait for updates during this 9.5-hour surgery. Karen expressed that she was happy to finally be able to receive the donor heart God had chosen for her, one that God brought in His perfect timing. She was comforted in these truths. As we parted, she wanted me to know that she loved me and that whatever happened, God was in control; His way is best. I said, "I love you too," and "If God does take you, be there to meet me at the pearly gates."

Survival Nugget: Back in November 2012, I felt like I almost went to Heaven, but it seemed God wanted me to wait a while longer before joining Him there. Much of my previous apprehension of death is gone. After nearly dying, I now think of death as just a passage to Heaven to see my Savior. Thoughts and songs of Heaven are not of a place I will go in some far distant future, but more of a cherished delight where I long to go. Philippians 1:21-24, "For to me to live is Christ, and to die is gain. But if I live in the flesh, this is the fruit of my labour: yet what I shall choose I wot not. For I am in a strait betwixt two, having a desire to depart, and to be with Christ; which is far better: Nevertheless to abide in the flesh is more needful for you." This verse expresses how I felt when I became aware of the state of my body with the many machines needed to keep me alive. I did not want to be a burden to my family. I told God that I was willing to go if He so chose; I was ready. But I love my husband and my family; I am willing to remain in whatever state He decided. I am grateful to be left here on earth for this time to be able to enjoy my family and friends and serve God on earth longer.

Chapter 15
KAREN'S NEW HEART!

Karen: The Heart that Became Mine

*M*any people received transplanted hearts at the University of Colorado Hospital during the nine months I waited. However, those hearts were not my blood type, or the antibodies did not match mine, or someone in a more critical condition needed one. In August of 2014, Gary determined that I could be without a caregiver for many hours a day; it was a significant milestone for me. I was the best physically that I had been since the coma. It was satisfying that I had progressed to this stage, but also scary, for I had not been alone in almost two years. I had numerous battles with my mind and my emotions that week. I kept forcing myself to not dwell on negative thoughts but instead to think about God and His characteristics.

I wanted to finish Andrew's quilt before my transplant in case I did not make it through the surgery. I finished it on Saturday, September 6, unaware that the call was coming the following day. The next morning at church, a friend asked me if I could help her with a project on Monday. I told her that I could "if I did not get the call." We chuckled, as I had said that so many times during the last several months.

Later that day, the call did come at about four o'clock. We all went to the hospital as we had done before. The preparation began. This time things were happening quicker. I gave hugs and kisses and told my family, "I loved them." Just before I rolled out of sight, with tears in his eyes, Gary said that he loved me and that he would see me in a few hours or on the other side. I did not know if I would actually get the transplant this time or if we would wait longer. A University heart surgeon had gone to get the heart, and its condition was not yet known. I also did not know if I would make it through the surgery. The word had gone out, and many people were praying for everyone involved. I was resting in God's love and care. I knew His way would be best, and I trusted Him. I woke up the next morning from surgery and felt for my LVAD controller. It was not there; the transplant must have happened, and I was alive. I was surprised and pleased that I was not in as much pain as I had anticipated. The transplant had gone well! Soon, they had me up and moving around, which was quite a different experience from the first heart procedure. It was odd not to be wearing my controller and batteries anymore. They had become part of who I was and literally a part of me. As had been our past experience, the doctors and hospital personnel were very kind and positive. I am extremely thankful for the donor who had chosen to be an organ donor. I was told that seven organs were donated to various people in different hospitals from this one donor. I am also very thankful for the donor's family. I prayed much for comfort in their grief and for them to draw closer to God through this. Although we reached out to them through the Donor Alliance, we never connected. I am very grateful to Dr. Cleveland for performing my heart transplant.

Later that week, he did another one for a man named Gary. Gary and his wife Jolene became good friends of ours while sitting together, getting infusions to prevent infection, going to cardiac rehabilitation at University Hospital, and seeing each other at

it times. We went out to eat together and also spent a
their cabin in the mountains. We both have Randy for
int coordinator, the best at University. We have grown
dy as he coordinated the arrangements for us, guided
the myriad of steps, and has been a great resource, com-
couragement. Rehab at University was a couple of steps
at I had done before; the therapist/nurses there helped
e so much. My friend Gary had a stroke at the time of
heart incident, leaving him unable to get out what he
ay effortlessly. After our transplants, we learned ways
iicate. It helped him when I would ask him a question
tient to wait for his halting answers. I could easily talk,
not remember some simple things; I required prompts
er the details. By helping one another, we were able to
it questions the therapist asked, even though we were in
out our caregivers. Since we had been through almost
ing, we understood each other in ways that people, even
to us, could not, in ways that we could not express. It is
o have such a friend.

g and talking to other heart patients during cardiac
ed us. The common denominator in everyone's story
ey were at another hospital first, almost died, and then
iversity Hospital and survived; now, we were exercising
here was good camaraderie among the people in rehab
hen we graduated from cardiac rehab, the whole group
including the nurse and the therapists. The rehab nurse
aduate a red ball cap that says on the front, "University
Hospital," and on the back, "SURVIVOR." My friend
enjoyed wearing them at the same time, when, as cou-
ed away from the hospital. My Gary and Jolene, as care-
talking with each other as well. Neither had spoken
r caregiver, and each was encouraged.

Survival Nugget: I fortify myself by learning of God, memorizing and meditating on Scripture, and thanking Him for the dark times, for they came from Him as training for future ministry. I continue to receive the blessings of God. In the Beatitudes, Matthew 5:3-6, the Bible says that the following will be blessed: the poor in spirit, they that mourn, the meek, they that hunger and thirst after righteousness – all these descriptive phrases unquestionably expressed where I was, and I needed to be blessed. Amid my dark days, I was blessed with indescribable peace and satisfying joy. Isaiah 26:3 says, "Thou wilt keep him in perfect peace, whose mind is stayed on Thee: because he trusteth in Thee."

Allissa: Abundant Mercy

When the whole idea of a heart transplant was considered, it almost seemed that God was saying, "Yes, dear Karen - I am with you - I have brought you this far, I will take you further." There were so many things that Karen had to overcome before it was possible for the heart transplant, but God got her through to His honor and glory. Now, it was a great courageous step for Karen to decide to go through with the transplant. She was doing so well with the heart pump that had been given to her and the LVAD system - but that wasn't enough. She wanted to go for something that would make her life more normal again. The week before the transplant, I saw Karen in the secretarial hallway at church. I commented to my husband that she looked the best and seemed like her old self as I viewed her then. We were so pleased that she was doing well! Little did we know that very shortly, she would get a new heart!!

We received the call on a Sunday afternoon before evening service that Karen had a match. So we prayed, and our church prayed. Will and I did not go to the hospital until about 7:00 the next morning. There we found Gary and sons patiently waiting as we had come to expect. They had been there all night. Gary was a rock through the whole situation from the beginning to the end. I will always think that those days were some of the most challenging days of his life and were handled with a great amount of fortitude and faithfulness. When we got there, Karen was still in surgery and would remain until around noon or a little after. I was amazed at what was being done in those moments. Dr. Babu was in the hospital and worked with Karen through the earlier part of her healing process. He came in with a smile to report that He had been in the operating room and that Karen now had a new heart! We all thanked him for his part in her recovery, but I found it interesting that he gave credit to the power that is outside of himself and ourselves and Karen. Our faith in our God can make all the difference!! I was beside myself when the doctor gave his report! It was a long surgery and a hard one, but it appeared that God was honoring Karen's faith and was giving her new life!! What a wonderful God we have, and I am so glad for the faith and trust that He so graciously gave to Karen.

"Blessed be the God and Father of our Lord Jesus Christ, which according to his abundant mercy hath begotten us again unto a lively hope by the resurrection of Jesus Christ from the dead." "That the trial of your faith, being much more precious than of gold that perisheth, though it be tried with fire, might be found unto praise and honour and glory at the appearing of Jesus Christ," I Peter 1:3 and 7.

Debbie: We Serve an Amazing God!

Many of the exact spans of time, the dates, and the details of each conversation during Karen's hospital stay are now quite vague, but the effects of Karen's miraculous journey are profound. God's loving hand carried her from death back to life. For those, like me, who witnessed Karen's still, comatose, machine-dependent body (described by her doctors as possibly tremendously neurologically compromised), to her awakening, to her slow progression toward independence, to her release from the hospital and eventual welcome back to work (her acute mental recall intact) with near full function in her fingers; we will never be the same. We have seen God's love and grace at work and will never cease to give God the glory for the gift He's given us in Karen.

Now that Karen has once again gone through heart surgery, this time to replace her mechanical heart with one of flesh, we are once again looking to God on Karen's behalf. We watch in awe as our Lord and Savior provides for her needs and for the needs of her family through her family members, her church family, her friends, her physicians, pharmacists, and therapists, as well as the many other people He has chosen to bless the Prices (and be blessed through their efforts) during her time of recuperation.

Let there be no doubt – we serve an amazing God! May His name be praised!

Karen: With a New Heart

I came home from the hospital, needing each day to take over fifty pills, including the vitamins. Slowly, as symptoms diminished and as I got farther away from the transplant, pills were eliminated. In the hospital, I set alarms on my phone to remember to take them at the appropriate times and show that I was cognitively well enough. I also had to answer many questions to demonstrate to an evaluator that I was not in the same cognitive state I was in when I was in the hospital in 2012. I passed; the evaluator was impressed that soon after surgery, I performed better than most people can do on an average day in life. I thought back to how far I had come in that area since the coma of 2012. Benjamin went on a trip to Alaska in 2013 and brought us each back a souvenir; mine was some painted shot glasses – painted pill cups. I had a difficult time looking at the many pills and thinking about swallowing all of them. With Ben's thoughtfulness, I then did not have to <u>look</u> at the pills and feel nauseous. I could get them down with less difficulty. As of 2020, I take eighteen pills a day, just seven different types!

I knew that after the transplant, when I went home from the hospital, Gary would be with me for a few days, and then I would not have a caregiver all day as I was used to having. I was in the hospital for just over three weeks, thankfully much less time than the three and one-half month hospital stay before. I smiled when I received a plant from a long-time family friend with a card that said, "A plant for a transplant."

I was glad to be without the LVAD and be able to take care of myself. It was a transition for me, though. After I acclimated to being back at our home, I started inviting ladies to our home for lunch two days a week. Some would bring lunch, some would help get out what we had, and some helped with other household chores. Mostly, I just wanted them there for the company. I listened to so many stories; the encouragement went both ways. I am also thankful for all the people who brought us meals during that time and those who gave me rides to cardiac rehab.

One thing that surprised me was that whenever I heard a beeping sound, I was startled and sometimes panicked; when it was the loud, persistent smoke alarm, I would burst into tears. It was similar to PTSD (Post Traumatic Stress Disorder). The beeping of my LVAD controller meant I had to have my batteries or other parts changed within a half hour to continue living. It also beeped when I was plugged into the machine, and the power went out. In the middle of the night, that beeping was very loud and demanding for a good reason. I was not aware of how much I lived in anticipation of the beeping to begin. After the transplant, I would tell myself that it is okay, reminding myself that I do not have my batteries anymore. My family comforted me, and after many months, I learned to have calmer reactions to various beeps. I still do not like beeps of some frequencies and dislike all loud ones.

I went back to the surgeon in the spring of 2015 with pain at the bottom of my ribs. Some tests he ordered revealed that the outer sheath of the LVAD driveline was still in my body and causing the irritation. Rarely do any pieces remain, but if they do, a body usually does not mind it. My body <u>did</u> mind, and the inflammation was painful. We learned why the driveline site did not heal as quickly as it does for most people - these pieces were still in me. During my transplant, the doctors saw that my LVAD cord was stuck against my lung. The surgical team took the time to carefully separate them without causing damage to my lung. Meanwhile, it was vitally important to get my new heart in me and attached it as soon as possible. Now we learned that my body had grown around and attached itself to the driveline. The pieces encased in the scar tissue needed to be removed to relieve the pain and inflammation. My transplant team reminded me that I could have no surgery until a year post-transplant. So I had to wait until September. At that September's doctor's appointments, we learned of the positive results from the many tests that were performed. We celebrated my first anniversary with my new heart.

I was then able to have the surgery to remove the piece of the driveline that was still in me. The operation was shorter and very minor compared to many others I had experienced, so we had not asked anyone to come to the hospital this time. Bethany (Matthew's girlfriend, now wife) came to be with Gary at the hospital during my surgery, bringing him a flavored coffee. We knew all too well that things do not always go as planned during surgery; therefore, I was delighted that Gary would not be alone. I woke up from that surgery in more pain than after the transplant. The cord's outer skin had to be dug out of the scar tissue; the underside of my ribs was scrapped. The healing time from this surgery was another experience of accepting pain and enduring as I had before. But this time, I was not an invalid in a bed; I was suffering as I tried to do much around the house. By December, I was tired of the pain and told my doctor at a clinic visit. He sent me to a department of University that was new to me – pain management. I was nervous and unsure of what would be involved. After the interview and talking with that doctor, we determined that I should have a nerve block in an attempt to reduce my pain. If it worked, I was to go back, and they would do the same thing again, but with stronger medication, so the results would last longer. I never had to get the second one; the first shot of numbing medicine near the nerve worked; it eliminated the intense pain!

I was able to return to church and do more things around the house. My body was able to work on recovering once again. This time I was sent to Kaiser for physical therapy. It was more of an individualized program than the other rehabs. During my appointment, my excellent therapist would talk to me and give me exercises to strengthen those muscles to help me now do a specific task again or eliminate some pain. I would work at those exercises, increasing time and repetitions, as I was able. Then in two or three weeks, I would return for adjustments and additions. I progressed much over the several months of physical therapy under his guidance.

It was interesting getting to drive again after several years of not driving. My family had a difficult time getting to the place where they allowed me to start again. They were used to chauffeuring me places and caring for me in so many ways. When I first came home from the hospital, I sat in the back seat with my LVAD and batteries; we did not want the airbag to hit me. I also did not have the energy to drive; my muscles were weak; my neck and other muscles were stiff. At a clinic visit in March of 2016, I asked the doctor for permission to drive. He was surprised that I had not already been driving. Gary agreed to help me renew my driver's license and take me for a practice drive in the church parking lot. Then I drove home the short distance. I also drove with a couple of our sons. They did not expect that I would remember and drive as well as I did. I agreed to make right turns at corners that did not have lights, so I received my husband and sons' approval to drive again cautiously. I would rather be chauffeured everywhere, but it was a welcome thing to be able to go to church, the grocery store, the library, or other places within a couple of miles when I wanted, and not wait for someone to take me. Driving was another accomplishment for me; I achieved another milestone.

I may not always have excellent health; that is all right with me. It is God's decision; I try to do the best I can with the strength and abilities He has given me. I agreed at the time of my heart transplant to do a series of annual tests; the most invasive test is a heart biopsy and the second a heart catheterization. One doctor explained that my new heart is a foreign object in my body due to its different DNA, so my body using its typical defense mechanisms would send an army to attack and destroy it. Therefore, I take the immune suppressant drugs to essentially put blindfolds on enough of the army, so it does not see my new heart and attack.

I try to do the best I can with the strength and abilities He has given me.

These immunosuppressant drugs keep my immune system low enough to prevent rejection. But this also means that I can get sick more easily and have a more difficult time fighting off sicknesses. The heart catheterization is the most conclusive way to determine if my body is rejecting my new heart. Each time I am asked to sign the waiver for surgery and willingly submit to a test similar to the failed angioplasty that began my severe heart issues. It is always an emotional struggle and an opportunity to practice the deeper trust I learned. Whatever happens is okay because God is in control, His way is best, He loves me, He is all-powerful, and His grace <u>is</u> suffi-cient! I have eternal life, and God is always with me! I have had the privilege to share many times these truths, giving God the praise for being alive. Now, I actually look forward to going and talking with my hospital friends. It is rewarding to let them see the improve-ments in me. Regularly I come in contact with someone who remembers caring for me when I was a patient in the hospital. They are eager to hear and see how I am doing. I enjoy telling them and others briefly of what God did and what He is doing. So far, there has been no measurable rejection!

Andrew, Gary, Karen, and Benjamin – 2016

Survival Nugget: When we lived in California, a situation out of our control happened in our church, and overnight some close friends rejected us. We prayed and felt God's presence and guidance through the whole mess. We learned that God is all that we need. We also learned more deeply about His love. I John 4:16, "And we have known and believed the love that God hath to us. God is love; and he that dwelleth in love dwelt in God, and God in him." That confidence in God's love, learned from experience, was a strength to us throughout my heart trial.

Chapter 16
GOD IS
IN CONTROL

Karen: Opportunity to Trust God Again

In the spring of 2017, I had another opportunity to exercise my growing trust in God. Gary was having chest pain, then shoulder pain, then jaw pain, then pain down his arm, and then back spasms. He hurt in different places at various times during the week. He would rest, and they would go away. It got to the place where there was pain even when he was lying down. So, Gary called his cardiologist, and they had him go to Kaiser's RADAR (Rapid Acute Diagnostic and Referral) Department. Those evaluating him were surprised that he was not having a heart attack with all his symptoms he had now or had during the last week. It is thought that the medication he began taking three years previously was now the reason he was still alive. I wish he had gone to the doctors with the first symptom. The doctor told us to go directly to St Joseph's Hospital and not to stop anywhere. It felt like we were told, "Go directly to jail. Do not pass GO!" St. Joe's is an excellent hospital; it was the second hospital I was in – the one I do not remember and barely survived while there. When they wheeled Gary away for an angiogram, I turned and started to sob. I knew in my mind that God was in control, but it had to be a conscious effort to trust God with my husband, my caregiver, and my best friend. I prayed, telling God that I trusted Him and that I knew His way was best, and then God flooded me with overwhelming peace.

God chose for Gary to make it through the test fine, as most people do. We had a special experience when two of the three heart surgeons that worked together came to see Gary in his hospital room. On different days, Doctor Ammons and Doctor Miller did the same thing: explained what would be happening once tests came back, looking directly at Gary and never glancing at me. While trying to reassure him, one surgeon said that there are risks, but they are low. And then said something like, "I know your wife ..." and glanced over at me, then a big smile came across the surgeon's face saying that he knew I had survived, but he was astounded at how well I looked. Just seeing me was an encouragement. The other doctor did almost the same thing the next day before surgery. I was very pleased to have met them and be able to thank them for their part in keeping me alive. Dr. Miller had done my bypass surgery, and Dr. Ammon was the one who took over after three days and strongly recommended I be transferred to University Hospital immediately. Gary had a four-way bypass and recovered for a few days; then, we brought him home. We were thrilled with his recovery and his progress in cardiac rehab. It was, thankfully, a completely different experience from mine.

Three weeks after surgery, Gary and I were sitting on the couch with Matthew, Bethany, and Andrew all in the living room. They were telling jokes, showing clips on their devices, enjoying time together. Suddenly, Gary told me to call his doctor. Dr. Miller was on call, and he said to give him a nitroglycerin tablet and call 911 and then call him back from the ambulance. As I was on the phone talking to dispatch, it was like the classic heart attack on a movie was taking place in our living room. Gary's breathing changed; he gripped his chest, he could not speak, and his eyes rolled back into his head. Despite having the bypass surgery to avoid a heart attack, he was now having one. We were all terrified and yet calmly doing what needed doing. Everyone helped, moving the recliner to clear a path to the door for the ambulance stretcher, getting Gary's medication list, gathering what I would need at the hospital, calling Timmy and Benjamin, etc. I stayed at Gary's side until the paramedics arrived in an ambulance and a fire truck. They calmly told us they would be taking him to Good Samaritan Hospital. Gary started to panic, and we all said, "No!" I called one paramedic over to the side, and he told me they were required to take him to the closest hospital. I told him that if they did, that they would lose him on the way from panic and agitation. I said that any other hospital in the world would be acceptable because I had almost died of heart issues at that one. He noted how Gary was very agitated and told the driver that Lutheran in Wheat Ridge would take about the same time on a Friday evening. Gary relaxed, and they put him in the ambulance. I rode in the front with the driver. The rest followed in cars. The first moment I sat in the ambulance, I thought, "I may never see him again alive." I texted our pastors asking for prayer; then, I called Doctor Miller back. He was very helpful to me, asking questions and explaining things. I was shocked at how calm I felt as if being carried along, trusting God to take care of us even if we would lose Gary soon. Prayers were answered again that night; Gary survived, was stabilized, and was given some medication. Not knowing the new hospital or the doctors there, we were reassured when we learned that these doctors could see Gary's previous health records at St. Joe's and Kaiser and that they were in communication with his heart doctors at those medical facilities. Dr. Miller kept in contact with me about the details and also reassured me.

An interesting fact to us was that Gary's heart doctor could watch the angiogram live at St. Joe's Hospital, as it was being performed at Lutheran Hospital. He called the heart cath. lab at

Lutheran to talk to that Lutheran doctor. Tests were done, but with the pictured angles, the team could not see what had caused the heart attack. Electronically, the doctors at St. Joe's, Lutheran, and Kaiser met and compared the films of this angiogram and the one before his heart surgery. They determined that one of the smaller graphs from the recent bypass surgery had failed, but it could be treated with medication and therapy. Going the ten miles back and forth to this hospital to visit Gary was the farthest I had driven since 2012. I was happy that I could drive. I do not like having Gary be the patient, especially a critical one. Watching him suffer was much harder than being a patient myself. Gary came home and rested, then returned to cardiac rehab. We are very thankful for how well he improved; none of our health issues prevented us from a few weeks later attending Matthew and Bethany's June wedding!

Survival Nugget: The peace and trust I learned in the past were exercised again and again. I was grateful Gary's heart attack was not my first test of faith. As a teenager, I had a head-knowledge of God and His attributes, but I had to learn by experience truthfully to know what it means to trust Him. When growing up, life had been relatively easy for me. I knew a lot of spiritual truths in my head. I trusted Christ as my Savior and committed my life to Christ. But the first major test was in 1984 when I was required to have surgery. Going into surgery, I did not know if I would ever be able to have children or if I had cancer. God spoke to me through a verse, John 14:27, "Peace I leave with you, my peace I give unto you: not as the world giveth, give I unto you. Let not your heart be troubled, neither let it be afraid." He gave me indescribable peace that day as I rested while trusting Him. I did have surgery, but a hysterectomy was not required, nor did I have cancer. The following year, God answered our prayers for a child. But three months later came the second major test; when I went for my first ultrasound, our baby was not alive. I named our baby Tracey, and I look forward to seeing this child someday in Heaven. About two months later, I was told I had developed a condition, and a hysterectomy needed to be performed. I was still grieving Tracey's death; I could not imagine life without having children. I had always wanted to grow up and be a mommy; God promised that He would grant me the desires of my heart. So, this did not make sense. I prayed over the story of Hannah in I Samuel 1:10-11, begging God for a child and promising to give him back to God. I prayed that He would give us a son that He would use, even as a missionary to Africa or China or wherever He chose. A couple of months later, God gave us baby Timmy! I was so afraid we would lose him as well, and we were moving across the country away from my doctor, my church, and my mom. We prayed much for Timmy's life and for me to trust God and His way completely. Right before we left New York, I had an ultrasound, and we heard Timmy's heartbeat! I praised God; our baby was alive! After college, Timmy was a missionary in China for two years teaching English. He went to Africa in 2018 for a ten-day mission trip. After that trip, Timmy was excited to learn of the prayer I prayed before he was born. God answered each aspect of my prayers. I learned to give a hard situation over to God and trust Him for the outcome.

Karen: More Milestones

We routinely flew "BC" a few times a year to visit our family in upstate New York. For years after the coma, I was not strong enough or well enough to fly, and also, we wanted to be close to home when my heart became available. We had a special time with each of several family members who came out to visit while I was waiting for a heart transplant; some previously had not been to visit us in Colorado. My mom, mother-in-law, Gary's brother Sam, and cousins Frank and Linda came from New York, and my older brother, Kevin, from New Jersey. I resumed flying with my first flight in April 2016 with

Gary and Andrew to New York. I wore a mask over my nose and mouth on the plane to protect myself from getting sick (potentially seriously ill) and rode in a wheelchair. Wearing the mask reminds me of something I did not enjoy, for I had to wear one every time I left the house during the first year after the transplant and when I was around sick people after that. At first, it was suffocating, but I would remind myself that this was part of being alive and now part of being able to go and see and do. After my major incident, I did not think I would be able to travel again, and because of that, I would never be able to see most of my extended family again. When I was well enough to visit, I was overwhelmed with gratitude to be able to see some of the people I love and be back in the home where I grew up. Each time I saw something familiar, blocked memories would come flooding back, especially when looking around my mom's home. I think of it as my brain forming new paths back to the memories that happened, or things said while I was looking at that picture years before. I had to close my eyes for a while because the memories were returning so fast. It was fascinating to learn how memories are cataloged in my brain by the sight, a smell, or something I memorized about the time they were made.

I took piano lessons from second grade through when I was in college. I have little natural talent but worked diligently and loved to play. When my mom no longer wanted the piano in her home, Gary brought it to Colorado! All our sons took lessons, and I enjoyed playing. At various times during 2013-2016, I tried to play the piano again. When I first tried, I could only play a few notes since I was so weak, and my fingers could not bend enough to play. The next time I tried, I requested a chair to replace the piano bench as I could hold myself upright for only a few minutes. I could play notes, but not the songs that I had memorized and could play right before going into the hospital. My brain and my fingers had forgotten them. The feeling I experienced was like grief over losing a friend. Later I tried again; I remembered some, but the brain-to-finger response was slow. I was excited to be able to play better. I played regularly for a while, stopping due to minor injuries, or surgeries, or just the busyness of life. It makes me happy to see the piano in our living room and know I can play.

I could not wear dresses when I had my batteries. Mom gave me a very thoughtful gift after my transplant – a red dress. When she visited me in Colorado, we had a picture taken together in front of the piano she gave me years ago.

Karen and Her Mom

I enjoy serving with Gary helping homeschoolers again with curriculum, organization, and advice. I was excited to go back again to the local homeschooling conference to help as I had from 1996 to 2012. The positive and friendly people at the conference were an encouragement to me. Although these accomplishments of mine seem small to many people, to me, each was another sign that I was getting better, and I relished each milestone as a victory, another illustration of what God accomplished and what He continues to do.

Several times while in the hospitals and after, medical personnel suggested that I go somewhere in my mind to be able to handle a medical procedure or to help me relax. It helped me to go to what I began to think of as my happy places. They were each a place I went to in the past and felt happy and peaceful. I would pray and go in my mind to these places; the most common location was in Oahu, Hawaii overlooking the beach and the ocean waves. Another site was in the woods just off the path behind my Grandpa and Grandma Lilyea's home in Penn Yan, New York. I had written a few English papers, hidden there, looking down on flowers, plants, and trees, and hearing the creek a short distance away. Another place was the Chapel of Transfiguration, in the Grand Teton National Park. It is a tiny rustic church with a cross at its front. The cross is not on a wall like at the front of many churches; it is in front of a large window that frames the Teton Mountains! I had seen this gorgeous sight when I was nine years old and again at sixteen. Gary took the boys and me there a couple of times as part of vacations. Mom and I enjoyed a trip in 2005 to the Tetons, and we saw the chapel. I never thought I would be able or have the opportunity to revisit any of these places. But I did! In August of 2017, we went to Oahu, Hawaii! In October of 2018, Gary and I went to the Tetons to write a part of this book. I was excited that we were able to visit the Chapel of the Transfiguration! This spectacular site is on the front cover.

People often said to me things similar to: "I would have never responded as you did," or "I'm amazed at your attitude, after all, you've been through," or "Why are you not bitter and angry at God?" or "God allowed you to go through this and not some others since He knew you would respond in the right way." While all of these may include some truth, I am not some super Christian. God gives grace tailor-made to one's specific trial, and the grace He gave me was sufficient. These comments did make me ponder why I had the responses that I did. I never once questioned God's sovereignty or His love (those had been ingrained into me years before), nor did I become angry or bitter. That was God working through me. People tend to share their individual trials with one who has been through trials. I longed to meet with each person who had shared with me their complex issues, pray with each, and try to help each, pointing them to God, but I did not have the energy to do this. I realized one day that much of what I knew to be true and what had helped me was contained in one Bible study I had done years before, *Quieting a Noisy Soul*, by Dr. Jim Berg. I was concerned that I would not have the health and energy to lead this class well, but God provided Heather, one of my friends, to assist me. Facilitating this class to a group of ladies during the summer and fall of 2017 was a privilege. God helped me with health, energy, and clarity of thought as I led this class. It was another milestone for me, and I was also excited to be teaching again. I was blessed that through our study, the ladies who attended regularly and did their homework had some significant changes in their lives and grew to become more like Christ.

Survival Nugget: I am now trying to encourage others and learning how vital encouragement is. It can be a smile, a word from a janitor, a wave from a child, a hug, a prayer, a flower, a Scripture verse, a card, a visit, listening, paying attention, a meal, a ride, and so many other things. All these were lifelines for me to continue to try to get back to reality, recover, and heal. I have taken the time to go back to the hospital and visit nurses who took care of me and thank them. Visiting hospital personnel encourages me as well as them: my therapists, CNA's, technicians, ambulance drivers, and others. I am very thankful for them.

Chapter 17
EMOTIONAL TRAUMA

Karen: God, as Promised, Was With Me in the Waters

I had completed writing this book, and it was in the editing process. We chose the publisher, and the contract was signed. Then God made it clear that I needed to write another chapter; hopefully, this will help others traveling a similar path. Inserted here is my experience and what I have learned; I could have used some advanced warning before February of 2018. Many books are already written, and many counselors, doctors, and therapists are available to help with each person's specific needs. The waters I navigated then perhaps should not have been so baffling, unexpected, and troubling, but I had never personally faced anything like this.

We rejoiced that my heart still showed no measurable rejection during my annual battery of tests in September 2018. I was four years out from the heart transplant, and overall, I thought I was happy, content, and doing well. Starting in December, I experienced a series of losses, one that affected me deeply. Over the next few months, additional losses and other hurtful situations were coming rapidly and close together. Some were minor, a couple huge, and all affected me emotionally. Some cut deep, causing real, excruciating pain. The losses took the form of people, expectations, work, what could have been, and relationships (ones I perceived as close). These crutches that helped prop me, that I had relied on to heal and become "normal" again, were falling. Some of these losses I am still grieving. They were piling up, weighing me down, so even tiny things felt significant. There were unkind, unrealistic demands made of me that I could not have fulfilled even if I was well. It became undeniably clear that I was not as well emotionally as I thought. By then, even happy things were affecting me, adding to the emotional load I was carrying. I was raised with four brothers; I have four sons and a husband. Except for when my dad passed away and the subsequent months, I do not usually have emotional swings or express many emotions. People often disappoint or are unkind, and I had accepted that as part of life. But now, things did not just slide off; it was as if my oil, like a duck's oil, was gone. Things seemed different now, and my reactions were altered. Much of what I thought was reality was now shattered, I felt. I had been asked to assist, but some of what I had been doing to help others was rejected, criticized to others, or ignored, yet no one came to me to discuss it. I wondered, "Where do I fit anymore?" I was having physical issues now as direct results of all this upheaval. What was wrong?

Several upsetting things happened a few days in a row that seemed more important and more significant than they actually were, and the accumulation of items weighing on me took its toll. Wherever I was, I could not stop the deluge of tears. Then in our living room, I felt like the walls were closing in on me and the room going dark. I screamed and pushed my hands outwards, trying to stop the walls from crushing me. It seemed very real; I was not sleeping. I prayed and cried, shared with Gary what I was feeling. I thought I was about to have an emotional breakdown that I had heard others talk about. I no longer felt grounded. I was scared and did not know what to do. None of the people were available to whom I typically would turn if having a problem. Of course, Gary was there and supportive, but he was as confused as I was about what was happening. I did not go out around people without Gary. An appointment with one of my transplant doctors was in two weeks. During that time, I cried much and begged God for help; I forced myself to eat well, made sure I was getting enough sleep, and of course, drank enough water. I read the Bible and told God I did not know what was happening, but if it was His will for me to go to a mental facility, I was willing. All I wanted was for Him to get the glory and accomplish what He wanted through me. I could not think about much; I felt stuck, empty, hopeless, and losing control. I had facilitated the class, *Quieting a Noisy Soul,* and God used me to help others; I knew information, but I could not get to it. I thought I was doing so well but then realized how very broken and weak I still was. I talked little and was very sad, desperate for some help but not knowing where to turn or what to do.

Although I had not seen them for a while, I called Pastor Bishop and Cheryl to ask some questions about emotional issues they had experienced and had helped others. They invited me to their home; I went and just sat – very sad, very unlike my usual demeanor. I told them what I was feeling and some of my recent experiences. I know they took me seriously, listened, talked, and prayed with me that evening. They encouraged me to rely heavily on God and quoted many Bible verses to me. The only two specific things that got through my foggy brain that evening were, "There is <u>HOPE</u>," and "Karen, you are going to be okay." I played both of those phrases over and over in my head, wanting to believe them. I got a couple of books they recommended and read them. I began listening daily to several sermons or teaching podcasts. I started a journal of all the encouraging, helpful things I read or heard. I wrote out the words of the verses that spoke to me. I immersed myself in God's Word. I came to the place where I accepted the fact that I may need medication to help me. It was a hard place to get to since I had seen adverse effects on others. But things were not getting better. This condition I was in was not like a cold that one endures for a couple of weeks, and then the person is better. I take medicine when I need it for other issues, so why not this one. I needed help.

Meanwhile, I went to church and performed other needed activities and put on a good act that all was okay. Gary and I agreed that I should pull back temporarily from my volunteering and avoid most interaction with people. Most people with whom I shared some of what I was enduring did not understand, nor did they react in a helpful way. When people said, "Hi, how are you?" I did not want to lie, nor could I tell them, for what I was experiencing was deep, and even I did not know how to express it. I simply said, "God is good."

I felt like there was a cloud hanging above me, slightly off to the side, threatening to descend and envelop me. I carried a big load on me that weighed me down. I was afraid if one more thing happened, it would put me over the edge, into what I did not know, but it did not look pretty. The Bishops brought me flowers and checked on me regularly through texts and calls. These contacts were lifelines for me.

It came time for my semi-annual checkup with one of my heart transplant doctors. Initially, I was very disappointed to learn that instead of having an appointment with one of the doctors, the nurse practitioner would see me. I wanted the more senior doctor that had more experience, who maybe could help me. God knew better; the nurse practitioner was doing her doctoral thesis on anxiety and depression in heart transplant patients. She was the <u>best</u> person for me to see. She has found that 30% of people between four and a half to five years after a transplant experience anxiety or depression, and most do during the first fifteen years. I was four and a half years out. After my initial trauma and then again after my transplant, I had much cardiac therapy, occupational therapy, physical therapy, and cognitive therapy. No therapy sufficiently addressed the emotional part of me that was damaged. She recommended that I be evaluated for EMDR therapy (Eye Movement Desensitization and Reprocessing) as there has been much success with that therapy among transplant patients. But first, she told me to schedule a complete physical with my PCP to be sure there was not another cause. It was good to learn that this was not a unique thing and that there may be an explanation, and I could get help. EMDR therapy was designed to resolve unprocessed traumatic memories in the brain - to help get the brain past where it is stuck and move on to processing the trauma. My trauma was not as severe as others, not like a war veteran experiencing PTSD. I learned that all people who get emotionally stuck due to a trauma are treated in the same way; some just have more layers to work through.

My PCP listened to me, ran many tests, and said I was healthy. He referred me to the behavioral health department. My chiropractor of many years also thought that I should have the EMDR therapy to see if it would help me. I shared with our four sons and our daughter-in-law some of the issues with which I was struggling. They were very supportive, encouraging, and helpful in each one's distinct way. There was a time back in 2012 when no one thought I would get my cognitive abilities back. But I did, and everyone thinks I am doing well. Yet now, I was going to the mental health section at Kaiser. Submitting again to whatever God had for me, I went (though it was difficult) to see what help, if any, I could receive. The process took much longer than I wanted, and it frustratingly seemed not much was happening. My assigned therapist listened to me, verified I was not suicidal, and had me come back. Appointments were an hour long and two to three weeks apart. I went, and I cooperated with the activities and reading homework, but some were strange and did not seem to address the root problem. I questioned within myself if I actually needed this. I asked, "Aren't

Christians just supposed to trust God, turn things all over to Him, then get better?" "Am I a lesser person because I am not getting better because I am so weak?" I renewed my commitment to trust God even in the middle of this cloud, even if things never improved and even if they worsened. I know His way is best, and this was another opportunity to put that knowledge into practice. Could I be well again? God reminded me of a verse Isaiah 42:3, "A bruised reed shall He not break, and a smoking flax shall He not quench." God cares for me. He did not allow me to break, nor the circumstances to snuff me out. He is with me and allowing whatever is best for me and His purposes.

At my therapist's recommendation, I went to a trauma management class and learned much. My words expressing what I was experiencing were the same ones the teacher used to describe how people feel after trauma. I took many notes and soaked up what she taught, learning much. She told us that undealt with trauma is like having a live tiger that we have locked in the attic. We function in the house but continually glance at the attic door, wondering when the latch will break and the wild tiger will get out and overcome us. This illustration precisely described how I felt, and the trauma I had not processed was using quite a bit of my limited energy. The cloud had moved farther away, but I could still see it out of the corner of my eye. God stayed the avalanche of hurts, disappointments, and losses, but I wondered when the next one came, what would happen to me. My teacher explained that we might not deal with the daily effects of trauma, but we are still looking through the lens of trauma to see everything else. That lens needs refocusing, and I needed help refocusing it. I clung to her

"Trauma produces a depth of character and wisdom that cannot be obtained any other way."

reassurance that there is hope for recovery, a happier life, and healing. I attended the series of three classes, and I think she said at each one, "Trauma produces a depth of character and wisdom that cannot be obtained any other way." I am still pondering that statement.

I learned how to cope for the moment: listening to soothing, uplifting music, taking naps, feeling soft fuzzy things, looking at pleasing, pretty, encouraging things, and having pleasant things to smell. I implored all my senses to help. I did not watch the news. We followed suggestions and watched comedies when I could focus on them since laughter or even a smile can help. I spent much time crying; I am not traditionally a crier. The tears seemed to be always a second away. As advised, I avoided potentially toxic situations and negative people. We were careful not to say too much to others, as most people treated me differently when they heard I was having behavioral health issues. They do not understand. I listened to some people brave enough to admit to others that they were on medication or struggling with emotional problems. We talked with Pastor Senn. He was and is a big encouragement; his counsel and actions on my behalf grounded me. He told me that it was okay to cry, even in church. After all that I had been through, the bigger wonder was that the emotional struggles had not happened sooner. I drew strength from him. What I read and heard reminded me repetitively to keep my eyes on the Lord and not on the problems. Even though Pastor was going through multiple testings of his own, I so appreciate that he still made time for me, listened attentively, and gave me biblical help.

Psalm 27:4 says, "Wait on the Lord: be of good courage, and he shall strengthen thine heart: wait, I say, on the Lord." I tried to wait patiently, keeping my eyes and thoughts on God. Through listening to preaching and teaching, reading, the Bishops, my pastor, and my therapist, I learned many necessary things. I learned to set boundaries, and I learned some strategies that helped. I tried to let go of the things I could not control; they belong to God, for they are in His bucket; I have enough stuff in my bucket that is my concern. Someone told me not to look at all the things going on around me but to focus on only what God has given me to do – my responsibilities. I learned that it is acceptable to be sad about losses or circumstances but not be unhappy about who I am. I am still me and valuable. God created me in His image for His glory. I need to meditate on the Bible and its truths and not replay the crushing hurtful things people have said to me and turn from negative thoughts. Reading about others who have struggled and survived was so informative and encouraging. Mostly, I immersed myself in Scripture reading, writing out verses, and memorizing many. Years ago, Pastor had preached on lamenting, but it was a distant truth at the time. In my struggles, I learned to lament with Jeremiah and the Psalmist; the words God had them write struck cords deep within me.

I was getting an education on mental and emotional health while being immersed in the issue. The things I learned and experienced changed how I now view behavioral health. When I was still physically weak in the hospital and had difficulty processing concepts, a visiting person told me that my condition was the result of sin and that I should search for it and confess it. At the

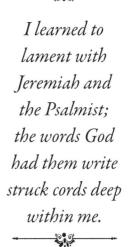

I learned to lament with Jeremiah and the Psalmist; the words God had them write struck cords deep within me.

time, I could not even grasp what sin was. Fortunately, talking to Gary and Pastor Robbins helped me with that troubling accusation and focused my attention on God and the Bible. I think that each person faced with a trial should examine his life to see if he has unconfessed sin. If there is one to be confessed, God will bring that sin to the forefront of the mind. Guilt can cause emotional, mental, or even physical issues, but it is not always the case. God has a myriad of reasons for allowing a trial.

Just as physical sickness is dealt with by medical personnel and perhaps medication, one should seek help from people trained to assist with the relief of emotional and mental issues. My doctor or therapist told me that I needed to explore my trauma response to the point of understanding what happened and thus get some clarity. This inner contemplation would lead me to a place of resolution. As I thought about what happened to me in 2012 and what affected me in 2019, I came to two conclusions. I don't fear them or fixate on them; it took a long time for me even to be able to put them into words. One is that I trusted the hospital and its doctors to make me well, to fix a small problem, but instead, they irreversibly damaged me. Secondly, I don't want to be useless, unable to care for myself, unable to help others, and unable to make a difference. I want to be able to be completely happy again, to be able to grow thick skin again where things don't bother me as much, and to be more stable and grounded so that I can be a help to others. The feelings common to 2012 at the beginning of this trauma and 2019 when I emotionally hit a wall were unfulfilled expectations – People/institutions not living up to the trust I placed in them and the feelings of being useless or my help unwanted. Identifying these helped my therapy to be more effective.

I returned for more visits with my therapist while I waited for consideration of my case to allow me to have the EMDR therapy. I waited for a medical team to determine if the EMDR therapy would be beneficial to me. During that time, I had chances to witness to some people I would never have met if I had not gone to that department. My therapist said some things that made me think. He said I was too much of a fighter to be depressed. I thought about all that I had fought through and the strength that God gave me for those years. "When thou passest through the waters, I will be with thee; and through the rivers, they shall not overflow thee: when thou walkest through the fire, thou shalt not be burned; neither shall the flame kindle upon thee. For I am the Lord thy God." I felt like I was drowning; these verses in Isaiah 43 reminded me that God is still in control and will take care of me. God is still God, and He understands even this.

I was encouraged by hearing that this current emotional state was not permanent; it will not last; it will continue to lift. My therapist's confidence gave me hope. He urged me not to focus on others and what they think but to give myself credit for what I have accomplished. He asked me to think of the facts and to recognize the value of who I am. Although it may take effort and time, I can be confident. I remind myself to think about what God has accomplished in and through me and my value to Him as His child. My therapist expressed to me that people try to put others into a box to become similar to themselves, but that I should not force myself to conform to other people's expectations. I do not have to feel bad about not being like others. As strange as it sounds, it was like he gave me permission to be me and to be happy about it. I know God made me who I am with my unique gifts and experiences to do the unique tasks that He is molding me to do well. What is important is what He thinks of me.

My therapist encouraged me to expand who I am instead of staying the same as I was or getting back to "BC" (before the coma). In many ways, I am different and have learned much, so I should use those things. He also asked me to step out of my comfort zone. The uncomfortable things he suggested include going back to visit the convalescent hospital and face the feelings I had when I was there. Also, I was encouraged to try to do new things, reread things I have learned, and grow hopefulness. I did some of these, including starting to learn Portuguese, one of our daughters-in-law's heart language. It is also okay to tell people, "No," especially if I am not up to it or feel it would not be wise for me to participate, and I do not have to think that I need to explain the "no." It is wise to tend to my own needs, have a balance, let go of some responsibilities. "Moving forward is what it takes to go forward," I heard. I determine to keep taking a step, even if tiny, to keep moving forward. I learned to purposefully gravitate toward safe people, instead of taking everything that is dished out to me, to work at building healthy relationships that go both ways.

Clarity of what I was experiencing began to form as I started to understand the balance and connection between emotional connectivity and brain processing. People respond in different ways to similar situations, and that is normal. Most people seek treatments that treat the symptoms: headaches, lack of ability to sleep or stay asleep, irritability, exhaustion, confusion, sadness, anxiety, agitation, mood swings, numbness, disconnection, confusion, or a variety of other symptoms. When we've been traumatized, we can spend a lot of time in the PAST and the FUTURE. But it is only in the PRESENT that we can control our reactions, thoughts, feelings, and behaviors. A superb technique to help prevent a panic attack or lower anxiety levels is to go in my mind to a peaceful place I had thought about before, using all my senses to explore it. In my mind, I went back to the happy places I previously had visited during difficult times. I was encouraged to know that many of the recommended things for coping and healing were things I already was doing due to God's promptings.

I learned that it is easier to sink back into depression or have other symptoms reoccur when another loss or disappointment occurs, even though the most recent loss may be much less in intensity. My thinking and emotions may slip back into previously formed ruts. The beneficial side is that I now have the tools and awareness to help navigate through it. I learned to pay attention to my triggers to prevent a reoccurrence and stay far away from the road that may lead to another near collapse. Sometimes, I need to take a step back and reach out for help on how to handle a new stressor. I was encouraged to stop at regular intervals, three to six months, to evaluate myself, think about what I need to remember to practice, go over coping strategies, and get a follow-up treatment if required. These things will buffer, reinforce, and help in my recovery.

In August, I did two sessions of EMDR therapy. It seemed too simple to work. I had learned the theory behind it and heard of cases of people helped by the treatment, and I wanted to try it. The committee approved my case thinking it would help me. As I understand it, this therapy is similar to how the brain processes things in REM sleep. Sometimes after trauma, one gets stuck and cannot get beyond the trauma. I watched a series of lights going on and off, giving the appearance of traveling up and back a slanted light bar, and at the same time, thinking of the details at the time of the initial trauma. I thought of how I felt when I woke up after the coma, the expectations that did not happen, those that treated me poorly, the things that frightened me, the frightening, warning beeps of my LVAD machines, etc. The doctor who administered the test watched me closely, periodically stopped the lights briefly, and then began again asking me to think about the answers to a couple of questions. Toward the end of the session, she asked me to think about the positive things that happened due to this trauma and to remember that the bad things were over - in the past, not in the present. When the test finished, I felt sick to my stomach (bright lights do that to me usually since the coma), and I felt drained. I felt like I had been back in time, reliving the events.

When I left the office, I found myself being surprised that the world was still the same, that things outside seemed unchanged. It seemed like much time must have passed; I felt different. The sun was shining brighter, and I felt lighter. I went home and slept. A couple of days later, I realized that I could no longer see the dark cloud. The fog that I had been living with for almost seven years had cleared considerably. I felt hopeful for the first time from within, not just because others told me I would get better. I had more energy than I have had since the previous December. Later, when I began to work on this story again, I was able to concentrate longer. As I edit, I still get caught up in the experiences and feelings I had when the events happened. In some ways, though, it is different. It affects me less, and my responses are less pessimistic.

My second EMDR therapy session ten days later was shorter and less intense. This time I focused on the long-term effects of the initial trauma, the transplant, the process of making the difficult decision to have it, the waiting ten months for my new heart, and the effects of that surgery. The results were less dramatic than they were after the first session. I felt more settled, less apprehensive, and ready to tackle some projects enthusiastically. When a disappointing, discouraging event occurred shortly after that, I handled it better than I would have before the EMDR therapy. It still hurt, but it did not shake me off-center. I am not entirely well, but I am more aware and have safeguards in place. We live in a fallen, cursed world that affects all of us. Are not we all broken in some way?

I have in my journal things that helped: books I read, what I learned from them, many verses, songs that helped, quotes from people, and lists of suggestions. I have already referred to this journal when discussing with individuals things that have helped me. My therapist shared that he could see that I have a teacher's heart. He encouraged me to pursue that by leading a support group, teaching a small group, or helping others in another way. I now lead a Bible study and occasionally teach in another one, I had the privilege to speak at a ladies' event, and I may tutor again. I have also done much editing. Following my therapist's advice has produced some beneficial results for me. I surmise that I will continue to have emotional struggles, but I am content with that. I desire to be in whatever state God chooses to bring Him glory and assist others in their journey. God says in Isaiah 41:10, "Fear thou not; for I am with thee: be not dismayed; for I am thy God: I will strengthen thee; yea, I will help thee; yea, I will uphold thee with the right hand of my righteousness." I cling to those promises and do not fear what is next. I rest in the knowledge that God knows, and He is in control; He loves me; He is all-powerful; His grace is sufficient for me. I am so grateful that the Bible is rich with all we need in every situation.

My survival journal of 2019 has sections entitled: Verses for Meditation, Things to Ponder: truths heard that I need to learn and practice, Things That Helped: practical, tangible things to do, Books: read and suggestions for future reads, Podcasts listened to, and Songs. I even recorded sayings from plaques; one said, "The measure of an achievement is marked by the difficulties and barriers you overcame to reach your goal." I encourage you each to make your own journal of what God teaches you along your journey. Mine was a stabilizing force at the time and has been a useful reference. In the verse section, I wrote many passages from the Psalms. Other verses that were especially helpful are:

- Philippians 4:5-9, "Let your moderation be known unto all men. The Lord is at hand. Be careful for nothing; but in every thing by prayer and supplication with thanksgiving let your requests be made known unto God. And the peace of God, which passeth all understanding, shall keep your hearts and minds through Christ Jesus. Finally, brethren, whatsoever things are true, whatsoever things are honest, whatsoever things are just, whatsoever things are pure, whatsoever things are lovely, whatsoever things are of good report; if there be any virtue, and if there be any praise, think on these things. Those things, which ye have both learned, and received, and heard, and seen in me, do: and the God of peace shall be with you."

- I Peter 5:6-11, "Humble yourselves therefore under the mighty hand of God, that he may exalt you in due time: Casting all your care upon him; for he careth for you. Be sober, be vigilant; because your adversary the devil, as a roaring lion, walketh about, seeking whom he may devour: Whom resist stedfast in the faith, knowing that the same afflictions are accomplished in your brethren that are in the world. But the God of all grace, who hath called us unto his eternal glory by Christ Jesus, after that ye have suffered a while, make you perfect, stablish, strengthen, settle you. To him be glory and dominion for ever and ever. Amen."

- James 1:2-4, "My brethren, count it all joy when ye fall into divers temptations; Knowing this, that the trying of your faith worketh patience. But let patience have her perfect work, that ye may be perfect and entire, wanting nothing."

- I Corinthians 1:3-4, "Grace be unto you, and peace, from God our Father, and from the Lord Jesus Christ. I thank my God always on your behalf, for the grace of God which is given you by Jesus Christ." II Corinthians 12:9, "And he said unto me, My grace is sufficient for thee: for my strength is made perfect in weakness. Most gladly therefore will I rather glory in my infirmities, that the power of Christ may rest upon me."

- II Timothy 1:7, "For God hath not given us the spirit of fear; but of power, and of love, and of a sound mind."

• Jeremiah 29:11-13, "For I know the thoughts that I think toward you, saith the Lord, thoughts of peace, and not of evil, to give you an expected end. Then shall ye call upon me, and ye shall go and pray unto me, and I will hearken unto you. And ye shall seek me, and find me, when ye shall search for me with all your heart."

I underlined words in the journal that I should be doing and circled words like hope, joy, and peace. There are many other verses I wrote out. I recommend each person search the Bible for verses that specifically apply to the current need.

Some of the books I read and from which I drew strength, teaching, and encouragements are: Walking with God through Pain and Suffering by Timothy Keller, It's OK to not be OK by Sheila Walsh, Trial by Fear by David Pennington, Walking on Water When You Feel Like You're Drowning by Tommy Nelson and Steve Leavitt, Dark Clouds, Deep Mercy by Mark Vroegop, Calm My Anxious Heart by Linda Dillow, To Fly Again by Gracia Burnham, and You Can Trust God to Write Your Story by Robert and Nancy DeMoss Wolgemuth.

From these and many sermons, I made numerous entries in my journal. I am known for my lists and organization. In my attempt to gain back some structure, I wrote lists in my journal of things to do regularly to help me be better prepared to deal with future losses, things to do when struggling, things to do in a crisis, and things I did for long term help. My plan is to turn to this easily accessible, guiding aid when needed for direction and assistance, especially if I ever get back to a place emotionally where I can barely think or function. These emotional struggles were not a part of the journey that I would wish on anyone, but I know it is what God chose for me. He made Himself very real to me, comforted me, and taught me much. Blessed be God, even the Father of our Lord Jesus Christ, the Father of mercies, and the God of all comfort; Who comforteth us in all our tribulation, that we may be able to comfort them which are in any trouble, by the comfort wherewith we ourselves are comforted of God," II Corinthians 1:3-4. I am extremely appreciative of those that walked with me and helped. I hope now to be more sensitive, compassionate, and also better equipped to help more struggling individuals when the paths of our lives intersect.

Gary: Testimony of a Caregiver

All people will provide caregiving to someone else, to some degree, at some point in their lives, although we do not always know when. As children, we may care for our siblings; as parents, our children present us with a huge caregiving opportunity. Some people will care for their parents, and some of us care for our spouses. Over seven years ago, my wife (who was in good health, not overweight, low cholesterol, and no family history of heart failure) experienced a little chest pain, then failed a stress test, and then a failed angioplasty procedure. This failure resulted in a heart attack that permanently damaged her heart. She was then transferred to a second hospital to have immediate bypass surgery and placed on life support. After four days, she was transferred to a third, more specialized hospital. Because of Karen's dismal neurologic condition and the inability to bring her to a conscious state, termination of life support was recommended. We were cautioned that if she became conscious, she would not have the ability to talk, walk, or feed herself. She remained in a coma for ten days. She spent almost four months in four hospitals, receiving multi-faceted care from numerous caregivers. After being discharged to home, she continued to receive outpatient treatments. Life had changed. After my normal workday, I spent hours each day caring for my wife, both in the hospital and later at home.

Other caregivers that helped include our immediate family and our church family. During the first few weeks of hospitalization, people from our church were at the hospital continuously during normal hours. I was greatly encouraged initially by their presence and later by their willingness to provide care: prayers, gifts of money or gift cards, transportation to medical appointments, and many meals. One lady continued to send in meals long after the others did, only stopping when her kitchen caught on fire and sustained some damage. When Karen was still in a coma, three ladies from church joined by our friend Dona sang. Our neighbor Gwen displayed her love and faith by anointing Karen with oil and praying for her healing the day before Karen came out of the coma. Pastor Whitcomb sang solos to Karen in two different hospitals. We are truly thankful for all these expressions of love, which were types of caregiving.

Caregiving is not always easy or fun. It is difficult to see a close loved one struggling. These struggles include clinging to physical life, suffering intense pain, losing cognitive and physical abilities, enduring emotional difficulties, or a combination of these. Caregiving is demanding – demanding of time and energy. The caregiver does not always feel appreciated. God, I believe, uses these trials to perfect us individually. He can perfect or build or grow the love we have for Him and others as we recognize that He orchestrates these events for our good. Then, as we allow God to give us these opportunities (caregiving included), God is successful at maturing us. The care we give to others is a demonstration of the love God is producing in our lives.

A couple of people, who had been caregivers for their spouses, encouraged me by telling me they could somewhat understand and that they were praying for me. Others sent encouraging emails indicating that people were praying in most states and in a few other countries. Included here are excerpts from some of the emails.

"I don't know when you will read this, but I wanted you to know that my family & I are praying fervently for you & your sweet family! I know that God is at work & none of this was an accident to Him & that He will accomplish His will in your life. Thank you for your sweet testimony & Godly example to me over the years that I have had the privilege to be your friend!"

"The progress is incredible, and obviously, God is willing that it will continue that way." "It's been a bumpy ride till now, and all the family is surely very proud of you and Karen. Please give her a big hug and a kiss from the cousin she has never met and remind her we send our love and prayers and very best wishes for her continued miraculous recovery." This note was from Karen's dad's first cousin.

"I have prayed so hard each day for Karen, as well as for her family. What a journey this has been for them all."

"I am so happy about Karen's progress. Her progress is nothing short of God's miracle. Praise God from whom all blessings flow."

"Hanging with her thru all this has been a Heavenly blessing for us." "We are all closer to God as a result, and I might add, a LOT MORE AWARE! Aware of family, aware of our own frailty, and aware of our dependence on our Heavenly Father."

"Thanks for the update. She is still amazing. So neat seeing God's presence. Being a part of this sure ups our faith."

"It is wonderful that Karen is home now; what a miracle. It shows what faith can do."

"We still have Karen on our prayer list at church."

"I thank God that she has continued to progress as far as she has. And you can be sure she will continue to be in my prayers. She certainly has been through an unusually difficult ordeal for one person! My heart goes out to the whole family."

"We rejoice in the continuing improvement."

"She has come a long way in less than a year."

"Wow, what a long walk Karen is going through. And to think she still is in good spirits."

"I am so happy to hear that Karen is still moving forward and continuing her progress. I know of no one who has ever had a tougher hill to climb. May God bless her efforts. I know he will."

"Again, we have seen a miracle; we have seen God's working. It makes one know there is always HOPE. Think and pray for you all often."

"I especially love hearing of how God sovereignly orchestrated events in your life to prepare you for your health difficulties." Keep in mind II Corinthians 4:16-18.

"We will continue to pray for you. I know how long the days can seem when you can't get up and do all the things you used to. But God has shown that he can do ANYTHING, so we'll just pray that he keeps on healing!"

"Praise the Lord for answered prayer on your behalf! Keep pleasantly surprising the doctors!"

I appreciate all of the encouraging emails and all the people that were praying. I am thankful that God provided me the compassion and desire to show love by providing the physical and emotional support my wife needed. Caregiving opportunities may be of short duration. One may only have a short period of time to provide care for the needy person and demonstrate love before it is too late. If long-term care is required, then we can ask God to give us the needed patience and endurance. There are no iron-clad guarantees despite how we may interpret Scripture. If we try to be engaged, do our best, and view all outcomes as God's will, without becoming complacent or bitter, I believe that God will then be pleased and provide additional blessings. I do not know why God allowed healing for Karen and not others mentioned in this book, despite the clear evidence of faith they displayed. However, I am thankful that God did provide healing for my wife and a caregiving opportunity for me.

Conclusion

Karen: Thankfulness and Trust

I hope the people mentioned in this book and others that cared for me will read this book and that they will know how much we appreciate them and be encouraged by it. I also trust that all will learn from this book and be drawn closer to God, too, through reading it. I am confident in Christ and what He has done and can do. At the same time, I am humbled by what God did and is doing in and through me. More than just believing, I know now by experience the words of the Bible, which teach that He loves me, that His Way is best, and that I can put my complete trust in Him. The biggest thing for which I am thankful is that I heard the plan of salvation, trusted in His finished work on the cross as the only way to Heaven. I continue to trust Him. Serving Him is a big part of my life. I want to be found faithful until the very end of my life here on earth.

Survival Nugget: I could share many more words about the details of my dark days and the miracles that only God could perform. What I know to the very core of my being is that God's love for me does not change; He is always with me; I don't have to understand, only trust Him as He molds me to be more like Christ. Through all of this, I did not doubt His ways, for I know His Word, the Bible, is the final right answer, and He gave me sufficient grace as I needed it. His ways are above mine. I praise my awesome God for His wonderful works.

Steps I have used with many to explain how to put your trust in God and know you are going to Heaven someday!

- Romans 3:23 records, "For all have sinned, and come short of the glory of God." We have all sinned. We have all done things that are displeasing to God. No one is innocent. Romans 3:10-18 gives a detailed picture of what sin looks like in our lives.

- Romans 6:23a teaches us about the consequences of sin, "For the wages of sin is death." The punishment that we have earned for our sins is death. Not just physical death, but eternal death!

- Romans 6:23b says, "But the gift of God is eternal life through Jesus Christ our Lord." Romans 5:8 declares, "But God commendeth his love toward us, in that, while we were yet sinners, Christ died for us." Jesus Christ died for us! Jesus' death paid for the price of our sins. Jesus' resurrection proves that God accepted Jesus' death as the payment for our sins.

- Romans 10:9 states, "That if thou shalt confess with thy mouth the Lord Jesus, and shalt believe in thine heart that God hath raised him from the dead, thou shalt be saved." Because of Jesus' death on our behalf, all we have to do is believe in Him, trusting His death as the payment for our sins. Then we will be saved! Romans 10:13 repeats it, "For whosoever shall call upon the name of the Lord shall be saved." Jesus died to pay the penalty for our sins and rescue us from eternal death. Salvation, the forgiveness of sins, is available to anyone who will trust in Jesus Christ as their Lord and Savior.

∂• Romans 5:1 has this magnificent message, "Therefore being justified by faith, we have peace with God through our Lord Jesus Christ." Through Jesus Christ, we can have a relationship of peace with God. Romans 8:1 reveals to us, "There is therefore now no condemnation to them which are in Christ Jesus." Because of Jesus' death on our behalf, we never have to be condemned for our sins. We have a precious promise of God in Romans 8:38-39, "For I am persuaded, that neither death, nor life, nor angels, nor principalities, nor powers, nor things present, nor things to come, Nor height, nor depth, nor any other creature, shall be able to separate us from the love of God, which is in Christ Jesus our Lord." Once you have accepted Jesus as your Savior, you are secure in Him. Nothing can ever remove you from His Hand and prevent you from joining God in Heaven.

Although saying these words will not save you, here is a sample prayer you can pray if you would like to tell God that you are relying on Jesus Christ for your salvation, "God, I know that I have sinned against You and am deserving of punishment. But Jesus Christ took the punishment on the cross that I deserve so that through faith in Him, I could be forgiven. With Your help, I place my trust in You for salvation. Thank You for Your grace and forgiveness and the gift of eternal life! Amen!" Only faith in Jesus Christ can provide salvation!

The Four Stabilizing Truths

1. God's LOVE for me is unchanging.

   Jeremiah 31:3; 1 John 4:10, 16; Romans 8:31-32,35-39; John 15:12-13; Deuteronomy 7:7-8.

2. God's PURPOSE for me is Christlikeness.

   Romans 8:28-29; Colossians 1:28; Ephesians 4:11-13; 2 Corinthians 3:18

3. God's WORD to me is the final right answer.

   2 Timothy 3:15-17; Hebrews 4:12; 1 John 5:3; 2 Peter 1:3-4; Deuteronomy 6:6-9; 30:11-20; John 16:13-15.

4. God's GRACE to me is Sufficient.

   2 Corinthians 12:9; 2 Timothy 2:1; Hebrews 4:15-16; Titus 2:11-12; Psalm 116:5; Romans 5:20-21.

Pastor Senn: God's Amazing Grace!

When I review this whole story, all I see is God's amazing grace, His goodness, and His divine acts. I think of ten lessons that stand out from this ordeal.

- ❧ First is just the miracle of her life being preserved.

- ❧ Second, to see the healing of family relationships through the process and to see a family really come together where they were hitting on all eight cylinders in the care for their mom was very impressive.

- ❧ Third, to see the prayer support, the groundswell of Christians all over our state, and the country, and the world, praying for the Prices and for Karen, was amazing to watch.

❧ Fourth, the friendships within the church and elsewhere that were strengthened and the relationships that God has been building were again amazing to see.

❧ Fifth, we observed the witnessing opportunities for so many of us. They abounded then and still abound as a result of this story.

❧ Sixth, the provision of God to meet the exorbitant cost of the medical processes and time in the hospital with all the things that went on; to see God's care for the Prices was remarkable.

❧ Seventh, to see the Price family respond in such grace and mercy towards the doctor who caused this initial problem. The restraint they exercised not to sue her or the hospital or the various systems but to take the high road was again impressive to watch.

❧ Eighth, perhaps the most difficult prayer to pray for Karen was for her to get a heart transplant. The wait for a heart was nearly unbearable. To pray for a heart transplant, as we all did, we knew that the answer to that prayer would involve someone dying. That was a very difficult prayer request, but one we offered, and when a heart came and was a good match, we were all thanking God for the life that produced that heart and then the new life Karen would gain from it.

❧ Ninth, I would say another lesson we learned through this was the appreciation of life: every day is a gift, to appreciate the simple things, and that the little things we can do are really important.

∾ Tenth, to see Karen back in the office today, to see her back at church, to see her ministering, and coming alongside the staff in an administrative role again points to the abundant grace and mercy of our God.

We are just so thankful to have her back (we know her family is glad to have her back), to see God use her, and to realize that God was not done with her; He had more to do.

Survival Nugget: Pastor Senn preached through I Thessalonians in the fall of 2018. He included the following truths when preaching on I Thessalonians 5:8, "But let us, who are of the day, be sober, putting on the breastplate of faith and love; and for an helmet, the hope of salvation." These are three things all believers should do when experiencing a trial. The following three words became very precious to me.

1. FAITH - By God's grace, we put on the breastplate of faith and trust God through the trial one day at a time. The test is part of God's sovereign plan for our lives, and we embrace it gladly.

2. LOVE - By God's grace, we experience the sustaining love of God. We also want to be good stewards of the trial and redeem each opportunity to declare the love of God to others. We always want to be wearing the breastplate of love.

3. HOPE - By God's grace, we put on the helmet, the hope of salvation. Our hope is in the Lord. We have the absolute confidence that we possess eternal life and will obtain the

final aspect of salvation, which is glorification. We look forward to being with the Lord, free of physical and emotional issues, and sin-free!

ACKNOWLEDGEMENT: Thank you to all of you who gave us your thoughts or gave us the things you wrote and helped us gather information for this book. Thank you to all the people who told us, "You should write a book," or encouraged us in some other way to put our thoughts in print. Thank you, Timmy, for your diligence in helping us edit. And thank you, Xulon Press, for providing us with information and encouragement to write and for publishing this book. Most of all, we thank God, who, among countless other things, gave us life and helped us write this book.

Epilogues

Gary: More from the Stories

Day 2687 – March 20, 2020

Over seven years since the failed angioplasty
Five and one-half years since the heart transplant

K aren received many required heart catheterizations, as is the case for all transplant patients. These help determine the level of organ rejection and allow for a more precise dosage and type of anti-rejection medication. Karen has volunteered at the church office for a few hours a few times each week. She tires easily and requires a daily nap. Her attitude through all of this has been inspiring. She has chosen to give God the praise, be thankful for God's provision, and focus on the positives. She stated, "God is there during the dark times, so do not give up on God. He is still doing miracles."

Early in 2014, two of Karen's friends at church gave me some insight into what some people thought while Karen was in the hospital. Joyce Bromley stated, "This incident has brought the corporate body [of our church] together more than I have seen anywhere. It seemed like everyone was praying for Karen." Karen's Sunday School teacher, Cathy Major, said, "Pastor told us while preaching,

'Don't give up on praying for Karen, God can perform miracles.' That was a rebuke to me. We have lost other people [church members] and recently lost Debbie [Robbins], our music pastor's wife, and now we are going to lose Karen. I went home and prayed that God would perform a miracle. Three days later, Karen came out of the coma. Praise the Lord."

The following is my recollection of where some of the people I mentioned earlier were, last we knew. Although time and distance separated us, it is interesting to see where the paths of their lives have taken them after experiencing their own trials.

Mark and Mary Snyder continued their walk with God, despite losing their mother to cancer while still young. Mark married and has four children. He and his wife served at the Ross Corners church; eventually, he became one of the deacons. Mary displayed a friendly and polite attitude, served in a different church, married, and adopted children from another country. I always enjoyed being around her.

Ken Fagan's widow, Wanda, remarried and served the Lord. We know that one of Ken and Wanda's sons became a pastor. Our sons had his wife as a Junior High distance learning teacher.

Cinthy Midkiff's parents, Bill and Joan, still attend Tri-City with us. Karen regularly talks with them and hugs her mom. Joan and Karen became special friends while serving together over the years.

Jon Bixby struggled for a while as a single parent with seven children. Many miles south lived a widow named Christy with three sons. Her husband had left the pastorate to be a military chaplain. Besides being an encouragement to many military people and leading them to Christ, one of his goals was to be instrumental in ten men going to Bible college to be preachers after leaving the military. When he died in Afghanistan, only eight men had surrendered to God's call to be preachers. Christy was confused with why God had allowed her husband's death and for not completely fulfilling her husband's desires nor the desires God had put in her heart to have a big family, including girls and twins. In the few years after her husband's death, more military personnel came to know the Lord because of his testimony, and three more men dedicated their lives to be pastors, totaling eleven. Christy attended a Ladies' retreat where Amy Bixby, while in remission from her cancer, gave her testimony. Later, when Christy heard that Amy went to Heaven, Christy prayed for Jon and his seven children. She knew how she struggled with three children without a mate. Jon and Christy met sometime later and began dating. God brought beauty from ashes, giving Jon and Christy a love for each other. Karen was honored to be the wedding coordinator for their ceremony in September of 2012, which included Jon's seven and Christy's three children. God fulfilled Christy's desires; she and Jon have ten children between the two of them, three girls, and three sets of them are the same age. The youngest two act like twins.

Pastor Robbins started meeting with other widowers. He led many sessions of a GriefShare group, a class/support group for those that have lost loved ones. He eventually remarried a retired Spanish teacher who had taught his children in high school. They continue to be an encouragement and help to all, especially the senior adults at church.

Byron Pollock finished college and changed jobs from the Deck Superstore to being a medical technician. He remarried; his new wife also served as a nurse at Camp Eden.

Phil Price and his sister Mary Morgan wrote this testimony, entitled "Each Step of the Way," specifically for this book.

My story began in Europe in 2012 while celebrating my twenty-fifth wedding anniversary with my wife and daughter, who was studying abroad. On Palm Sunday, my wife's mother died suddenly of a heart attack in our hometown of Creston, Iowa. Unable to get back in time for the funeral, we had no closure for her passing. Later that year, my father was placed in a nursing home in Florida. My siblings and I went for a family gathering in November while he was still living. Upon my return home, my wife came down with a respiratory illness, which turned into an asthma attack, and then she succumbed to a coma. She was placed on a ventilator, and after much prayer and deliberation with her medical team, we released her to God in January of 2013. That shook me to my core.

Four short months later, my father died, as did two other close friends. Losing five individuals with whom I was so close, dealt me too many stress points, and took a toll on my body. On May 15, 2014, I suffered from transverse myelitis. In layman's terms, I had a stroke resulting in an interruption of messages that my spinal cord nerves could not send throughout my body. I had no feeling on the left side from my chest to my foot and from my right knee to my foot. Within days I had a myriad of tests done on my heart, nerves, brain, and back to determine what had happened.

At that same time, hereditary PAD - Peripheral Arterial Disease, manifested itself, leaving me with ten percent blood flow from my carotid arteries to my brain. I had hypersensitivity to any touch and a drop leg, making walking almost impossible. My primary care physician, as well as specialists in Des Moines and Iowa City, told me I'd never walk right, to go home, get my affairs in order and enjoy the last month of my life. Shaken to my core, I wondered what my life would consist of in those thirty days.

My foremost thought was - what this would mean for my two daughters. The older was married with two toddlers while the younger was finishing her college education at Iowa State University. I met with a lawyer, drew up a new will, dividing my financial and physical assets. I pastor a rural church in Orient, Iowa, so I informed the congregation what the future might look like for them. Then I talked to my six siblings for what I thought might be the last time. Physically, I was down, but spiritually, I remained strong. I knew, at my death, I would be with the Lord, my wife Diana, my parents, and others who had been a big part of my life.

At the end of the first month, I was glad to be alive. I went for a recheck with the specialist who informed me again I'd never walk without dropping my leg with each step. I couldn't accept that diagnosis and told him I'd be walking in six weeks. I did not want to just sit in a chair, waiting to die. Neighbors and people from our church came by with food, mowed my country yard, and cut up a tree that had fallen during a storm. I was not allowed to lift anything heavy or bend my head forward for fear of having another stroke. I could walk with the aid of a cane or hang on to the edge of a counter or a piece of furniture. Down deep, though, I knew I had to remain strong for other people. Each week I continued to study for a sermon, and because I had a bit of feeling in my foot, I drove the country roads to church on Sundays to deliver it. I had two little grandsons who missed playing with Papa, and that really got to me.

Faith helps you move forward. When people tell me they can't figure out how things will change for them, I tell them, "You can't ask God for things and not do your part." Since my brain had disconnected from my body, I decided to focus on reconnecting it as much as I could. I sat and stared at my feet and told my toes to move. At first, nothing happened. Weeks went by, and one day, I saw a wiggle in my big toe. It happened again. I got so excited, I put on my shoes, and I drove into town to show my father-in-law. At first, nothing moved, and he doubted that I had seen my toe wiggle. Then waves of electric shock went from my foot to my brain. Then there was a twitch. He saw it happen! The miracle was beginning. My brain was once again able to send messages, and my body responded.

On day 100, I changed my mindset. I told myself I was going to start doing things for myself. I was going to mow my own yard, plant my own flowers, and be strong for other people. I was tired of waiting to die. I knew God had a reason to heal me, and people needed to see it. I gave it totally to Him to plan how it was going to happen.

I understand when people say, "I have nothing to look forward to." I tell them to find a new mission. Don't look at what was; look at what you can be doing or should be doing. Choose to think differently and make yourself do it. It is on you to figure it out. I was determined with the Lord's help to make a difference for others – even if it meant going at a slower pace than I was used to going.

My mission became my church and my grandchildren, who needed their Papa to be a caregiver while their mother went back to nursing school, and their father was in the National

Guard. The two boys were toddlers, and I'd have them sometimes twelve out of fourteen days. They were thrilled to be once again at Papa's house, and their energy brought new life to me. It wasn't too long before another brother joined us, and eventually, a sister was born. All the while, I took on the challenge of helping to make it work for all of us. We developed a system of doing things, and they adapted to it. It kept me busy and kept my mind from focusing on things I should not.

My focus turned outward rather than inward, and it carried on over to the church. In addition to pastoring, before my stroke, I owned my own construction company. I had to close up shop. Little by little, I was able to use my building skills by doing small jobs and then moved on to bigger things like installing a chairlift in our church's entry. Growing flowers continued to be a passion. Throughout the summer, I graced the altar with varieties of fresh flowers and gave them away after the service. I even grew all the flowers used in my younger daughter's wedding held at that same church in 2016.

I am a living testament to the healing power of God. I accepted the possibility of death, but my desire to live and be used by God in the lives of those I love was great too. I desired to give witness to my faith in God, which became evident in January of 2019 when I needed hernia surgery. My surgeon refused to do it until my specialist in Iowa City gave me clearance. Imagine the doctor's shock when he walked into the exam room and saw me sitting there five years after he had said I had a month to live. He said he knew I was a man of faith who believed in God's ability to heal and that it had worked for me. But more amazingly, imagine more shock when they did a nuclear scan of my carotid arteries, and found the three that were fully dead now had new ones next to them pumping blood to my brain. The one with ten percent blood flow was at 100%—just another miracle without an explanation.

But wait – there's more: another problem surfaced. The surgeon doing my hernia operation told me in order to have the surgery, I needed to feel pain in my left leg so that afterward, I would not overdo it with any activity. So, I asked my church to pray that I would feel pain. A week later, I woke with such pain, I knew their prayers were answered, and I was able to have the surgery. Believe me, after the surgery, I felt pain, and I did not overdo anything!

In 2018, I began a new chapter in my life. Via Facebook, I reconnected with Marsha, a former classmate from the Christian school I attended in New York. She had become a widow several years prior, so we had Facebook chats on finding a new normal. We began a long-distance relationship, which resulted in many flights from Des Moines to Binghamton and vice versa. This led to our wedding in June of 2019. We are settling into a new normal with both of us now in our 60s. Each of us has seen God work in amazing ways and look forward to what lies ahead.

My life's verse, Jeremiah 29:11, says it all. "For I know the plans I have for you,' declares the Lord, 'plans to prosper you and not to harm you, plans to give you hope and a future'" (NIV). I have a future because my HOPE is in the Lord. He has been there every STEP of my way and will continue to keep my STEPS steady wherever the path may lead.

We praise God that He brought beauty from the ashes in these people's lives. **We, as a family,** *have been significantly affected by these events. We are stronger now as a family and as individuals. Our four sons are married to godly women. We, as parents, are very blessed!*

Family 2021

Karen: God Loves Me Now

On February 22, 2020, I spoke at the Anna's Hope Luncheon, our church's ministry to the widows. As always, I was grateful for the privilege to tell my story and what God has taught me, pointing people to God. "God Loves Me Now" is the title of my talk that follows.

Many of you know parts of my story, but for those that do not, I want to start by summarizing what happened to me beginning in 2012 that helped me to know God's love in a fuller sense. I experienced a little pain by my collar bone, so I went to the emergency room. During an angioplasty, a major artery to my heart was severed. The result was a heart attack, two strokes; I had to be revived several times, then hung on the edge of life and death for ten days in a coma. A brain scan showed that my brain was barely functioning; the best-case scenario was that I would never walk, talk, or be coordinated enough to feed myself if I ever woke up. I was on total life support, my fingers and toes had turned gangrene, my muscles were atrophying, and my family was told to think of when they would terminate life support. Many people prayed often, and God performed a series of miracles, evidenced by the fact that I stand here today. After ten days, I did wake up in an enormous amount of pain, could barely see, couldn't talk, had no strength, and could remember very little of my past. I was confused as to why I was in that state, but I confidently knew that God loved me and that I could trust Him. Through the long years of healing and recovery, I have come to know God better than ever before. God loved me even then, and God loves me now.

God loves me now! Who really is God? He is my creator, the one who made me. God also is my protector, my provider, my healer, my everything - all I need. He is all-knowing, in control of all, all-powerful, and unchanging. There are many more attributes of God we could consider. Today, we will focus on the fact that God loves each of us all the time.

God **loves** me now! How can we know God loves us? He demonstrated it by creating us, desiring fellowship and communication from us, most of all, by providing salvation for each of us. I John 4:10, "Herein is love, not that we loved God, but that He loved us, and sent His Son to be the propitiation for our sins."

All each one has to do is to believe that you are a sinner, believe Jesus paid the penalty for your sin when He died on the cross, and accept His free gift of salvation. He rose from the grave, so each of us who trust Him can have eternal life with Him. Jeremiah 31:3, "I have loved thee with an everlasting love: therefore, with lovingkindness have I drawn thee." If you are not sure you are loved and going to Heaven, please talk to me later. God also demonstrates His love through His tender care for us, teaching us, and molding us to be more like Jesus Christ.

Not only does He show us His love, but also, God is love. In preschool, I learned a verse for every letter of the alphabet. The one for "G" is, "God is Love," John 4:16. I enjoy Math because there are absolutes you can count on; they are always true: they stay the same. 1+2=3. A mathematical word problem: *Sisters Joy and Hope are going to buy their mom some Valentine's candy. Joy has one dollar, and Hope has two dollars. How many dollars do Joy and Hope have?* "And" means plus, so in a mathematical equation, $1+$2=$3. Another math equation is: *Charity made ten paper hearts. She gives half of her hearts to her sister, Faith. How many hearts does Faith have?* Half of ten is five. Since "of" means multiplication and "is" means equal, the equation is ½ X 10 = 5. So, when the Bible says, "God is love," we can write it like a math equation. God equals LOVE, Love = God. This truth is not to be questioned or debated. It is a definite; God is love, or God = LOVE, Love = God, they are one - the same; God **is** love. He cannot be separated from love; it is who He is.

God's Love for Me is Unchanging. I had learned about God's love when I was very young. It was something I knew and did not question. I have never felt God's love more than during a crisis. Psalm 18:1-3, "I will love thee, O Lord, my strength. The Lord is my rock, and my fortress, and my deliverer; my God, my strength, in whom I will trust; my buckler, and the horn of my salvation, and my high tower. I will call upon the Lord, who is worthy to be praised." I lived out every part of this verse. God was faithful, and my strength, rock, fortress, deliverer, and high tower. This crisis was to be the biggest of my life. Through it, God showed me His unchanging love.

God loves **me** now! God tells us He loves us in many verses. I suggest you look up verses about love in the Bible and read them. In John 3:16, you can put your name in place of "the world," for you are part of the world, "For God so loved, Karen." Think, "God loves you." No matter what happens, I can rest on this fact. God loves me. People will disappoint, including family and friends; some will hurt. Some will gossip or tell lies about you; that can be devastating. Life does not go the way we planned; events may crush you, but God always loves you. Even when we fail, God loves us. No one completely understands what you are going through, except God, and His love is there. Being alone is hard to bear; many health issues can be a heavy load; being in pain is difficult (I know). Sometimes life is just hard. Psalm 13:5, "But I trust in your unfailing love; my heart rejoices in your salvation." God's love can always sustain. He understands.

I had not yet reached the age of most of you when I began this trial, but overnight I became very old. Gary told me I appeared to age forty years in just over a week. Even when I came out of the coma, I was told if I worked hard, I could get strong enough and learn how to sit up, but it was indicated that I would remain in a wheelchair and need someone to care for me. Knowing that a loving God was in control was the great thing that got me through that time. I had a surgery (no one knew if I would survive it) to put a machine inside me to pump for half of my heart that was forever damaged. I lived by being plugged into a wall or by the batteries I wore for almost two years. I knew there was a high risk of the machine failing. I remember laying in the bed in the hospital room, thinking, "Why did God leave me in such a state?" "Why did He not just take me home to Heaven?" God brought to my mind that years before I had dedicated my life to Him to be used for His glory. These events were His plan for me, and He would get the glory through it. God decided to heal me, and I praise Him for that. If

God had not healed me, we would still know that God remains good and loving. His way is best.

Almost two years later came the opportunity for me to get a heart transplant. The decision was an act of faith to exercise our trust in a loving God. On September 7, 2014, I received my third call about a potential heart. I did not know if I would get the transplant that time either (a University heart surgeon had gone to get the heart, and its condition was not yet known), nor did I know if I would make it through the surgery. The request had gone out; many people were praying for everyone involved. I was resting in God's love and care. I knew His way would be best, and I trusted Him. I woke up the next morning from surgery and was surprised and pleased that the pain was not as much as I had anticipated. The transplant had gone well!

I am not a widow, although I almost lost my husband twice due to heart attacks and other heart issues. I had to come to terms with THE THOUGHT, "Could I trust God if He allowed my husband, my best friend, my caregiver, my support, my strength to die?" In the midst of my sobbing, I told God, "I love You, and I know You love me. I choose to trust You even in this." Proverbs 3:5&6, "Trust in the Lord with all thine heart, and lean not unto thine own understanding. In all thy ways acknowledge Him, and He shall direct thy paths." We have many opportunities to exercise trust in our loving Father God, but it is not easy. It is a choice we must continually make.

I agreed at the time of my heart transplant to do a series of annual tests; the biggest one each year is the heart catheterization. It is one of the most accurate ways to determine if there is rejection occurring. For me, this is willingly submitting to a repeat of the same test that began my severe heart issues. It is always an emotional struggle and an opportunity to practice what I have learned – to trust God, who loves me at this moment. Whatever happens is ok, because God is in control, His way is best, He loves me, He is all-powerful, and His grace is sufficient! I have eternal life and a God who is always with me! I now look forward to going to the tests and talking with friends who work at the hospital, letting them see the changes in me. I also enjoy telling the hospital workers and others briefly of what God did and is doing.

God loves me **now**! No matter what happens, no matter how I feel today, no matter what I can no longer do, no matter anything. God loves me now. Romans 8:38-39, "For I am persuaded, that neither death, nor life, nor angels, nor principalities, nor powers, nor things present, nor things to come, Nor height, nor depth, nor any other creature, shall be able to separate us from the love of God, which is in Christ Jesus our Lord." All the time, His love is there for me. Nothing can take His love from me. My emotions may feel like I am not loved, but I will choose to believe what I read in the Bible, John 15:9, "As the Father hath loved me, so have I loved you: continue ye in my love."

Through this trial, we learned more fully that God is all that we need, and we learned more deeply about His love. A recent church memory verse was I Thessalonians 5:8, "But let us, who are of the day, be sober, putting on the breastplate of faith and love; and for an helmet, the hope of salvation." By God's grace, we experience the sustaining love of God. We do not want to waste our trials, whatever they may be, but be good stewards of the suffering and redeem each opportunity to declare the love of God to others. We always want to be wearing this breastplate of love. God can perfect or build or grow the love we have for Him and others as we recognize that He orchestrates these events for our good. Then, as we respond correctly to these God-given opportunities, He will mature us.

The care we give to others is a demonstration of the love God is producing in our lives. Many people here at Tri-City provided meals, rides, cards, gifts, acts of service, and encouragement, and prayed.

These were sustaining for us during this time. I trust we will all look for opportunities to share God's love through our words and actions.

I could talk for hours about the details of my times of testing and the miracles that God performed. I believed before my trauma that God is love. Amid these events, I experienced God's love, as I had not previously. What I know to the very core of my being is that God's love for me does not change; He is always with me; I don't have to understand, just trust Him as He molds me to be more like Christ. Please, all of you say it with me, "God loves me now." Just as we said that today, say it to yourself as often as you need to hear it. <u>God loves me now</u>!

ABOUT THE AUTHORS: Gary and Karen Price grew up in rural New York, living a mile apart in the town of Vestal (about seven houses). After Gary graduated from high school, they met at church. They were married in August 1980 and moved to South Carolina to continue their college education. They also lived in Tulsa, Oklahoma, and New York State. Two of their sons were born while they were living in Fremont, California. Finally, in 1990 they settled in Colorado, where their other two sons were born. They all enjoy the view of the gorgeous Rocky Mountains. Gary is a dedicated husband and father; he works as a building maintenance mechanic. Karen is foremost a wife and mother; she has taught and edited for many years. *A Way Higher Than Ours* is their first book.

CPSIA information can be obtained
at www.ICGtesting.com
Printed in the USA
FSHW022052051121
85968FS